About the Author

Kennedy Lindsay was born in Saskatchewan, Canada and grew up in Ulster. He was educated at Trinity College, Dublin and the universities of Edinburgh and London. (Studied under Richard Pares, Dame Lillian Penson and Sir Lewis Namier and has a doctorate in modern history.) He has served on the staff of the Royal Military College of Canada; has held a senior appointment with the Canadian Department of External Affairs and has held various university appointments. In addition, he did a stint with the Canadian International Development Agency which is the equivalent of the British GVSO or the American Peace Corps. He was elected to the short-lived "Northern Ireland Assembly" in 1973 and to the Northern Ireland Constitutional Convention in 1975. He was involved at first-hand in many of the events described in this book.

DUNROD

THE BRITISH
INTELLIGENCE
SERVICES IN ACTION

KENNEDY LINDSAY

DUNROD

First published in the Irish Republic
by The Dunrod Press

2nd impression, June 1981,
by The Dunrod Press,
28 North End, Ballyclare, Co. Antrim

Copyright © *Kennedy Lindsay*

Printed and bound in Ireland

BL *British Library Cataloguing in Publication Data*

Lindsay, Kennedy
   The British intelligence services in action.
   1. Intelligence service — Great Britain.
   I. Title
   327'.12'0941   JN329.16

   ISBN 0-86202-111-1
   ISBN 0-86202-112-X Pbk

Secret intelligence methods *corrupt not only the spy, but those who employ him and those who give official approval to his use.* Adlai Stevenson when U.S. Ambassador to the United Nations.

There is a very strong temptation in dealing both with terrorism and with guerilla actions for government forces to act outside the law, the excuses being that the processes of law are too cumbersome, that the normal safeguards in the law for the individual are not designed for an insurgency and that a terrorist deserves to be treated as an outlaw anyway. Not only is this morally wrong, but, over a period, it will create more practical difficulties for a government than it solves . . . Functioning in accordance with the law is a very small price to pay in return for the advantage of being a government. Sir Robert Thompson, KBE, CMG, DSO, MC, anti-insurgency specialist and for four years head of the British Advisory Mission to Vietnam.

To the courageous
men and women
who wished this book well
and helped me with information

Contents

Illustrations

Preface

This book focuses on the immense influence and unaccountable power of the British intelligence services and describes specific cases of intolerable excesses by them. These have been chosen because the author was involved with each at some stage. All raise profound constitutional issues.

It sets out how intelligence men have been allowed and encouraged to usurp to themselves a dominant role in policy-making in one region of the United Kingdom and have deliberately condoned and initiated violence, crime and racketeering in order, in the long term, to alienate both terrorist and political opponents of the government from their host populations and, in the short term, to provide agents on the ground with operational facilities and advantages.

It recounts how law enforcement and justice have been perverted and manipulated.

It draws attention, for the first time, to the revolution in defence strategy caused by advances in technology which make nuclear attack from the Atlantic a defence nightmare for Britain and reveals how the response has been an immense intelligence covert operation against the policies and current government of a neighbouring, officially friendly country.

Finally, this book underscores that these things are possible in the United Kingdom because of the immunities given by British libel and *sub judice* law, "Crown privilege" in the courts, Official Secrets Acts and oath, the power of the Attorney General to waive prosecution for criminal acts and the convention that intelligence organisations may not even be referred to by name in Parliament.

1 I Knew I had Wronged No One in my Life

I did not even attempt to walk quietly. I was so sure that there was nothing wrong. When I reached the top of the stairs, I just turned round the little bannister rail intending to walk straight into my daughters' bedroom. (This is the room where the boys thought there was a light.)

That was as far as I got. There was a belch of flame towards me. I felt searing pain in my mouth and side. I knew that I had been badly shot. In the light of the flame I recognised what I knew to be a Sterling machine-gun. I was also able to see a very dim outline of a man. This man at no time made any sound that I could hear. Everything happened so quickly I could not tell whether he was in uniform or civilian clothes. As I fell, the shadow of the man seemed to go back further into the room and I could no longer see it.

After I fell, I found myself lying almost in the corner of the top landing between the wall and the small room door. (This room is unfurnished, but there is a sun bed stored in it.) The blood was pouring out of my mouth and I was in great pain all over. I called out to whoever was in the girls' room for them to help me. I was sure that I was going to die and could not understand why this had been done to me for I knew I had wronged no one in my life. After I called, I got no answer from anyone.

I don't know how long I lay there, but while I lay in the same place, I saw from the corner of my eye another dim shadow of a man in the doorway of the big upstairs bedroom, but, whether it was the shock of my injuries or the darkness of the landing, I cannot say whether he was in uniform or not. The man [pushed me with his foot and]* moved back very quickly into the big bedroom again without a sound. I suppose whoever it was thought I was dead.

*The incident recorded in brackets was omitted in error from the statement as provided to the police.

18

I lay there trying to reason things out. As I lay huddled up in the corner, I felt my own sporting gun lying under me. I realised that, if I didn't get help soon, I was finished. Somehow I managed to get to the top of the stairs. I never bothered about my gun though I feared for it falling into the wrong hands. I could not let it hold me back from trying to get help.

Somehow between rolling and sliding down the stairs, I managed to get to the open front door. I pulled myself round the doorpost to the left expecting to get shot in the back to stop me from getting away. I headed out towards my car in the yard. When I got to the yard, I saw no one about. My car was there, but no use to me as the other car was in front of it blocking the gate.

I struggled out on to the road and looked up and down to see if there was any car coming to get help. At the same time I remember hearing myself calling out, "Someone, for God's sake, help me. I am dying."

Then I remembered Mr. Seawright, who lived in the house down the lane on the left-hand side of the road on the way to Saintfield. I staggered down the hill on the road. I suppose it was natural instinct that I hid behind what wall there was, then the hedge. At the bottom of the hill, the road starts to rise up again. As I staggered on up this hill, I heard the sound of the Sterling machine-gun. I was able to see the bullets hitting the road about me. At this time I don't know whether I was hit again or not, but I reached the lane, which was on the left-hand side of the road, and staggered on towards the house. The blood was pouring out of me all over. I reached the house and called out to Mr. Seawright to help get me to the police station in Saintfield for I knew that, if I got there, the police would do everything possible for me.

The above is an account of the shooting of William Black, which he himself wrote in hospital. A police officer asked him to write down everything he could remember and exactly as it happened. It was a slow, stubborn task. By that time he had been transferred to a semi-convalescent hospital, but was still too weak to write more than a few sentences at one time.

Black was a law-abiding, God-fearing citizen. He was a member of the Plymouth Brethren Church and, in keeping with its teaching, was conscientious in Sabbath observance; drank no alcohol; and took no part in politics. He was forty and married with three sons and two daughters, who ranged in age from twelve to eighteen.

He was a skilled fitter employed by Short Brothers and Harland, Ltd., the aircraft manufacturers in Northern Ireland. He had been with the company for nine years and was highly respected by management and fellow employees.

He was a member of the Ulster Defence Regiment, which is a locally recruited, part-time, volunteer regiment of the British army, used mainly to relieve regular troops of routine guard duties and patrol work. His other interest was a youth club. He started it when he found that his own teenage children had nothing to occupy them in the evenings. He had been granted funds towards equipping it from various charitable sources, including St. Martin's-in-the-Field, London.

A special unit of army intelligence shot William Black in his own weekend cottage near the small town of Saintfield in Co. Down. It had lain in wait for three days and two nights and was operating as part of the British undercover organisation in Northern Ireland.

He was shot because he was an honest man with a keen sense of public service. He had unwittingly stumbled on happenings which could most seriously embarass "the authorities" and an order had been given that he had to be silenced and discredited.

2 Now I Find that the Army is Doing it

William Black was shot on 26th January 1974. Eighteen months earlier, the night of 18th August 1972 was warm — much too warm for his wife, Margaret, who had a weak heart. Heat affected both it and her breathing. She was unable to sleep and sat on the side of the bed close to an open window, trying to make the most of the cooler night air which came through it.

The house was 61 Black's Road on the south-west outskirts of Belfast, the capital of Northern Ireland. It had been the Blacks' home for twenty years. The majority of the residents of the district were Protestant, but less than a mile distant was IRA-dominated Lenadoon. The windows commanded a clear view down a short cul-de-sac street called Trenchard.

A little before 2 a.m., Mrs. Black heard movements outside. She came closer to the window and saw three men tampering with a small, 7cwt. van, belonging to Thomas Shannon, a butcher. It was parked on the driveway of his house which was the first on the left side of Trenchard. Two wore anoraks with coloured stripes down the arms. The other had a dark anorak. All had long hair.

Mrs. Black awakened her husband. They saw the intruders force open the rear doors of the small van. One entered it and two moved to a larger, 15cwt. van, left parked on the road by the owner, Seán McNamee, who lived in 4 Trenchard. A few minutes later, the man in the small van climbed out and followed the others to the larger one.

At this point, William Black sent his wife downstairs to telephone the police. While she was on the phone, he noticed for the first time a large, dark BMC 1800 saloon car sitting nearby at Trenchard.

She completed the call and returned to the bedroom. The three men began to push McNamee's van towards Black's Road. Black sent her to telephone a second time to urge the police to hurry if they were to make arrests. He assumed that he was watching IRA terrorists stealing the van for use as yet another "car bomb", the device with which they were wreaking havoc across Northern Ireland.

Although a member of the part-time Ulster Defence Regiment, Black had no military weapon in the house. However, he did have a light, .22 calibre, sporting rifle. He seized it and ordered the men pushing the van to halt. One man drew a pistol, but Black's house was in shadow and he could not locate his position. Black ordered his wife to the floor. The engine of the BMC 1800 started up. All three men ran towards it. Two climbed in as it moved off. The third was dragged for some paces, fell on the road and rolled into hiding behind the van.

Black fired at the tyres of the car, but it sped on down Black's Road. McNamee's van was left in front of a flourescent street light. Black could see the feet and ankles of the man hiding behind it. He ordered him to stand up and to remain with his hands raised under the street light. He did as instructed, but began to attempt to lower his hands. Black could see what looked like a gun in his belt and warned him to keep his hands up or he would fire. He obeyed, but repeatedly called out in a strong English accent, "I am security", and, "I will show you my I.D. card". Black remained firm that he keep his hands up and hoped that the police would come quickly.

Soon a police car arrived with two policemen and a soldier who was substituting as a policeman. They stopped their car close to the van. Black pulled a pair of trousers over his pyjamas, threw on a coat and dashed over to meet them. At that moment, the escaped BMC 1800 drove past, turned at nearby Ornmore Park and came back and stopped at Trenchard.

The man under the street lamp made a dash and scrambled into it. Black shouted to the policemen that these were the van thieves and that they were armed. A policeman with a Sterling sub-machine-gun sprang into the car, covered the occupants and disarmed them.

On receiving Mrs. Black's telephone calls, the police had asked a local army unit for support. The result was the arrival at this juncture of soldiers in an armoured personnel carrier. The four arrested men were manhandled into it and it left, followed by the BMC 1800 driven by a policeman.

The policemen asked Black to come, too. He travelled in the police car. It proceeded to Garnock House, an army centre, which, as it chanced, was also on Black's Road although some distance away.

In the army centre Black saw the BMC 1800 sitting parked. The men who had been arrested at Trenchard stood nearby chatting. As he passed them, he saw that two had wigs in their hands and that both wore their hair cut short. They, in turn, recognised him and abused him crudely for his interference.

Suddenly, Black realised that the men were not IRA terrorists, but British army personnel. He was perturbed. He sensed that the military authorities would be furious at his intervention. Also, that the shots and commotion at Trenchard would focus attention on him and it would become widely known that he was in the Ulster Defence Regiment. The IRA frequently singled out UDR men for attack and the best protection was to conceal that one was in the regiment.

The two policemen who had made the arrests took Black aside and asked him to wait to see the commanding officer, a captain in rank. After a few minutes, he appeared. He said that the four persons who had been surprised taking the van at Trenchard were Special Investigation Branch men [the army's "plain clothes" military police] and were under his command. They had, he said, to do certain things at times in order to go into certain areas for information.

Black, indignant and worried, exploded, "I am out of my bed two or three nights a week patrolling roads and lying in hedges to stop people from robbing and stealing and now I find that the army is doing it." Also, he pointed out that he himself was now in danger from the IRA as everyone in the area would know that he was in the UDR.

When the captain heard that Black was a member of the Ulster Defence Regiment, he immediately adopted a strongly authoritarian tone. He told him that, as a member of the regiment, he was bound by the Official Secrets Acts and must not speak to anyone of what he had seen. He then again explained, "Certain vehicles are known and are accepted in certain areas. When we want to go into them, we have to lay hands on those vehicles."

Back at No. 61, Mrs. Black, tense and anxious, was watching for the return of her husband. Windows of the house commanded both Trenchard and the entrance to Tildarg Avenue which was opposite Trenchard on the Blacks' side of Black's Road.

An army landrover with four men drove past and stopped. Two were in uniform and two wore civilian anoraks with coloured stripes on the sleeves. The men in civilian dress jumped out; broke into a white Vauxhall car; pushed it a little distance; opened the bonnet and started the engine. One then rejoined the landrover and the other drove the car along Black's Road in the direction of Garnock House.

Mrs. Black knew that the car belonged to a young married couple called Darrem. She immediately telephoned Dunmurry Police Station and again spoke to the duty sergeant. He told her not to be alarmed and that her husband would explain everything when he returned home.

At Garnock House, Black had just asked permission to telephone his wife to say that he would soon be home when the duty sergeant phoned and asked him to phone her. He did so and she began to describe the stealing of the white Vauxhall. He told her to say no more on the telephone and that he would explain the situation when he reached home.

Black also telephoned a senior officer in the UDR and said, "I apprehended what seemed to be four terrorists stealing vehicles." He cut in, "Great news! How did you do it?" Black continued, "But, wait till I finish. It turns out that they are four army men in civilian clothes." The officer replaced the telephone receiver without saying another word. Black had had his first practical indication that in this matter authority at no level would wish to know.

At home, Black and his wife discussed the events of the night. Mrs. Black was indignant that the young Darrems should have had their car stolen. The husband was a milk roundsman and needed it to travel to work early in the morning before buses began to run. She remarked that she at least was not bound by the Official Secrets Acts and was resolved to do something about it.

Next morning she crossed to the Darrems' house and told them, "I know who stole your motor car. Phone Dunmurry Police Station and tell them that I saw it being stolen and that if they come to my house I will give them a full statement."

The Darrems did as advised, but no policeman visited Mrs. Black for a statement. However, in the evening the car was discovered in a nearby street with more petrol in the tank than when stolen.

A cover-up operation was quickly launched after the SIB's attempted vehicle theft at Trenchard. It consisted of three separate exercises to allay the misgivings of, first, McNamee, the owner of the van; second, the residents of the Black's Road district; and third, the wider public.

The exercise to reassure McNamee took place at once. He and his wife were awakened when Black fired at the escaping BMC 1800. He opened his front door to see what was happening and she telephoned the army. He saw the man in civilian clothes standing with hands up and shouting that he was "security". He watched subsequent events and finally returned to bed.

An hour and a half later, a police sergeant from the Dunmurry Station knocked on the door. He told McNamee that he was not to be alarmed at the attempt by plain clothes army men to remove his van. It had appeared suspicious to them and they had decided to take it into custody until they could check it out.

McNamee retorted that the van was properly taxed and registered and had been parked outside his house each night for a long time. He added that, if it had not been for the UDR man, there would have been another mysterious assassination in Andersonstown [Belfast's large IRA-dominated district].

The exercise to reassure the Black's Road residents took place on the following day. Royal Military Police arrived at Trenchard. They took numerous photographs and measurements and spoke to various residents. One of Black's bullets had ricocheted on the road and passed through the upper section of a window. The broken pane received concentrated attention from the photographers and measurers.

No attempt was made, however, to contact the Blacks although they were the key witnesses and were standing on their front doorstep watching the commotion.

The exercise to reassure the wider public was relatively simple. The army press office released a news item which duly appeared in the Belfast press. A terrorist, it said, had fired shots into a house in Black's Road, but no one had been injured.

Excluded from the cover-up operation, and still to be dealt with, was the stubborn Plymouth Brother who abhorred crime and cover-ups and whose wife had a compassion for their young, recently-married neighbours greater than her respect for the Official Secrets Acts.

It is clear that the SIB needed McNamee's van plus at least one other vehicle. Their first task at Trenchard was to break into

Shannon's small van. Presumably, it was to be driven off at the same time as McNamee's. The theft of Darrem's white Vauxhall came three-quarters of an hour later. Did they need a third vehicle or was it a substitute for one of the vehicles which they had failed to steal in Trenchard?

The vehicles had been selected with some care. McNamee's wife, Ester, when going to bed about midnight, had seen from the bedroom window a man with long hair moving around in Trenchard. He failed to break into a car on the opposite side of the street from her house. He then crossed to her husband's van, succeeded in opening it and walked away.

Andersonstown appears to have been the area of the intended SIB operation. McNamee's van was well known in the district. He owned a light engineering works and most of his workers lived in Andersonstown. Morning and evening the van conveyed them from and to their homes. Also, his mother and relations of his wife lived in that district and he frequently used it to visit them. This fact, too, agrees with the remark which the officer made to Black at Garnock House. He had said, "Certain vehicles are known and accepted in certain areas. When we want to go into them, we have to lay hands on those vehicles."

McNamee appears to have been closely linked with the Provisional IRA. His neighbours at Trenchard and Black's Road knew nothing of such an association, but British intelligence could have been otherwise informed. The Official IRA was sufficiently confident that he was a key figure in the Provisionals to have him assassinated during an open feud between the two organisations some months later.*

If the SIB vehicle theft exercise had been by the Provisional IRA, the explanation would have been as follows: one van was needed to carry a bomb; the second van for the "getaway"; and Darrem's car as a "clean" vehicle to which the bombers could switch once they should be clear of the immediate vicinity of the target.

Was this also the explanation of the SIB operation? Particularly significant and sinister could be McNamee's assumed association with the Provisional IRA. Was the object to sow contention between

---

*Charles Anthony Fitzpatrick, a member of the Official IRA, was convicted for the murder of Seán McNamee on 7th June 1976. He lodged an appeal against the conviction, but it was rejected by the Northern Ireland Court of Criminal Appeal on 8th October 1976.

Provisional and Official IRA or between rival wings within the Provisionals? Was it something else? It is essential that a judicial inquiry establish the truth.

3 The Family which Would Not Emigrate

The Blacks were in a dilemma. Neither wished to take any step which might hinder the army in searching out IRA killers and bombers. At the same time, they were most unhappy that it was resorting to the theft of vehicles from law-abiding citizens and for purposes that were unknown. There was also at the backs of their minds the recollection of another vehicle theft some months earlier.

William Black and his eighteen-year-old son, Tom, both belonged to a company of 9th Ulster Defence Regiment based in Thiepval Depot, the large army complex in Lisburn. When on duty, the men left their cars in the depot car park, which was inside the heavily guarded main gate. One evening in the previous winter, he and his son left his car in it as usual about 8.00 p.m. They joined their unit for ninety minutes of drill and basic training and then left on a landrover patrol through the town of Crumlin and the country area between Lisburn and Aldergrove Airport. The patrol returned between 2.30 and 2.45 a.m. for a cup of tea and a rest break. About 4.00 a.m., it left on a further routine landrover patrol to either the Northern Ireland Electricity Service sub-station at the top of Glen Road overlooking Belfast or the Ulster Television transmitter on nearby Black's Mountain. It was back in Thiepval Depot about 6.00 a.m. and the men prepared to return home.

In the car park Black found that his car had been entered by someone who had forced the quarter-light on the driver's door and that the mileometer registered twenty additional miles since the previous evening. One or two other UDR men also found that their cars had been forced open, but they had no way of knowing whether they had been driven in their absence.

Black was certain about the mileage. He was a trained and meticulous motor mechanic. He had installed a new engine in the car and was carefully recording the mileage during the first five hundred miles "run in" period. He had noted the exact figure on the mileometer when he parked. A small, expensive, portable radio had been stolen from the car, but he was less concerned about it.

The other UDR men left for home, but Black and his son waited a further three or more hours in order to take up the matter with the army authorities. Officers of the military police eventually arrived for day duty and they had an interview with one in civilian clothes.

The officer tried to minimise the incident. Black became furious and stormed at him. He pointed out that, if the army had needed a car for a lawful purpose, it had plenty of its own from which to choose. If it had to steal one, the purpose must have been unlawful. He said that he had been "angry and afraid" when he discovered the additional mileage. Also, that he hoped he would not hear of anyone being shot down in the street from a red Zephyr, but, if he did, he knew where to send the police when they would come to his door. (The car was maroon, but the Black family had fallen into the habit of referring to it as red.)

Black's tempestuous interview appears to have worried the military authorities. A day or two later, a sergeant-major in the UDR was sent to his home to reassure him. He pointed out that no car could have been removed from the Thiepval car park as it would have had to leave and return by the main gate. On each occasion the driver's pass would be checked and the registration number of the car telephoned through to his unit as a further safeguard.

Black replied that that was exactly why he was so concerned. His car could have been removed and returned only with the approval of the military authorities.

On 29th August 1972, eleven days after the vehicle stealing episode at Trenchard, the Black's doorbell rang twice about 2.15 a.m.

Tom Black, the eldest son, was completing his final year at school and had more time to spare than persons in normal employment. His UDR company commander knew this and sometimes, when a private failed to report for duty, he would send a messenger to ask him to stand in for the absentee. Often these requests came late at night.

Black assumed that the double ring on the doorbell was a last moment request for his son to do a stint of UDR duty. He got up, came downstairs, walked towards the front door and called out, "Who is there?" At that instant a strange, instinctive impulse made him suddenly step to his right into the open sitting-room doorway. As he did so, a gun was fired outside the front door. Black's half-formed intention had been to look through the bay window of the sitting-room to see who might be the caller. It was a precaution which he seldom took even at such a late hour.

The bullet came through the door at chest height and would probably have killed him but for his impulsive step into the sitting-room doorway.

He immediately telephoned the police station at Dunmurry.

A moment or two later, a number of soldiers under a sergeant arrived in an armoured Saracen. They said that they had been passing along Black's Road; had heard the shot and had turned back to investigate. The soldiers found the bullet embedded in the wall at the back of the hall and dug it out. A police sergeant and constable arrived shortly afterwards and took measurements where the bullet had pierced the door and wall. Neither then nor subsequently were the Blacks asked for a statement.

The Blacks thought it probable that the shot had been fired by an IRA gunman as he and his son were members of the UDR. At the same time, they resented that neither army nor police had asked for a statement about the incident. They felt that the authorities ought to have shown the same concern for the safety of members of a UDR family as they would have shown for ordinary members of the public.

The Blacks were also conscious of two strange aspects of the incident although they did not let their minds dwell on them at that time. No "getaway" car was heard speeding off as would be normal with an assassination attempt by IRA terrorists. In addition, their house was directly on Black's Road. Passing traffic was always clearly audible in it and heavy vehicles shook the entire building. Saracens are large, heavy and with multiple engines. The family was familiar with the distinctive sound and the vibration in the house when they drove past. They are confident that no such vehicle was passing along that section of Black's Road at the time of the shot.

Shortly afterwards, William Black received a letter from the Ulster Defence Regiment stating that his services were no longer required. He saw his company commander and asked for an explanation. The latter said that he had been informed that the dismissal was because he had failed to perform sufficient periods of duty and that the decision was final.

Black next wrote to the colonel who commanded the battalion and who, like all senior UDR officers at that time, was a regular army officer on temporary secondment.

He pointed out that he had a consistent record of duties in excess of the minimum required, except for a recent period of sick leave for which he had supplied the regiment with the required medical certificates. He asked for an interview with the colonel, but received a reply stating that the decision could not be rescinded.

During a visit of the Black family to relatives in the country, an eight-year-old niece had discharged a shotgun accidentally. Part of the charge had caught Black on the arm and shoulder. He had been on sick leave from both his normal work and UDR duties while he recovered from the injury. Black had informed his UDR superiors of the injury and supplied the required medical certificates. At no time had his doctor suggested that his arm and shoulder would do other than make a complete recovery. The regiment had provision for absences due to illnesses or injuries and there was no precedent for someone to be discharged for such a reason.

Black had an excellent attendance and service record. Prior to the injury, he had performed many more duties than the minimum required. In fact, he was so well in excess of the minimum that he was entitled to a special annual service bounty and was excused the requirement to attend the annual camp. He was promoted to lance-corporal within a few weeks of enrolling and held that rank until dismissed. Also, he had completed the course for promotion to full corporal. At no time had he been subject to any disciplinary charge or admonished in any way. In addition, he had at an earlier period served in the Territorial Army Volunteer Reserve and had left with excellent testimonials.

It was not possible to go beyond the commander of the battalion in the quest for an explanation. The vetting of applicants for the UDR, and the discharge of members, were at that time entirely in the hands of the Northern Ireland Army Headquarters, Lisburn.

The British Government had established the Ulster Defence Regiment in 1970 as a non-sectarian, local auxiliary to the regular army. It had emphasised and re-emphasised in the Westminster Parliament and elsewhere about the care taken in selecting recruits to ensure that they were tolerant, fair-minded persons of good standing in their communities.

Perhaps this is the key to the dismissal. Not only did William Black "know too much", but he had too much good standing for his word to be dismissed as easily as certain interested persons might have wished. One way to reduce it was by the sudden and unexplained dismissal from a reputable body.

Black, however, did not as yet see it in that way. He was only mystified and indignant.

The Black family decided to move to a new area after the 2.15 a.m. shot through their front door. It was the best way to foil further assassination attempts, assuming that the Provisional IRA had been responsible.

Houses were difficult to discover. Eventually, they secured 174 Ainsworth Avenue in west Belfast and moved in on 9th October. The remainder of the year passed without incident.

On the evening of 20th January 1973, the family was watching television in the living room. Suddenly, there were bursts of machine-gun fire outside the house. They threw themselves to the floor with the eldest daughter, Anne, holding down Honey, the dog, with her arm.

William Black went outside to investigate after a short interval. The house directly opposite his own had been struck by numerous bullets. The occupants were an inoffensive Roman Catholic family who had lived in it for a number of years. As it happened, they were not at home.

Police soon arrived. While they were examining the house, Black and his son, Tom, collected a number of empty cartridge cases in the street and handed them over. Next morning, they found additional ones which they had not seen in the dark.

Black, with his Territorial and UDR experience, noticed that the cartridges had been standard British army issue. The cases had copper percussion caps and were stamped with the date of manufacture. If they had been other than army issue, they would have had coloured percussion caps of anodised metal and no date stamped on them. The possibility that an IRA gunman would have had British army ammunition was remote.

Later in the morning, a police sergeant from Springfield Road Police Station called. He did not appear to know the family's name, but asked if a UDR man lived in the house. Mrs. Black replied that her son, Tom, was in the regiment. He mentioned the shooting of the previous evening and Mrs. Black pointed out the house which had been machine-gunned. He then explained that the police had received a telephone call stating that the house directly across the road had been shot at by mistake instead of the UDR man's house.

The sergeant drew attention to two concidences which could have misled the gunman. Black's house was number 174 and the other house number 147. Both had yellow doors. He advised the Blacks to be on the watchout for further attacks and to live as much as possible towards the back of their house.

In the evening, a captain from a guards regiment called with similar remarks and advice as the police sergeant. The Blacks were most perturbed. The machine-gun attack had been a traumatic experience and the warnings to be on guard against further attacks highly worrying.

They were even more worried by the knowledge that the gunman had used army issue ammunition. They began to see a logical relationship between it and the mysterious aspects of the shot through the front door of their former house and the inexplicable dismissal from the UDR.

If it was the Provisional IRA which was hounding them, they could secure safety by moving house to a new area. If it was the British undercover services, there was no safe place in the whole of the United Kingdom. The only ameliorating consideration was that the house fired on had been in darkness with no one at home. Perhaps, the purpose had been to intimidate rather than to kill.

Black and his wife considered emigrating to Australia and only dropped the idea when the older children resolutely refused to leave Northern Ireland. Emigration is the normal reaction of persons who have their lives threatened by a terrorist organisation. In fact, it would be unusual for a family not to emigrate which had been subject to two shooting incidents in different areas within a few months.

This may well have been the underlying motive in the harassment of the Blacks. Not only did Black "know too much", but his wife and children "knew too much". Why not ensure that they, one and all, departed for good.

The Blacks decided to remain in Northern Ireland. They were also conscious that the children had been restless and unhappy in Ainsworth Avenue. They missed the surroundings in which they had grown up and their old playmates. This factor was decisive when it was learned that 16 Horn Walk was vacant. It was close enough to the old home to enable the children to rejoin their friends and to attend their familiar schools.

Horn Walk was in a small Protestant enclave on the Lenadoon and Roman Catholic side of the Stewartstown Road. From the enclave green one could look up a hill and see six hundred comparatively new houses from which Protestant families had been driven. The outgoing family at No. 16 was Protestant. The previous one had been Roman Catholic and had been forced to leave by the communal tension. Mrs. Black subsequently explained the decision to go to Horn Walk in these words: "We decided that if we were going to be shot, we might as well be shot in a district where the children would be happy and contented."

The Blacks moved to Horn Walk in May. A week or ten days later a police sergeant from the Lisburn Station called. He said that the police had received a letter threatening the lives of the UDR men who had moved into Horn Walk. Also, that a distressed woman had called on the telephone and urged the police to stop the UDR men from moving into Horn Walk as she did not want more murders in the district.

Black, of course, was no longer in the UDR, but the use of the term would make the threats appear like the work of the IRA and link them with the previous incidents so that the family would feel truly hounded from pillar to post.

The new threats were worrying, but the Blacks decided to push them to the backs of their minds and to rely on the police for protection.

4   I Meet William Black

The present writer met William Black for the first time in August 1973. I had been elected to the short-lived Northern Ireland Assembly in a general election in the early summer. The Provisional IRA had renewed their harassment of the enclave in which Horn Walk was situated and I was on a visit one evening to talk with members of the local tenants association. The residents of the district had installed a hooter to warn of attacks. About ten o'clock it sounded.

For once the Provisionals were not the problem. A taxi had been stoned by teenagers. An army patrol had come on the scene. The stone throwers had disappeared around a corner and scattered. The patrol followed in hot pursuit around the same corner. They spotted four boys sitting on a wall who made no attempt to escape. The soldiers seized them, tossed them roughly into an armoured personnel carrier and took them to Garnock House army centre.

The children were innocent. The parents were worried and furious and the residents as a whole very indignant.

The army patrol belonged to the Queen's Own Hussars. It was nearing the end of a tour of duty and, unlike previous regiments, was unpopular with the local people. It had several officers who did not inspire local confidence; it had the reputation of being scarce when wanted for protection and had made a number of arrests of Protestant children for stone throwing on the edge of the enclave while ignoring Roman Catholic stone throwers.

Stone throwing at such a flash point was dangerous to the survival of the enclave and even one-sided arrests would have caused only limited resentment had it not been for the treatment of some of the children after arrest and especially of five arrested on July 5th.

On that occasion they were aged 12, 14, 15, 16 and 16. They were taken to the army centre at Garnock House; left standing in the open in intermittent drizzle for two and a half hours; subjected to medical checks; and photographed with a board held under the chin on which was written name, address, age, etc. They were then interrogated one by one for about fifteen minutes each by a stout man in civilian clothes with black-rimmed glasses. His language was interspersed with obscene adjectives. The interrogation room was in the basement of the building. It was draped around with black cloth and each child had to sit below a polished metal plate, approximately three feet by two feet, on which a bright light shone. Finally, the army handed over the boys to the police who promptly released them to their parents.

The army was again to impound and interrogate in the same way a boy aged 13 and three others aged 16 on 2nd September and two boys aged 12 and 14 on 12th September.

Garnock House army centre was one of the places where IRA suspects had been subjected to the special interrogation techniques when the United Kingdom government introduced detention without trial for terrorists in August 1971. Interrogation was carried out entirely by personnel from army intelligence and the detainees assigned to it were the only ones to claim before the European Commission of Human Rights that they had been forced to swallow pills. The special interrogation techniques had been exposed in the press in the following months and in early 1972 the British government had given an assurance that they were no longer in use in Northern Ireland. I heard of no case of adults being subject to the treatment which the local children received. It is probable that the basement room, draped in black, was a relic from 1971 which was kept in good order in case a change in circumstances should again permit its use. The interrogation of the children in it was probably intended to frighten them. In terms of the army's relations with the local community, it was madness and did much to explain the strong reaction by the residents to the mistaken arrests of the four children on the evening of my visit.

The hooter brought the residents quickly together. They formed a large, orderly gathering outside the nearby Woodburn army base on the Stewartstown Road and told the lieutenant-colonel in charge of the district that they would not disperse until the children were released. Some time after midnight, he informed the gathering that the children were being transferred to the police at Lisburn. The parents and several others immediately left for Lisburn which was a few miles away. I was asked to accompany them.

At the police station there was a delay while the police questioned the boys about their treatment in the custody of the army. On this occasion, no one had been subject to interrogation gimmicks. Nevertheless, several parents lodged written protests at the arrests. This caused further delay.

I spent part of the time chatting to the parent of a sixteen-year-old who had been one of the boys arrested. His name was William Black.

He was indignant at the arrest and had been much worried about the possibility of the boy being roughly handled. He mentioned that sections of the army were involved in activities which no decent person could condone. I asked him if he had first-hand knowledge of any such activity. He replied that he did have. I asked if I could meet him and hear in detail what he knew and he agreed. A day or two later, I telephoned him and arranged to call at his house.

I was convinced of the need to document at least one undercover excess of the intelligence organisations in order to demand an independent, judicial inquiry with the legal power to subpoena witnesses and to take evidence on oath. I was confident that they were sometimes operating with as little respect for the law as Al Capone. I knew that well-informed members of the Royal Ulster Constabulary were most unhappy about information which they had on their activities. Also, there were other indications pointing to the same conclusion although some had to be treated with rather more caution. One such was the revelations of Kenneth Littlejohn, the British undercover agent,* who was convicted in the Irish Republic for participating in an IRA bank robbery.

William Black told me at his home in Horn Walk the story of the attempted thefts of the vans belonging to McNamee and Shannon at Trenchard and the subsequent events which had befallen himself and family. He also described the earlier removal of his motor car from inside Thiepval Barracks. His wife, Margaret, was present. She left most of the recounting to him, but once or twice intervened to describe a particular event. On one occasion, the sixteen-year-old son, William, entered the room; remained for a short time contributing the additional detail to his father's story; and then left to meet a few of his teenage friends.

*Lord Carrington, secretary of state for Defence, admitted on 7th August 1973 that the brothers Kenneth and Keith Littlejohn had been British undercover agents.

I was impressed by the apparent honesty of the story. I heard Black retell it several times on later occasions and there was always a consistency in detail which would have been impossible if he and his family had invented it.

The police were able to confirm the incidents where they had been involved. The McNamees subsequently confirmed the accuracy of Black's description of the attempted theft of their van and gave additional information. The Darrems, too, confirmed Mrs. Black's account of the stealing of their white Vauxhall.

5 The Aim Must be a Judicial Inquiry

As already noted, three vehicles is the standard arrangement for a car bomb expedition. If that was the purpose of the vehicle thieving episode at Trenchard, it was a shocking activity for officers and men in the pay and under the orders of Her Majesty's government and, if made public, would have profound repercussions at home and abroad. On the other hand, if that was not the specific purpose, knowledgeable persons who might learn of the incident would nevertheless assume that it was.

Black had fired shots and wakened up the neighbourhood. He and his wife had talked to others. He had told his UDR superior at once and had reacted strongly and unhelpfully when ordered by the captain at Garnock House to keep secret what he had learned. His wife had told her neighbours, the Darrems, and his five children knew and were likely to talk to others. The Blacks had communicated everything to the police, a disgruntled body, full of resentment and disquiet at army domination of law and order and with numerous family and other contacts with the press and Ulster politicians, loyalist and republican.

The authorities had, in addition, the frightening question of what else William Black and his family might know. He had shown abnormal agitation when on the earlier occasion his motor car had been removed from Thiepval Barracks during his absence on the UDR night patrol and he had asserted forcibly that it could have been used for an assassination. The authorities at that time had been sufficiently alarmed to take the exceptional step of sending a sergeant-major to his home to talk to him.

The simplest way to kill the story of the Trenchard episode or to prevent confirmation, if it did spread in the locality, was to get the Blacks out of the area. At the initial stage, it was probably assumed that a shot through their front door would cause them to transfer post-haste to a healthy distance. Possibly no great thought went into the matter and the decision is likely to have been made in Ulster. It is probable, too, that, if Black had been a different type of person and had given an assurance that "he would not breathe a word", the decision would still have been to intimidate him and his family out of the district. Why risk catastrophe when a shot into a building would make everything safe?

After Black came into contact with the present writer, the authorities undoubtedly assumed that they were moving towards serious trouble. A Dublin newspaper some months later quoted a senior RUC official as saying that I was "the most dangerous of all the Ulster politicians" and the persistent covert surveillance to which I have been subjected has been ample proof that the government intelligence services in no way underrate me. During the preceding months, I had made several public references to illegal government undercover activities and had attempted to speak on the subject at the inauguration of the Northern Ireland Assembly in July 1973, but was prevented by the chairman.

Also, by a coincidence, in the same month as I first met William Black, Seán McBride, chairman of the International Executive of Amnesty International and recipient of the Nobel Peace Prize, expressed disquiet that bomb explosions in the Irish Republic could be the work of the British intelligence services. He specially singled out an explosion at Liberty Hall in Dublin and remarked, "I cannot conceive that anybody would want to destroy Liberty Hall, but that it was engineered by the British secret service to force the government to take action against the IRA." "Secret services," he commented, "often are dangerous. They are not responsible to their governments and act on their own initiative."*

No persons anywhere in the world could be more sensitive to the significance of the information which the Blacks carried around with them than the United Kingdom intelligence services nor to the consequences for themselves as individuals and as organisations should it become known and emerge on the political scene. Their core function is the acquiring and evaluating of information with political implications and phrases such as "question in parliament", "commission of inquiry" or "European Commission of Human Rights" can

*The Irish Times, 9th August 1973.

cause their alarm bells to sound before almost anyone else would sense danger.

Intelligence men work continually in dread of the project which goes wrong and embarrasses the political masters of the country. The consequence can be the end of a career (possibly in middle-age) and with minimal pension rights. The history of British intelligence has many examples. It can equally have serious consequences for the organisation itself. DI6's* *Ordzhonikidze* incident, which acutely embarrassed the prime minister, Sir Anthony Eden, during the visit of Premier Khruschiev and Marshal Bulganin in 1956,† was followed a little later by the appointment of Sir Dick Goldsmith White (an outsider from DI5) as director-general and a spate of unwelcome, internal changes.

They also know that the consequences of an embarrassment can be out of all proportion to its importance. Major-General Sir Vernon Kell, director-general of MI5 [later renamed DI5], was dismissed in 1940 following an internal administrative fiasco with secret files for which he had no personal responsibility.

It must be emphasised, too, that when an intelligence organisation has a "slip up" subordinates are as likely to have their careers destroyed as the men at the top. For instance, 212 senior agents of covert operations were dismissed in the "Hallowe'en Massacre" during the reorganisation of the CIA in the aftermath of Watergate.

Nor should it be forgotten that 1973 was the year of the Watergate verdicts. The American CIA, the most impressive and wealthiest intelligence organisation of any country, had its influence, resources and activities curtailed and a number of its officials sent to prison. The British SIS (DI6) played a mother role when America's first international intelligence organisation, the Office of Strategic Services, was established during World War II. The OSS later became the CIA, but person-to-person and operational contacts with DI6 were maintained and expanded. Miles Copeland, the former

---

*See appendix, "The United Kingdom Intelligence Organisations", for explanations of the names and functions of the intelligence services.

†Khruschiev and Bulganin arrived at Portsmouth in the cruiser, *Ordzhonikidze*. A retired naval officer, Commander Lionel Crabb, was sent at night to check if the hull had a hatch for dropping atomic mines. He was middle-aged, short-winded, needed flippers to swim any distance, unstable, eccentric, talked too much and was given neither plan nor guidance. He was not seen again alive.

senior intelligence official in both OSS and CIA, has described the relationship of the CIA and DI6 as that of a team and believes that they are closer and better co-ordinated with each other than the CIA is with the FBI.*

The Watergate proceedings were watched with intense interest by the senior officials of the British intelligence organisations. Some were on first name relations with their CIA counterparts and all would know that the revelations in Washington could be more than matched if their own organisations were to be subject to a similar scrutiny.

The British government (and its various intelligence services) was at that time hypersensitive about the European Commission of Human Rights. On 9th August 1971, it had interned without trial 230 persons suspected of being IRA terrorists. During the next few days, a number of key suspects were subjected to long periods of standing against walls, high pitched noise, lack of sleep and little food or drink in order to make them more amenable to interrogation. The cases of the maltreated internees were taken by the government of the Irish Republic to the European Commission of Human Rights at Strasbourg.

Tens of thousands of man-hours were spent on the matter by persons, ranging from the British prime minister and foreign secretary down to ordinary soldiers and policemen who had taken part in the arrests. Many of the senior men in army intelligence were closely involved as it had been responsible for the preparatory planning and for the arrests and interrogations.

The most intense activity was from the late summer of 1972 to the conclusion of the hearing of witnesses in May 1974. The oral hearings of the admissibility of the application on behalf of the internees was from 25th to 30th September 1972. The SIB vehicle thieving episode at Trenchard was on 18th August 1972 and thus came at the beginning of a period of heightened apprehension about the Strasbourg proceedings.

The Irish Republic was pushing the cases of the maltreated internees with determination. It could be assumed that it would be no less resolute if it were to have the opportunity to lay before the Commission a case of officially approved vehicle stealing for a suspected car bombing. William Black had seen only the attempted theft of two vans and his wife the theft of a motor car. But, as the

*Miles Copeland, *The Real Spy World* (1974), p. 93.

authorities had blocked any possibility of successful remedy through the courts by their decision to deny the occurrences, they had seen enough to enable the Irish Republic (or even an affected individual) to indict the United Kingdom at Strasbourg under Article 1 of the First Protocol to the Convention for the Protection of Human Rights and Fundamental Freedoms. It reads: *Every natural or legal person is entitled to the peaceful enjoyment of his possessions. No one shall be deprived of his possessions except in the public interest and subject to the conditions provided for by law and by the general principles of international law.* In addition, when the United Kingdom signed the Convention in 1950, it undertook under Article 28 (a) to provide the Commission with "all necessary facilities" for such an investigation. The wording reads: It [the Commission] *shall, with a view to ascertaining the facts, undertake . . . if need be, an investigation, for the effective conduct of which the States concerned shall furnish all necessary facilities, after an exchange of views with the Commission.*

The Commission would thus have both the duty and the acknowledged power to disect methodically the British intelligence organisations to establish the facts and motives and to apportion responsibility. It would concentrate on the fundamental questions: for what purpose were the vehicles to be stolen that night at Trenchard; who issued the orders for the operation; and what type of organisation and authority enabled such orders to be issued. It would be a development which no country has ever permitted, unless defeated in war.

The British and other governments are today rather less apprehensive about the Commission than they were at that time. The cases of the maltreated internees showed that a ruling by the Commission could be delayed for up to six years and by the Court for a further year even in the face of vigorous presentation by a signatory government. (In cases presented by individuals the delay has sometimes been up to nine years.) Cases which do not have the backing of a signatory government, or lose such backing along the way, are liable to be swept under the carpet by the Committee of Ministers to whom the Commission and Court report. Such has been the fate of the case brought against Turkey by Cyprus in connection with atrocities committed during the Turkish invasion of 1974. Most important of all, the governments (including the United Kingdom) have been able to circumscribe the effectiveness of the Commission by restricting its budget. Seventeen nation-states have subscribed to the Convention for the Protection of Human Rights and Fundamental Freedoms. They stretch from Iceland to Turkey and from Sweden to Malta. The Commission has money to employ only twenty trained lawyers to deal with the ever-increasing number of cases submitted to it. Twenty is probably fewer than is needed for the cases from Ulster at present in its files if they are to be processed within "a reasonable time" — a fundamental right spelled out in Article 6. The Commission is keenly aware of this financial limitation and is increasingly cautious and conservative in admitting new cases.

The signatory governments have been specially concerned at the threat which the Convention poses to traditional defence and intelligence arrangements. For instance, Article 9 makes official secrets acts and oaths almost useless in practice. It underscores the right of the individual to freedom of conscience and the main value of these devices is that they impose silence on the individual regardless of his conscience and are enforceable in court. Under Article 9, William Black had the right and duty to tell others of the criminal activities which he had witnessed at Trenchard. Under British law (as yet unchallenged on the matter at Strasbourg), he was committing a serious offence if he did not remain silent.

The Commission has not been unmindful of the signatory governments' apprehensions on defence and intelligence. In fact, it may now have reached a point where it operates in a manner not dissimilar to most national departments of justice* and evades taking up or runs into the sand any case which would touch on either. This is relatively easy to do with the widely drawn general principles of the Convention and the frequent use of a Nelsonian blind eye. There is, in addition, evidence that the Commission metes out the same fate to any case which would cause serious political embarrassment to a signatory government unless it is pushed by another signatory one (which is a rare occurrence) or is backed by widespread public opinion assisted by influential institutions such as Amnesty International. It is rationalised that the Commission is young, frail, deliberately starved of funds and absolutely dependent on the tolerance of the signatory governments. Attempts to use the huge

*Among such national departments of justice was the American Justice Department until the post-Watergate reforms. Prosecutions likely to reveal "classified" information were dropped by it. One consequence was that intelligence officials were in effect freed from personal criminal liability.

powers assigned to it under the Convention, it is urged, would not advance human rights and freedoms, but lead to the extinction of the Commission.

A new non-governmental, international movement (possibly similar in structure to Amnesty International) is needed urgently, first, to rally public opinion within the signatory countries for adequate funding of the European Commission of Human Rights; second, to monitor the pressures by which governments endeavour to curtail and thwart its activities; and, third, to scrutinise its proceedings and, in particular, the rationalisations and devices by which it limits its responsibilities.

I was convinced that the story which the Blacks told me in their home in Horn Walk was true. The immediate problem was to find the best way in which to have it raised at Westminster in a manner so that it would be the lever which would open the door to a wide-ranging judicial inquiry into the activities of the British secret services. There was also the problem of protecting in the interval Black and anyone else who might take up his cause.

I assumed that the more persons who had a detailed knowledge of the case, the less likely that British undercover would strike at Black or others. On the other hand, there was the fear (shared more by others than by myself) that, if his name became public knowledge, the Provisional IRA might murder him in the expectation that the action would be attributed to British undercover and make the case against it appear even more damning.

I decided to begin by bringing a lawyer into the picture and asked David Trimble to come with me to Black's house to hear the story of his experiences. He was a lecturer in law at Queen's University, Belfast and was subsequently to be a member of the Northern Ireland Constitutional Convention.

I called at Trimble's office at the university in the morning on Saturday, September 15th. We arranged to make our visit to William Black in the early evening. I telephoned Black to confirm that he would be at home and then left the university to attend a meeting with the Northern Ireland Potato Seed Marketing Board Committee.

Trimble and I travelled together to Horn Walk. We parked the car at the nearby Methodist Church on the Stewartstown Road and were immediately confronted by an army patrol. The officer, probably a second-lieutenant, asked our business. I told him my name; said that I was a member of the Northern Ireland Assembly; and that I had come with a friend to visit William Black, a constituent, in Horn Walk. The officer, young, courteous and helpful, replied, "Ah, yes, we knew that you were coming. We were looking out for you. Let us show you where Horn Walk is."

My telephone call to Black was the only way in which the army could have learned that I was coming to visit him. The most likely explanation is that the telephone line had been tapped. The patrol had then been ordered to watch out for us, but had been given no explanation and the young lieutenant had innocently blurted out the fact.

Tom Black, William Black's eldest son, had entered the Royal Ulster Constabulary after successfully completing his school examinations in the previous January and was in training at the police college at Enniskillen. On the same Saturday as Trimble and I visited his parents, he returned home on a weekend leave. In the evening, he walked in civilian clothes to Finaghy, a shopping centre, made a few small purchases and began the return walk home. As he drew level with a secondary school called Larkfield, he saw the brake lights glow on a passing car and a man with a gun lean out of the window of the forward door on the passenger side.

Tom Black instantly hurled himself over a low railing which fronted the school. The gunman fired four shots, but missed each time. As the car accelerated away, Tom whipped out a .22 calibre pistol which he, being a police cadet, carried for his own protection. He fired one shot, but the light bullet was unlikely to have penetrated the car.

It is improbable that a Provisional IRA gunman could identify a nineteen-year-old police cadet in ordinary dress when approaching from behind in a motor car on a public road. Also, the Provisional IRA forbid their members to travel armed, except when on a specific mission, as long prison sentences await them if caught with weapons in one of the frequent roadside searches by police and army.

Taken in conjunction with the various preceding incidents, the shooting at young Tom Black would seem to indicate that British undercover was again turning up the pressure on the Black family — the family which would not emigrate.

Six days later on Friday, 21st September, I brought Ernest Baird, a fellow member of the Northern Ireland Assembly, to William Black's house to hear his story. (He is now leader of the United Ulster Unionist Party.) Afterwards, Baird left to attend a function in Whitehead and I spent the evening at the house of Rev. Robert Bradford, who was to be elected member of parliament for South Belfast a few months later.

I arrived back at my own house at half-past midnight. It was in the country between Belfast and the village of Templepatrick. The avenue to the house is bisected by a small secondary road. I could see a car sitting with headlights extinguished at the junction of the main road and secondary road. Being involved in politics, I was sensitive about strange vehicles near my house. I continued past my avenue; turned into the secondary road suddenly and without signalling; and accelerated away quickly.

The car was a BMC 1800 of the kind used by the Military Police and SIB. It appeared to contain three men. A fourth was standing on his own some paces away. He wore a pale blue suit of a cut and colour more likely to be seen in one of the less socially salubrious districts of London than in sedate Ulster. When I returned ten minutes later, car and occupants had gone. It could have been a coincidence that it had been sitting parked so near to my house at that time on that particular night, but I was not completely happy about it.

However, I was already alert to the danger that government undercover might strike at any one who endeavoured to take up the case of the Blacks in order to achieve a major investigation. I had decided that the best protection would be if it realised two things. First, that various people were well versed in the details of it and other undercover excesses and, second, that much of the information had been provided by well-placed persons who would turn to some other spokesman if I were not around. Thus, it could be hoped that the undercover organisations would conclude that no one individual had information which others did not have and that to eliminate one person might trigger off an inquiry rather than prevent one.

I also decided that it was an occasion when attack was a good form of defence. Prior to meeting Ernest Baird at Horn Walk, I had distributed to the press an attacking statement designed to raise the wider issues and to remind those who controlled the intelligence organisations that the Blacks were only one of a number of possible exposures with which they were threatened. I hoped that the more they grasped this point the less obsessed they would be about the Blacks.

The statement was used by *The Irish Times, Belfast Telegraph, Irish News, Irish Press* and several Ulster local newspapers. The key part read: *The Littlejohn affair is the tip of an iceberg. The greater part of the activities of British undercover agents has been in Ulster and not in the Irish Republic. They have been aimed as much at undermining and discrediting the loyalist cause as at opposing the IRAs. They have frequently been as unlawful and outrageous as the Littlejohns claim.*

The men who control the British undercover operations in Ulster learned their trade as younger men in occupied Germony and similar areas during the cold war of Stalin and his successors. The experience of those years conditioned them to think of bomb, arson, assassination, burglary, theft, and intimidation as normal expedients. The British secret services are under anonymous heads who are responsible solely to the prime minister . . .

Edward Heath and William Whitelaw* are responsible in constitutional theory for the full story of the British undercover activities in Ulster and any serious inquiry will lead as surely to their doorsteps as the inquiry into the burglary at the Watergate building led to the doorstep of President Nixon. Nor will the constitutional and political implications be any less than those which followed in the United States.

John Morrison, the most respected of the columnists who write for Ulster newspapers, gave valuable support in the *Sunday News* two days later. He wrote: *There are strange stories going around and strange speculations current. What about those men with wigs and English accents who have been reported as doing peculiar and rather illegal things? Are not the Littlejohns only two individuals out of quite a throng? Who really did the dirty work last spring on the occasion of the weekend Vanguard and UDA demonstrations and strike? Who is really responsible for some of those explosives so expertly placed in certain religious buildings in rather unexpected*

---

*Secretary of state for Northern Ireland, March 1972 to December 1973.

48

areas of the province and so neatly calculated to bring discredit on a section of the community? Who fired that shot?*

The present generation of British secret agents will stand in the dirtiest traditions of the cold war of the 1950s. They will not boggle over a corpse or two so long as the desired effect is produced and the left hand does not know what the right hand doeth. The man at the top knows the result that he would like to achieve but he does not know and need not ask about the means that others use, even though a body such as "MI5" is supposed to be directly answerable to him . . .

Can we persuade those who have hard evidence to come out into the open and tell what they know? Not hearsay or speculation, but some hard facts? And are there those who are prepared to try to fit the pieces of the jigsaw together?

An obvious step was for William Black to record the various incidents in an affidavit. He himself felt that such a step was a civic duty. He recognised that British government undercover men might murder him. He felt that, if the affidavit were in existence, it should play a part in exposing them and their criminal outrages.

I was, in addition, keen to have one in order to remove the incentive for assassination. An affidavit detailing the story of the Blacks could be almost as effective in any court, or inquiry, as if Black were alive and present as a witness. Thus, there would be less to be gained by killing him.

I consulted William Craig, a former minister of Home Affairs in the old Northern Ireland Parliament and leader of the Vanguard Unionist Party. He suggested George Brangham, a young solicitor in his office in Lurgan, as a good person to draft an affidavit.

I introduced Brangham to the Blacks on 3rd October. He returned to Lurgan and wrote out a draft. He posted separate copies to Black and me on 10th October. (The postings are recorded in the outgoing mail register of the office.) Neither copy was received.

Brangham provided further copies of the draft affidavit. Black

*"Who fired that shot?" This is a reference to a shot fired at William Craig, leader of the Vanguard Unionist Movement, when driving his car in a safe, loyalist area near Lisburn on 4th October 1972. The loyalist paramilitary organisations and factory-based Loyalist Association of Workers had offered him the position of overall commander. Some suspected that the shot was by a government agent and was intended to discourage him from accepting.

found it too brief and the wording a little misleading in places. These defects were easily remedied and he affirmed it before Norman McSween, a justice of the peace, on the evening of 13th November. He affirmed it as he objected in conscience to swearing oaths even in a legal context. Such an affirmation is as valid in British law as the more normal oath. Quakers invariably choose to affirm rather than to swear and so do the adherents of a small number of other religious denominations.

Next day, 14th November, I told the story of William Black in some detail in a speech in the Northern Ireland Assembly and asked for support for an inquiry. I did not give his name as there continued to be the fear that the Provisional IRA might move in and murder him in the expectation that their action would be attributed to British undercover.

My account of the case was ignored by the press with the exception of the *Ballymena Guardian. The Irish Times* reported the speech in detail down to the point where I took up Black. It then moved on to the next speaker although my remarks on Black occupied five columns of *Hansard.* A factor may have been the "feed back" to the editors after my earlier statement. The middle classes and other large sections of the Ulster public refused to believe that any arm of their own British government could be guilty of criminal activities.

William Black's wife, Margaret, was the daughter of Robert Coggle. He was eighty years of age, blind and had been living alone in Belfast since the death of his wife five years earlier. At six o'clock on the morning after my speech, the old man's house was raided by soldiers. He asked them to call a daughter who lived three doors along the street, but the officer-in-charge refused. Subsequently, he had to receive medical treatment for shock. The soldiers searched the house methodically and left, admitting that they had found nothing. No other house was searched in the district.

It was a house most unlikely to contain anything subversive. Robert Coggle had had five sons. Each has had an impressive record of service to the state. Edward was in the Gordon Highlanders and had the rank of captain. Robert was a sergeant-major and Joseph a sergeant in the Territorial Army Volunteer Reserve. James served in the Royal Air Force in World War II and William was killed serving in the army in the same war.

Robert Coggle's house would have been a natural place for Margaret Black to leave documents which the family might not wish to keep in their own house. In addition, an unexplained house search at dawn by soldiers is a shattering experience and an age-old method of "leaning" on persons out of step with the wishes of a regime.

I immediately put out a press statement, giving details of the raid. The concluding sentences read: *I wish to emphasise to the authorities responsible for this scandalous incident that the family continues to be resolved that they will not be driven from Northern Ireland. Also, if the raid was an attempt to locate the sworn statements on the various earlier incidents, it was a waste of time. These statements are now safely lodged in a secure vault in a place well beyond the reach of British military and related agents.*

An inquiry into the excesses of the intelligence services could only be achieved by political pressure. The difficulties were formidable. Most Ulster people refused to believe that such things were possible. The same was true of a proportion of politicians and many of the remainder appeared not to care.

In the Northern Ireland Assembly, the Irish republican Social Democratic and Labour Party; a section of the Official Unionist Party led by Brian Faulkner; and the Alliance Party were waiting eagerly for William Whitelaw, secretary of state for Northern Ireland, to form them into an administration. They wished as much to see him or his regimé discredited as children on Christmas eve wish to see Santa Claus discredited. The only person among them to admit to any interest in the Black case was John Hume of the SDLP. During my account of it in the debate on November 14th, he went so far as to interject, "We will support you, too!"

A section of the Official Unionists led by Harry West; the Vanguard Unionists; and the Democratic Unionists were boycotting proceedings at the Assembly. Each was pledged to refuse to recognise it as a legislature or to recognise any administration which Whitelaw might form. The energies of the Harry West Unionists were expended largely in futile manoeuvres and negotiations aimed at detaching the Brian Faulkner Unionists from the Whitelaw alignment. They hesitated to be involved in joint undertakings with VUP and DUP lest it should interfere with the reuniting of the Official Unionist Party. A further difficulty was that Westite, VUP and DUP politicians were ultra-cautious in being associated with anything which might be construed as an attack upon army or police.

Political and community polarisation was even more intense in the country than in the Assembly. Any issue which was taken up by one side could expect to forfeit support from the other. If the SDLP, for instance, had moved to take up the Black case, the majority population would have tended to see it as an Irish republican plot to discredit the British government.

The VUP and DUP had formed themselves into the Loyalist Coalition. They were independent unionist parties and, unlike the Official Unionists, had no links with the mainland Conservative Party. They were led respectively by William Craig and Rev. Dr. Ian Paisley. I myself was associated with the Loyalist Coalition.

In practice most members of the Loyalist Coalition were not difficult to persuade to support a call for an inquiry into the Black case. At the same time, one realised that most saw it as yet one more among many calls for inquiries following street clashes with the army on similar controversial occurrences — calls which were made and forgotten almost as quickly by those who made them. Paisley was abroad for a week or more and there was a delay until he returned and confirmed that he supported the demand for an inquiry.

Ric Clark of the *Sunday News* was one of the few journalists with a sound knowledge of grassroot attitudes and happenings. He had built it up over the months by "on the spot" investigation and had a healthy scepticism for official explanations and assurances. On 9th December, his paper published the story that Craig and Paisley were backing a demand for an inquiry into the undercover activities of British intelligence agents. It spread across seven columns at the top of a page and carried photographs of both men. The text incorporated most of the details of the harassments of the Blacks which I had recounted in the debate in the Assembly. As in my speech, the name of the family was again withheld. Next morning, the *News Letter,* Ulster's main morning paper, carried a shorter, but substantial report.

The initial press coverage was satisfactory. Nevertheless, I was far from confident that the outcome would be an effective inquiry. The only ground for some encouragement was that Paisley was likely to see the wider implications and was a member of the House of Commons at Westminster. That was the one place where real pressure could be applied on the British government.

6 Ambush at Tully-West

Shortly after William Black and the present writer first met in August 1973 and we began the initial moves towards a public inquiry, British intelligence began its counter-move. It was based on the premises that Black "framed" as a criminal and dead would be the end of their worries and would make all demands for inquiries look foolish for a long time to come.

William Black at heart was a countryman. He grew up near Shaw's Bridge in County Down and most of his boyhood was spent on a farm. He and his wife for some years spent their holidays in camping expeditions to various parts of Ireland. In 1968, he rented a farm cottage in Islandmagee. Three years later, he decided that the shore was too dangerous for their growing children and gave it up.

He rented instead another farm cottage at Bow Loughs, Tully-West, near Saintfield, County Down. It was in a secluded spot. During the long absences of the Blacks, vandals would break windows and sometimes steal fishing tackle or other contents. On one occasion, the furniture was stolen, including the cooker.

The cottage was owned by Mrs. R. A. Morrow, a widow. She mentioned that she had a small, vacant cottage-farmhouse at 128 Middle Road, Tully-West. She pointed out that it was less isolated and had not been troubled by vandals. Also, it was within a short distance of her own house which was an additional protection.

William Black accepted the proposed exchange with alacrity. He and the family moved into the new premises during their summer holidays in July 1973. They returned on several weekends during the remainder of the summer and again for a long week-end holiday given annually in September by Short Brothers' aircraft factory.

The new premises included four outhouses. Black decided to let the largest one for the winter months as a storage place for caravans. He advertised it in the *Belfast Telegraph* on September 25th and had no trouble in finding a customer. He described what happened in the following extract from a statement which subsequently he was to make to the police: *A man came to my door and took the barn off me. I brought this man to the barn — he followed me in his own motor. I have given you a description of that motor. I had hoped to get two caravans into the barn. There was a discussion and this man told me he was going to put a caravan and an open trailer in the barn and that it was suitable for him. I had hoped to get seven pounds for each caravan, but, seeing it was the one man who was taking the lot, I agreed on twelve pounds which the man handed over in cash. This was rent up to the end of March 1974. I had a typed note with me for this man to sign stating that I would not be responsible for anything that would happen to the caravan at my barn. We signed it and put his address on it. I had only one key to this barn which I wanted to keep, but, seeing that I was not going to be there all the time, I gave him the key. I told him before he put his caravan in to move the old organ out and to put it into the old garage directly opposite this barn. After our deal he drove out the gate, turned left and I haven't set eyes on him since.*

The man who rented the barn was well dressed; of normal height and good build; he had no marked accent; his complexion suggested someone out in the open air much of the time; and his hair was short and neat — almost like an army haircut. Black thought that he might be a building contractor or of similar occupation, but did not ask him his profession. He signed the indemnity release note with the name, J. Thompson, and gave the address, 82, Farnham Street, Belfast.

Black did not know that a basic tool in intelligence work in all countries since before the First World War is the methodical and speedy reading of newspapers and especially the small advertisements. (The owner of a Provisional IRA "safe house" is unlikely knowingly to betray his passing visitors, but his little advertisement for a second-hand camp bed may do so very effectively.)

The Short Brothers long week-end holiday in September was warm and sunny. Margaret Black and the children returned home on the Sunday evening as the children had to be back at school next morning. Her husband remained on for a couple of further days to tidy up and potter around. He, too, then locked up and returned home.

William Black did not again enter the cottage until 26th January

1974, more than four months later. His description of that occasion is contained in the extract from his statement to the police with which this book began.

During the latter part of January 1974, Jim Birch, a fellow employee at Short Brothers, mentioned to William Black that he needed an interior hot water tank for his home. Black had bought one the previous summer for his cottage at Tully-West, but had decided not to install it. Birch expressed an interest in buying it. Black suggested that he visit the cottage a few days later on Saturday, 26th January, so that he could examine the tank. He himself intended to spend that day on the adjacent land shooting with his light rifle as it would be the last Saturday before the legal game hunting season closed.

On Friday, 25th, Jim Birch told Black that he had forgotten that he, his brother and a friend had promised to take a group from the Boys Brigade company attached to their church to a swimming pool on the following morning. A modified plan was agreed. Black would meet Birch as he was returning from the swimming pool at one o'clock and he, his brother and friend would make a brief visit to the cottage to see the tank before proceeding home for lunch.

The rendezvous was on the Belfast to Saintfield road adjacent to Forster Green Hospital on the outskirts of Belfast. Black arrived first in a Rover with which he had replaced his former maroon Zephyr. Five minutes later, Birch pulled his car, a Volkswagen, in behind him. Black started his car at once and led the way through Saintfield to 128 Middle Road, Tully-West. He stopped slightly past the double gates to the cottage yard; opened them; and reversed in. Birch then reversed in and left his car parked between Black's Rover and the gate.

Birch's brother was called, William, and his friend, Joe Patterson. Black had met neither man previously so introductions were made. He then said, "Hold a minute till I get the keys for the barn door." He opened the front door of the cottage; collected the keys to outhouse doors from a cabinet which stood close to the door of the front living room; and rejoined the Birchs and their friend. During the few steps he had taken into the building, he had noticed nothing unusual except a smell resembling cigarette smoke. He had dismissed it as that of a damp building which had been closed up for over four months.

Black opened the double door of the outhouse where the tank was stored. Jim Birch examined it and announced that it was exactly what he needed. (A stable separated this outhouse from the one sub-let to "J. Thompson".)

At that point, Patterson noticed a flicker of light in a small, upstairs window which overlooked the outhouses. Black laughed and said that it was unlikely. He could see a bright January sun streaming through the bare trees beside the cottage and was confident that Patterson had seen it reflected on the window. But the latter insisted that he had seen a light. Black then remembered the smell resembling cigarette smoke, but forgot about it again as Jim Birch brought the conversation back to the water tank.

"How much do I owe you, Billy?" he asked. Black replied, "Forget about the money in the meantime. Put the tank in your car and take it home. See if it will do your job. We can talk about it again on Monday at work." Black then explained that he was going to the field behind the cottage for a shot as there were foxes in it.

Black opened the door of his motor car and collected his light sporting rifle from the back seat. He loaded it at leisure, resting with one knee on the ground. The magazine consisted of a tube into which thirteen rounds are dropped one by one. The process took a little time and he chatted to the others during it. Finally, he secured the safety-lock as the police confirmed later.

He made one or two steps towards the gate which led into the field at the back of the cottage and then remembered that he had left the front door open when he collected the keys for the outhouses. He turned on his heel and retraced his steps. Jim Birch was still unhappy about the light which Patterson had seen in the window. When he saw Black walking towards the front door, he called out, "Are you sure everything is O.K.?" and suggested that he accompany him into the building. Black declined the offer. He knew that the Saintfield area of County Down had neither community nor terrorist problems and was as law-abiding as an English rural shire.

Black's intention was to close the front door, but, as he reached it, he decided first to examine the cottage for damp and to check the upstairs rooms for rain seepage in case the roof had been damaged in a violent storm a fortnight earlier. He had originally planned to make such an inspection on returning from hunting, but realised that it would be best to do it at once while the winter daylight was still strong.

Black walked straight up the stairs, holding his safety-locked gun casually under his left arm. He did not try to walk quietly as he was so confident that everything was in order. He was vaguely aware that the upper part of the house was dark, but the fact did not register fully on his mind. (The usual light was not coming through the bedroom doors which were normally left open to allow air to circulate.) As he reached the landing, he placed his right hand on the bannister post and was about to turn towards the "girls' room" which was the nearest of the two bedrooms. It was the one with the window where Patterson had seen a light.

At that instant gunmen fired from the doorways of both bedrooms. One gunman was seven metres distant; the other eight metres. He saw the dim outline of the gunman behind the flashes of his gun in the doorway he had intended to enter. (He recognised the gun as a Sterling.) He saw his smooth, disciplined movement as he showed himself to the minimum as he fired and swung back again into the room. He collapsed into the corner of the landing and, as he fell, the shadow of the man seemed to go silently back out of sight into the bedroom.

Black was in great pain and heavily shocked. Two bullets had passed through his neck and the floor of his mouth, breaking his jaw in three places, deeply lacerating his tongue and tearing apart the inside of his mouth, smashing out five front teeth and three molars and permanently destroying nerves connected with taste, hearing, speech and jaw movement. Two other bullets had ripped through his chest and stomach. One had struck him on the back. He was bleeding severely. He called out for help, but the answer was silence. He lay for a time where he had fallen. Then he saw the shadow of a second man appear in the doorway of the large bedroom at the front of the house. He pretended to be dead as he sensed that he might again be shot. The second man moved across to where he lay, pushed him with his foot as though to confirm that he was dead and quickly and silently moved back into the room from which he had come. He was the gunman who, unseen by Black, had also fired at him.

Black realised that he must find help quickly if he were to live. He struggled to the stairs and partly rolled and partly slid down them. He propelled himself on his back along the hall floor. At the front door he used the door keeper to pull himself to his feet. He left great smears of blood on the door post and a pool of it on the floor. He headed towards his car in the yard expecting to be shot in the back. It was blocked in by Jim Birch's Volkswagen. He struggled out to the road; looked up and down for a passing car. There was none. He then remembered the neighbouring farmer, Morrison Seawright. His house was down a short lane about three hundred yards along the road in the direction of Saintfield.

The road dipped down and then climbed up a hill. Black staggered along it, instinctively taking what cover he could from a wall and then a hedge. As he struggled up the hill, a man inside the front door of the cottage fired at least five shots at him from a pistol. Another emerged unto the public road and began shooting at him with a sub-machine-gun. (William Birch later described how "all hell seemed to let loose with shooting"). Black heard the bullets striking around him and saw the sparks from the nickel jackets of ones which hit the road surface. He heard the whine as they ricocheted. He did not look back at the men firing at him, but concentrated with desperate intensity on reaching Seawright's farmhouse.

Black reached it and found Seawright. He urged him to take him to the police station in Saintfield as he knew that the police would find him medical help as quickly as possible.

Seawright drove Black to the police station, but it was closed for lunch. He drove off uncertain what to do. He then saw a UDR landrover at a petrol filling station. He shouted to the driver who ran across to his car. He told him to drive to the Saintfield UDR post as it could provide first aid.

The UDR men on duty brought Black into the guardroom and began to do what they could for him. He handed over his wallet, firearm certificate for his sporting rifle and three key rings with all his keys. He saw that they could not understand his speech and signalled for pen and paper. Someone obliged and he endeavoured to write his home telephone number.

Dr. J. M. McKelvey, the district doctor in Saintfield, came quickly. (He arrived at 1.50 p.m.) He found Black sitting in a chair with the UDR men doing their best to staunch the heavy bleeding. He made him lie down on a stretcher on the floor and gave him oxygen from a cylinder.

In the prone position, Black saw a regular soldier come up close and stand looking down at him. He spoke no word, but the impression of hostility in his flint-like face burned into his memory.

He was the only regular soldier present and there was the striking contrast between his expression and that of the kindly UDR men. He was about six feet in height, well built and exceptionally fit with no surplus flesh. He had sharp features and wore combat green uniform (not camouflage green). He was a commissioned officer as he wore a pistol. His beret was blue or dark green and had a regimental badge which Black had never seen before during his years with the Territorial Army and UDR. It consisted of a Roman style sword supported by two upright hawk's wings.

An army doctor arrived in an army ambulance shortly after Dr. McKelvey. Black was lifted into the ambulance and the army doctor and a policeman, Constable John Savage, accompanied him. He asked to be taken to a Belfast hospital as his wife was in poor health and he did not want her to have to travel more than necessary. A little later he asked for pen and paper. The doctor gave him a wrapping from a bandage and he wrote something on it.

Constable Savage then gave Black a note book and he wrote, "Get my Rover home to Suffolk. Son policeman." He asked him if he had seen anything and he wrote, "Get my rifle. Hiding upstairs in house." The doctor asked if he had been shot before. He remembered the incident eighteen months earlier when his eight-year-old niece had accidently discharged the shotgun and wrote, "July". The doctor remarked that he had survived before and would do so again. Black replied on the notebook, "Christ is my Saviour". A little later the constable asked if he had seen any other cars. He wrote, "No other cars in sight". He then continued, "Break it to my wife easy — Suffolk".*

Looking back at a later date, William Black's main recollection of the journey was the ambulance bumping him as it went along the road and the dim shadows of people and their voices for what appeared to be a long time.

Six armed men were lying in ambush at the cottage at Tully-West when William Black, the Birch brothers and Joe Patterson arrived on Saturday, 26th January. One was armed with a sub-machine-gun

*Wm Black's remarks during the ambulance journey are recorded in Const. John Savage's statement of evidence.

fitted with a silencer. They had been waiting since the Thursday. Subsequently, the army acknowledged them as members of the SIB. Two were from the Special Air Service (SAS), the much-feared regiment specialising in undercover and commando operations. The army has declined to admit to this fact, but it has been confirmed from other sources. The remaining four were on secondment from the Royal Engineers. All six wore army uniform and some had army-issue, small, close-knitted woollen caps.

One of the unit was recognised as an army intelligence man seen at the Giant's Ring, which is also in County Down, following a mysterious murder a few months earlier. This last fact in particular was to cause one or two of the local police to have serious misgivings about their own safety when they came to investigate the shooting of William Black.

One SIB man was stationed in each of the two bedrooms upstairs; one in the working kitchen downstairs; and three outside in outhouses. They had plimsoll-type footwear, which explains the silence of their movements noted by Black at the time he was shot. The one in the "girls' bedroom" had the sub-machine-gun with the silencer. He was also equipped with a camera and was a good photographer. He was a chain smoker and had a candle burning from which to light cigarettes. It was the flame of the candle which had caught Patterson's eye when he had declared that there was a light in the window. The officer-in-charge was in the "large" bedroom. He had dark hair and sideburns and wore a dark-coloured beret.

SIB inside the cottage saw William Black and Jim Birch park their cars. They radioed to their contact centre the makes and registration numbers. They heard William Black open the door of the cottage and collect the keys for the outhouses from the cabinet. The photographer took several pictures from the bedroom window.* One shows the four men standing near the water tank and another them chatting while Black was leisurely loading his sporting rifle.

He may have followed the conversation of Black and his companions in the yard just below him and learned that they were discussing the purchase of a water tank and that Black intended to shoot foxes in the field behind the cottage. The present writer positioned himself at the window and followed without difficulty a normal

*The police subsequently obtained prints of the photographs from the army authorities. They are in colour.

conversation carried on at the same place. Black, the Birchs and Patterson were employed in noisy workshops and had developed the habit of speaking a little more strongly than average. Their conversation would have been easy to follow.

He would see Black take the steps up the yard towards the gate into the field and then retrace them as he remembered about the open front door. He and the officer-in-charge in the other bedroom would know from the footsteps that only one person had entered the house. They would see Black emerge up the short stairs with his back to them and with his sporting rifle held casually under his left arm.

Neither man challenged him and they fired as he laid his right hand on the top of the bannister post and began to turn towards the bedroom that he intended to enter. The officer fired four or five shots in rapid succession. He probably used an automatic pistol and, if so, he was a trained marksman as the bullet holes formed a tight pattern on the wall. The man with the weapon fitted with the silencer fired excessively and continued the burst as he swung back into the room as the door had holes where bullets had passed through it from inside the room. Altogether he fired seventeen bullets.

The man with the silenced weapon immediately crossed the bedroom to the window; broke a pane of glass and pushed his sub-machine-gun through it to cover the Birch brothers and Patterson.

They were standing close to the open outhouse astounded and shocked. They had seen Black enter the cottage and "five seconds later" had heard four or five shots and the scream as he was blasted. (They did not hear the seventeen shots from the silenced weapon.) Next, they saw a man appear at the window above them and the barrel of his "snub-nosed" machine-gun break its way through the pane.

They scattered into the outhouse and threw themselves to the ground near the front wall. The back wall had a small, two-pane window about one and a half metres from the floor. William Birch was the first to see it. He hurled himself through the lower pane although it measured only 51 cms. by 48 cms. The other two men quickly followed. All were absolutely terrified and ran through field after field without stopping. They assumed that the cottage was occupied by IRA gunmen.

The SIB in the cottage later stated that they heard Black slither and roll down the stairs and stagger from the front door. Possibly, the two upstairs were preoccupied with the problem of the escaping Birchs and Patterson. The one in the working kitchen may have been uncertain of the situation and waited for orders. At any rate, there was a moment's pause before one rushed to the front door and fired shots from a pistol at Black and another emerged unto the public road and began to empty his sub-machine-gun at him. Black was already about one hundred metres distant and forcing himself along in desperate determination. The range of the Sterling sub-machine-gun for accurate shooting is a little less than one hundred metres. The fleeing Birchs and Patterson, now some distance away, heard the renewed firing. As already noted, William was later to describe how "all hell seemed let loose".

The SIB watched Morrison Seawright's car — a dark green Ford Cortina — leave his house and assumed that Black was in it. They radioed the information to their outside contact. RUC District Headquarters, Newtownards, was given a description of the car and told that it was carrying a wounded man. It was asked to instruct all police to look out for it. It was also given descriptions of two other cars with their registration numbers. They were the ones belonging to William Black and Jim Birch. Both vehicles were sitting where parked in the cottage yard. Presumably, the confusion arose in the radio communication centre and was based on the earlier radio messages from the SIB unit. Newtownards RUC radioed the message to Saintfield Police Station where it was received at 1.40 p.m. in the middle of lunch.

Norman Dempster and Gary Nummy were rabbit shooting some five or six hundred metres from William Black's cottage. The former was a full-time member of the RUC police reserve, but in civilian clothes. His wife and her sister, Miss Ann Dickson, were strolling in conversation some distance behind them.

They heard harsh shots, a scream and softer sounding machine-gun fire. The sounds came from the direction of the cottage and the scream had an almost pleading note. The harsh shots would have been the pistol fired at Black from the front door and the softer machine-gun fire the weapon discharged at him by the man who stood on the public road. Black does not remember giving a scream at that stage, but agrees that he may have.

Dempster and Nummy were in front of the cottage and separated from it by a field of gently sloping, grazing land. Their view was partly obscured by a hedge. They walked rapidly towards it, crossed the hedge and were on the public road in front of it. A man in army uniform, with bare head and a rifle, was standing towards one end of the building. He pointed it at them and ordered them to drop their shotguns. They did as ordered. Dempster then said that he was in the RUC police reserve and produced his policeman's identity pass. His wife and Ann Dickson next arrived and he and Nummy sent them back to the Dempster home which was a short distance away.

Dempster and Nummy saw empty cartridge cases lying at the gate to the cottage where they had been ejected by the machine-gun as it was fired on the public road and a further five or so lying partly in a pool of blood at the front door.

Nummy went up to the front door. At that moment, one of the SIB began to come down the stairs and immediately pointed a black pistol at him. He held it with both hands in the manner of a trained pistol marksman and adopted a semi-crouching position as he completed the remainder of the steps. The man looked murderous and Nummy feared that he was about to be shot. Instead, he searched him roughly. He was the officer-in-charge with the sideburns and dark beret.

The SIB unit assumed that the Birchs and Patterson were still in the outhouse and that they might be armed. Part of the interior was hidden by the front wall and a closed half of the double door. They began to call on them to come out and that, if they did not, they would send in the dogs. The latter was a fictitious threat as the unit had no dogs.

A helicopter arrived after ten or fifteen minutes. It flew straight to the cottage as though the pilot already knew its location; banked around to select the best landing spot and landed. A man dressed in a tweed jacket and brown, outdoor trousers emerged. He wore a flak-jacket and pistol and was clearly a senior officer. He was forty to forty-five years of age, with slightly greying hair, and ran nimbly from the machine to the cottage. He quickly became involved in the exercise to flush out the non-existant Birchs and Patterson from the outhouse.

A little later regular soldiers arrived by road and a number of UDR. Dempster and Nummy left for home shortly after the latter arrived.

The Birchs and Patterson ran for fifteen or twenty minutes across fields after they escaped through the little window in the back wall of the outhouse. They eventually reached a farm house. It had no telephone, but the owner directed them to his son's farm which was nearby and had one. They telephoned the RUC station at Saintfield and told what they knew. The information was relayed to the station sergeant, Sergeant Ian Henry Brown, who was with William Black in the UDR guardroom. He immediately left with Constable Robert Patterson for the cottage in a patrol car.

A number of army vehicles were parked on the road close to the cottage. The army officer in charge was standing at the gate. Sergeant Brown asked him what had happened. He replied, "We have two cars here. There is stuff in the outhouse and my men have found a gun in the house. We have three men in one of the landrovers. You cannot touch anything and you cannot go into the house." The sergeant asked a further question and was told, "It will be made clear to you in due course. I am waiting for detectives and your chief."*

The three men to whom the army officer referred were the Birch brothers and Joe Patterson. Soldiers had collected them at the farm from which they telephoned the police. They had searched them "most vigorously" and were holding them in a landrover parked close to the cottage. Sergeant Brown and Constable Patterson walked across to them and they gave a brief account of their experience. The sergeant then went back to the patrol car and reported by radio to his base.

He returned towards the dwelling, but, at that moment, Chief Inspector D. A. McClintock arrived from RUC District Headquarters, Newtownards. He was accompanied by Detective-Inspector Desmond Browne and Detective-Constable James Beattie Wilson. The officer admitted all three to the cottage. The time was 2.45 p.m.

Five spent cartridge cases were lying on the doorstep from the pistol of the man who had fired at Black as he escaped along the road. In the room to the left on entering the hallway, the army officer raised the upholstered section of a bed-settee and showed Chief Inspector McClintock and his two men a parcel resting on the springs. It was wrapped in polythene and contained a semi-automatic Star pistol. On the landing there was a large pool of blood with

*The description of the arrival of Serg. Brown and Const. Patterson at the cottage is contained in their statements of evidence.

Black's light sporting rifle lying in it with the safety lock securely in position. Several holes made by the silenced sub-machine-gun were noted in the bedroom door. There were no spent cartridge cases in the room. A soldier admitted that he had them in his pocket. Detective-Inspector Browne asked for them. The soldier consulted his officer who ruled that they were not to be surrendered to the police, pending instructions from Brigade Headquarters.

Constable Wilson found a bronze-coloured tea caddy in a corner of the room where the Star pistol had been located. It contained sixty-five rounds of 9 mm ammunition in a plastic bag, one .320 revolver round in a discarded cigarette carton, two .32 revolver rounds, three .38 revolver rounds, six .32 auto rounds, twenty 9 mm rounds in a .22 ammunition carton, one cleaning brush, an envelope with six .177 darts and a pair of gloves.*

He also found forty-eight rounds of .22 ammunition in a drawer in the cabinet in the living room. They, however, had been left in it by Black when rabbit shooting in the previous summer and were for his legally-held sporting rifle.

At 3.05 p.m., the police were reinforced by the arrival of a finger-print expert, photographer and "scene of crime officer".

Attention was next focused on the outhouse which had been rented by "J. Thompson" and which, the army officer claimed, contained "stuff". The only window was in the back wall and was boarded up on the inside with the top of an old tea chest with the silver paper still attached. It was impossible to see into the building from the window.

The door had been made from corrugated metal by a local black-smith and was exceptionally strong. It was secured by an expensive, pick-proof padlock. One of Black's children had found it when playing on the site of a factory which was being demolished. It had probably been used to secure one of the factory's strong rooms. A single key had been in position in the lock when found and Black had given it to "J. Thompson" at the time of the letting.

The padlock baffled the police lock expert. The army was unable to help. Neither then nor later was it able to explain how it knew that there was "stuff" in the building when it had neither the ability to open the door nor to see through the window.

*The description of the police examination of the cottage is contained in the state-ments of evidence of Chief Inspector McClintock, Det.-Inspector Browne and Const. Wilson.

The police eventually brought metal cutting equipment and forced open the door. Inside were twenty-seven refrigerators, £1,500 worth of carpets and a quantity of wines. They were stacked to the roof and all were stolen property.

Daylight was beginning to fail by that time and Chief Inspector McClintock arranged for a joint, overnight guard of the premises by police and soldiers.

On the following day, a rifle was uncovered in a stone boundary wall at the rear of a fuel store outhouse and an air rifle in an old organ in the "J. Thompson" outhouse. The darts already found in the cottage fitted it.

The senior commanders of the regular army at Northern Ireland Headquarters, Lisburn, reacted decisively to the news of the shooting. They had the SIB unit at Tully-West arrested and placed in cells where they remained for one or two days. New troops from 23rd Royal Engineers were brought in from a distance to work with the police in the search of the premises. A brigadier travelled to the cottage by helicopter. He spent some time at it and showed the keenest interest in all details.

It is known that the regular army was most unhappy about the activities of army intelligence carried out in conjunction with shadowy civilians. Black's earlier harassments had received considerable publicity in the preceding weeks and particularly in the *Sunday News* article of December 9th. The senior commanders would note the press items and could easily learn his name from army sources. Possibly, they may have been rather expecting something to happen to him.

The assertion of authority by the regular army was temporary. The members of the SIB unit were released from their cells. One report said that they were transferred out of Northern Ireland shortly afterwards, but the present writer has been unable to confirm it.

In the late afternoon, the army press office in Lisburn issued a statement that an army patrol near Saintfield had sighted a man in the middle of a field aiming a rifle at them. He continued to aim it at them after being challenged and the soldiers had been forced to fire, in self-defence, wounding him. The BBC broadcast this version in each of its Ulster news bulletins during the following day. By Monday, the army press office had modified the story to an account of how a routine army patrol had arrived at a farmhouse when two cars with four men in them pulled up in the yard outside. The men got out of the cars and one was observed to be carrying a gun. The soldiers challenged the man with the weapon and, when he did not drop it, they opened fire hitting him in the body.

It is possible that the strange content of the army press statements arose from confusion and lack of information at army headquarters. The SIB unit were in the cells. The statements may thus have been based on such fragments of information as had been picked up by regular soldiers. The initial one that a man standing in a field had continued to aim a rifle at soldiers, after being challenged, and had been shot could have been a garbled reference to Norman Dempster and Gary Nummy who were rabbit shooting in the adjoining field. When the story was queried, the press office probably turned as a last resort to the radio operators for information. They would tell them that the radio messages indicated that four men in two cars had driven up to the cottage. Each army press office statement asserted that the soldiers only opened fire after a challenge had been ignored. However, it was common procedure for the office to add such a phrase to statements when soldiers had fired shots on the assumption that they always obeyed their "yellow card" instructions.

7 The Instruction was: "Kill Black"

Information has come from inside the officer corps of the Special Air Service Regiment that one of their number was sent across to Ulster with the instruction to kill William Black.

The assignment to assassinate an innocent, married man with five children and strong evangelical Christian beliefs caused intense indignation among certain army officers who subsequently came to learn about it from army sources. One is known to have declared that he never believed the British army could sink so low and to have considered resigning his commission. Nor was the officers' mess at the regimental depot of the SAS at Hoarwithy Road, Hereford, immune from the indignation. It is a small, elite regiment with a strong sense of regimental honour and professional integrity. It is suggested, too, that the officer given the task had it emphasised to him that Black was an exceptionally dangerous subversive and that he had no opportunity during his brief, special visit to Ulster to check the truth of what he had been told.

The fact that an SAS officer was assigned the "Saintfield job" raises a special question mark over the one who entered the guardroom at the UDR post as Black lay on the stretcher on the floor and stood looking down on him with a flint-like face.

The incident made a vivid impression on Black's mind. He told the present writer about it at our first long discussion after the shooting and was keen to draw a picture of the Roman sword and hawk's wings that formed the officer's regimental badge. There was no pen or paper convenient and I suggested that he leave it until another occasion. I added that, in the meantime, I would try to locate a handbook to regimental badges so that we could identify it. At that time, I suspected that the officer belonged to a regular regiment stationed in the area. A few days later, Black described the badge to Robert Fisk, the correspondent of *The Times*, and he recognised it at once as that of the Special Air Service Regiment.

The fact that the officer wore his SAS beret and badge is noteworthy. The Provisional IRA and other anti-British groups for sometime had been attributing various atrocities to the SAS. The government in reply had been asserting repeatedly that no SAS were deployed anywhere in Northern Ireland. The controversy was well known and the army and Northern Ireland Office were ultra-sensitive about it. No member of the SAS could have been in Ulster for any length of time without fellow-officers or someone more senior instructing him to remove all indications of his regiment. The beret and badge by themselves are strong evidence that he was a new arrival.

As has been explained, it is known from inside the Special Air Service Regiment that the shooting of William Black was a calculated assassination attempt carried out on specific orders. A critical examination of the details of the episode leads independently to the same conclusion. The answers to seven questions are particularly relevant.

Question 1: Why was the key gunman equipped with a sub-machine-gun fitted with a silencer? The presence of the weapon fitted with a silencer is a formidable pointer that the purpose was to assassinate and not simply to effect an arrest. The man equipped with it had the key role in the operation in that he was stationed in the bedroom with the window which commanded a view of the entrance from the road, the yard and the outhouses. The man in the other bedroom could see only fields and a section of the road to Saintfield. The one in the working kitchen and the three in the outhouses could see little or nothing.

Question 2: Why was Black not challenged? Black heard no challenge nor did the Birchs and Patterson hear one as they stood outside the building. The latter heard only four or five shots from the unsilenced weapon and Black scream.

Every soldier in Northern Ireland carries a code of instructions printed on a yellow card from which he is forbidden to depart. It is firm and explicit on the absolute necessity of a clear challenge in all confrontation situations.

If Black had been challenged by two men with guns at the ready and only seven and eight metres distant, he would have realised the hopelessness of resistance or flight and have surrendered at once.

Question 3: Why did the SIB fire instantly and excessively when

Black was not a threat to their lives? The yellow card instructions forbid a soldier to open fire in any circumstance whatsoever, unless his own life is in danger from a raised weapon or the life of another person. All other situations, including that of assumed hostile persons carrying firearms, are to be resolved by the minimum force necessary short of firing a weapon.

Black was cut down by the gunmen in total defiance of yellow card instructions. They were concealed in the doorways of the bedrooms and fired the instant he reached the closest point without seeing them. His sporting rifle was held casually under his left arm with the muzzle pointing downwards and was no threat to anyone at that moment.

In addition, the man who discharged some five pistol shots at Black from the front door of the cottage did so in defiance of yellow card instructions. Equally, the man who emerged unto the public road acted contrary to the yellow card when he discharged his sub-machine-gun at him.

Question 4: Could Black have been fired on through surprise or panic? It cannot be contended that the savagery of the onslaught on Black was because the SIB were taken by surprise. They saw the cars being parked; radioed the registration numbers and other details; heard him obtain the keys from inside the cottage; saw him open the outhouse; watched and photographed him as he talked at length with his companions and leisurely loaded his sporting rifle. The man in the bedroom overlooking the yard may have followed the conversation and learned the innocent nature of the visit. He would see him walk towards the gate of the field; change his mind and proceed towards the front door of the cottage.

The arrival of Jim and William Birch and Joe Patterson appears to have been unexpected and to have thrown the pre-laid plan into such disarray that Black was able to escape, but tactical confusion of that kind is totally different from the surprise confrontation that triggers the unpremeditated reaction.

Nor was there panic. Neither man showed panic or inexperience. Black noted the smooth, trained movement of the one whom he saw fire. The speed with which the same man turned his attention to the Birchs and Patterson indicated a cool, collected person. So, too, did the action of the second man in crossing to Black to push him with his foot.

Question 5: Could the SIB at the cottage have mistaken Black for

70

someone else? There was no indication of uncertainty on the part of the SIB in the bedrooms. The one with the weapon fitted with a silencer had ample opportunity to study Black in the yard just under him and to assure himself of his identity. Neither the police nor Mrs. Morrow, the owner of the cottage, was asked for the name of the occupant either prior to or during the three days of the ambush. This is firm evidence that army intelligence already had the information.

Troops in an arrest or ambush squad are supplied beforehand with photographs of the target person or persons and are required to memorise them as well as to carry them on the operation. It is one of the justifications for the immense collection of photographs of the Ulster public built up under Westminster "direct rule" by the ubiquitous army photographers, using their telephoto lenses, and is standard procedure whether the troops are regulars, Royal Military Police or SIB. In the case of William Black, photographs of him were easily available in his UDR and Territorial and Army Volunteer Reserve personnel files.

Question 6: Why were the police not informed of the ambush? The police were at no time informed that the SIB unit was in ambush at the cottage. This fact later caused much indignation within the RUC. Even at that period when army intelligence and SIB felt no obligation to liaise with the police, they normally asked them to undertake pre-planned arrests of civilians. In addition, there was the practical consideration that, if the police were not told of an arrest ambush, they were likely to intrude into it either on their own initiative or as a result of local people reporting the presence of strangers.

Question 7: Why were the SIB totally unable to explain, first, how they came to learn that there were weapons and stolen goods at the cottage and, second, why they were so confident that the latter were in the "J. Thompson" outhouse although they could neither see into it through the window nor were able to open the lock? At first they asserted that they were acting on intelligence information that the premises was a UDA hideout, but later dropped the claim when pressed to substantiate it.

The Black family were soon eliminated from suspicion of being involved. They made long and detailed statements and provided all the information they could to help the police. When these were checked and cross-checked, the latter were convinced that they were completely truthful. Policemen questioned numerous residents in the district around Tully-West about the cottage and the family. Afterwards one of them remarked, "There was not a person, but had a good word of William Black." Not a single fingerprint belonging to any member of the family was found on the stolen goods, illegal weapons, or ninety-seven items of illegal ammunition concealed in the tea-caddy.

The police sensed quickly that they were dealing with a "frame up" by British intelligence. Some were apprehensive about their own safety, but persevered with their work. They did not know about the earlier harassment of the Black family during the first stages of their investigations. A little time after her husband was shot, Margaret Black showed the RUC officer responsible for the case several items, including the *Sunday News* article of December 9th. He read them and remarked, "Most interesting! Most interesting, indeed! Now it adds up."

The Star pistol located in the settee in the cottage immediately aroused suspicion. It had the serial number 1127606 and had belonged to a man in Belfast called Todd. He had been authorised to carry it as he was in the Ulster Defence Regiment. A year earlier, he had been shot and killed during a confrontation between soldiers and local residents in the Shankhill district of the city. The weapon had disappeared at the time of the incident and had neither been handed over to the police nor returned to relatives for disposal to a licensed gun dealer.

The police were unable to discover the persons responsible for stealing the merchandise in the "J. Thompson" outhouse. (It is understood that some of it was traced to a motor van which had been hijacked in Belfast.) Possibly, it was obtained from ordinary criminals in Belfast or from mafia elements associated with one of the less-reputable urban paramilitary groups. As will be pointed out in a later chapter, British intelligence liaises closely with the criminal world, including stolen goods, drug pushing and brothels.

The members of the SIB unit at the cottage signed statements about the shooting and the army passed them to the police. They claim that Black was challenged to halt, but did not. They state that the men in the cottage heard him struggle down the stairs and escape from the front door. One man admitted firing a pistol and another a

Sterling as he was escaping on the road. They claimed that they fired in the air over his head. The statements assert that the three men who arrived with Black were apprehended, but later escaped through the window in the outhouse in which they were being held. They were not apprehended and this error of fact indicated that the statements were prepared for signing by someone who had not been present at the incident. Nor would such a procedure have been an innovation. There have been protests in courts in Northern Ireland at the presentation of statements on behalf of soldiers, which were so verbally identical as to raise the question of the extent to which signatories were responsible for them.

The army ambulance took William Black to the Musgrave Military Hospital in Belfast. He remembers a hospital ceiling. It consisted of white tiles with holes through which air was filtered. He remembers the rubber tubing of the blood pressure instrument being inflated around his arm. He remembers a woman's voice saying, "No blood pressure. No pulse." It was followed immediately by a panicky man's voice saying, "Heart massage. Quick!"

He remembers regaining semi-consciousness at a later period and a woman's voice saying that the police were outside, but not allowed in. He struggled to reason out why they should not be allowed in. She said that she had some questions which they had written on a piece of paper and could he try to give answers. He does not remember what they were except that one was about the water tank at the cottage.

He remembers his wife's voice saying that it was the army which had shot him. His mind refused to credit it. He believed that he was dying, but kept wrestling with the question, "Why should the army shoot me down in my own cottage?" The more he wrestled, the more improbable it seemed. He kept worrying in his semi-conscious state whether the Birchs and Joe Patterson had been shot.

As Margaret Black was waiting to be admitted to see her husband, a soldier approached her and said, "Your husband's clothes are in a terrible state and totally useless. Please sign this chit so that we can dispose of them." A young policeman, who was waiting in case Black should regain sufficient consciousness to be questioned, heard him and intervened. He told her on no account to sign the chit as the Royal Ulster Constabulary would require the clothes for forensic tests.

On the following day (Sunday), Margaret Black telephoned to tell the present writer that her husband had been shot. I had already heard on a BBC newscast the army press office statement that soldiers had shot a man in a field near Saintfield as he continued to aim a gun at them after being challenged.

We agreed that she must find a good lawyer as soon as possible. I consulted a couple of members of the law faculty at Queen's University and several other persons and reported back that there was a consensus recommending a particular solicitor. She telephoned him and he agreed to act.

By the time Black reached the Musgrave Military Hospital, his right lung had filled with blood and had collapsed. On the operating table his heart stopped, but the operating team managed to restart it. Over two days, he received fourteen pints of blood in transfusions. The surgeon was Colonel Boyd of the Royal Army Medical Corps. Black was much impressed by his dedication and kindliness and the civilian surgeons at the Ulster Hospital, to which he was transferred two weeks later, spoke highly of his skill. Part of the credit for Black's survival, however, must go to an outstandingly dedicated orderly from Wales, known as Taffy. He spent up to eighteen hours a day in attendance and even had his meals brought to him in the ward.

A month after the shooting, The Ulster Hospital permitted Black to return home. There was keen apprehension lest he should again be attacked, but, despite appeals to the secretary of state, the Northern Ireland Office refused to allow a police guard for his home. A short time later, he and his family transferred to a house in a district outside Belfast. When he had recovered a little from his injuries, he sawed in two his light sporting rifle and gave it to the police at the local station. When asked why he had destroyed a valuable gun, he remarked, "Rabbits, too, have their feelings."

8 Nobody Wants to Know

Following the shooting of William Black, the most urgent task was to endeavour to organise support for an inquiry. Rev. Dr. Ian Paisley of the Democratic Unionist Party was one of the few persons keen to help.

The shooting took place on a Saturday. On Monday, a meeting was demanded with Francis Pym, a newcomer who had replaced William Whitelaw as secretary of state for Northern Ireland some weeks earlier at the beginning of December. It was granted for the following day and a deputation was formed consisting of Dr. Paisley, leader of the DUP; Rev. William Beattie, deputy leader of the same party; Cecil Harvey, Vanguard Unionist Assembly member from the Saintfield area; and the present writer.

The deputation told the story of the harassment of the Blacks over the months and emphasised the various indications that the government's undercover organisations were responsible. In conclusion, a major inquiry was demanded and police protection for Black.

Pym listened impassively. I found myself wondering if he were really as indifferent as his expression and few comments suggested.

In Parliament two days later, Paisely asked James Prior, leader of the House of Commons, to permit him to make a statement to the House on the matter. Prior declined the request and pointed out that A. D. P. Duffy, MP for Attercliffe, Sheffield, already had a question on Northern Ireland on the order paper.

On Tuesday, 5th February, Duffy's question came up and was answered by Ian Gilmore, secretary of state for Defence. It was a general question on the operations of the army in Northern Ireland. Gilmore said, "The army has worked with the civil authority to bring about a reduction in violence and will continue to do so as long as it is necessary."

Paisley had to be in Ulster that day, but Kevin McNamara, MP for Kingston-upon-Hull, realised that the Black issue was being avoided and intervened to say that MPs were concerned about the serious allegations which had been made. He continued, "It is incumbent upon the government to refute them in the most absolute detail."

Gilmore replied, "I cannot do much more than say that what was said was absolute nonsense."

In his answer, Gilmore also took up and dismissed as totally unfounded a claim which Paisley had made several weeks earlier in the Commons that his own life was in danger from government agents. It had not been taken seriously by MPs or press and the Black case was discredited by being placed alongside the earlier claim. Paisley had based his assertion about the danger to himself on a warning from inside the security forces and this fact meant that he could not establish the credibility of it by revealing the source of his information.

In the meantime, on Saturday, 2nd February, an abridged copy of the police forensic report on William Black's injuries was secured. Paisley and I issued a joint statement spelling out that the authorities had made inaccurate claims about the shooting and referred to the information in the forensic report.

The local press and *Daily Express* gave reasonable coverage, but the state-owned BBC was a different story. I had given about half of the statement to a copy stenographer by telephone (a normal procedure) when a man with a southern or midland English accent intervened. He said that he could not have a girl's time wasted by taking down statements of that kind. I pointed out that it was a joint statement on behalf of Dr. Paisley and myself and that he was the best-known Ulster MP at Westminster and leader of a major Ulster party. He replied that he did not care and anyway he knew about the Black shooting and there was no truth in what we were saying. I asked to speak to the person in charge of the station. He replied that he was.

The local newspapers in Ulster printed our press statements, but did not follow up the Black story on their own despite the clear indications of sinister and dramatic happenings. Belfast has three dailies and a Sunday newspaper. As with most provincial newspapers, stories tend to be written in the reporters' office with a minimum of telephone calls to check facts and with one eye on the deadline for going to press. Much local news consists of accounts of terrorist and army activities and reporters rely heavily on the army press office* for immediate and up-to-date information. It was known that it could be unco-operative. There had been various cases of "blacked" journalists although usually as a result of pro-IRA stories.

On 7th February, I wrote to Derrik Mercer, assistant news editor, *The Sunday Times*, suggesting that the paper's Insight team should investigate the Black shooting and earlier harassments. A Westminster general election was in progress and newspaper staff fully engaged. Once it was out of the way, he sent across the correspondent, David Blundy. He arrived on Monday, 18th, and spent several days investigating the shooting. He received every courtesy from the army and a certain amount of information. It stressed that it accepted that Black had nothing to do with the stolen goods or weapons found at the cottage. This stance may have been the result of the influence of senior officers of the regular army, assisted by a warning from Black's solicitor that he would take legal proceedings should any new statement or comment on behalf of the army be libellous.

Blunay's report appeared in *The Sunday Times* on 24th February. Unfortunately, he did not have certain items of information such as the history of the Star pistol found at the cottage. He pointed out that the army version of the shooting prompted the questions: Why, if the army believed that it had caught three terrorists, did it let all of them escape? Why, if either Black or his friends were suspicious characters, would they first contact the police? Why was Black shot when the army's procedure explicitly states that soldiers should always try to handle situations "other than by opening fire"?

During the few days before Blundy came across to Belfast, Paisley contacted a legal friend who in turn suggested to Vincent Browne of the *Sunday Independent,* a Dublin newspaper, that he examine the Black case. Browne did so and from his own contacts within the RUC learned several pieces of information such as the fact that the Star pistol was assumed to have been in the custody of the army since the previous owner was shot a year earlier.

*The army press office was at Northern Ireland Army Headquarters, Thiepval Barracks, Lisburn. It was under a civilian chief information officer and at that time had a staff of forty.

Browne's story appeared on Sunday, 24th February, the same day as Blundy's. It was given a banner headline on page one and was continued on two inner pages. The *Sunday Independent*, however, does not circulate on the British mainland and so there was still no head of steam generated for an inquiry. In Northern Ireland, its impact was limited as the newspaper circulates among the minority community and has a reputation for anti-British bias. In the Irish Republic, it caused a minor sensation, but that was of slight value towards securing an inquiry in the United Kingdom. Next day, RTÉ, the state broadcasting organisation in the Irish Republic, interviewed Black, which was additional publicity for the case.

Paisley was optimistic that he would be able to have the Black issue raised in an adjournment debate in the House of Commons. He agreed that the aim should be a judicial inquiry. I sent details of the case to a large number of politicians in preparation for his move in the Commons. They ranged across the political spectrum from right-wing conservatives to left-wing socialists. Most of the Ulster MPs were included.

After some weeks, Paisley reported that he had been unable to persuade the speaker of the House of Commons to allow the Black case to be raised in an adjournment debate and that he was pessimistic of having it raised in Parliament in any other form. This was a most grievous blow to the hope of an inquiry of any kind. It meant, too, that other MPs were discouraged from themselves attempting to raise the matter. They assumed that, if a person with Ian Paisley's formidable powers of protest could not have it raised, they would have even less chance.

In a last effort to rally organised political support behind a demand for an inquiry, I had the Black issue placed on the agenda of a well-attended meeting of the Assembly members of the United Ulster Unionist Council. The UUUC had been formed in early December to bring together Westite Unionists, Vanguard Unionists and Democratic Unionists for electioneering and propaganda purposes. I had already discussed it with a fair proportion of them as individuals in the previous weeks. Paisley, one of the few who could grasp the larger issues brought into focus by the assassination attempt at Tully-West, unfortunately was absent at Westminster. Ernest Baird was absent also.

It was soon clear that few of those present could comprehend that it was not simply another shooting incident in the army's war against the Provisional IRA. The old reluctance to be critical of the army in public was evident. There were inter-party rivalries within the UUUC and inter-factional rivalries within the parties and, although Paisley and I belonged to different parties, the fact that we were both identified with the Black case was not necessarily always helpful. But, the greatest obstacle was the limited experience, confidence and education of the average Assembly representative regardless of party. Northern Ireland has a population of only $1\frac{1}{2}$ millions and the mediocrity of its representatives is similar to that of town councillors for a city of that size. The last straw was when a totally serious Westite Unionist remarked that, as it was a shooting matter, he recommended that it should be left to the army to investigate as it had a lot of experience of shootings of one kind and another.

I sent details of the Black story to key churchmen, ranging from the Archbishop of Canterbury to prominent Quakers. Both the Anglican and the Roman Catholic archbishops of Armagh were included. On each occasion, I pointed out that there were fundamental moral and constitutional issues at stake.

The response was disappointing. Few acknowledged my letter. A lay assistant wrote that the Archbishop of Canterbury would attend to it on his return to London from Canterbury, but no further communication ever arrived. The Quakers, who have championed so many humanitarian issues in the life of the nation in earlier years, were particularly disappointing in their apathy. An exception was Miss Evelyn Shire of the Westminster Quaker Meeting who clearly realised the underlying implications of the Black case and endeavoured to interest others.

The sole churchman to try to raise the Black issue in an effective way was Rev. Roy Magee, minister of Saintfield Presbyterian Church. Shortly after the shooting at the cottage at Tully-West, a man telephoned and asked to meet him. He declined to explain why or to give his name on the telephone. When they met, Magee discovered that he was a member of the security forces. He had not been on duty on the afternoon of the shooting or responsible for any of the aftermath investigations. But, he was well informed on the matter and admitted that he and others were worried about their own safety because of what they knew. He said that it was suspected that the SIB unit at the cottage was an army intelligence assassination squad. He gave the impression that he was most disturbed about the occurrence and wanted someone with whom he could discuss it in safety. Magee also received the impression that the man felt it to be his moral duty to warn a responsible person who might be able to do something about it.

Roy Magee learned of the efforts and frustrations of Ian Paisley and myself to secure political action. He decided to tell the story of William Black to the Down Presbytery which met monthly and consisted of the Presbyterian ministers of a substantial section of County Down together with one lay elder from each congregation. He hoped that it would express disquiet at the circumstances of the Tully-West shooting and would call publicly for an independent inquiry. He felt that such a call, coming from a church body, would be difficult for press and public to ignore.

At the meeting of the Down Presbytery, the first difficulty was innate sympathy towards the army and reluctance to admit that the shooting of Black was more than another of those unfortunate accidents which occur in war. One person pointed out that, if it was not an accident, there were serious political overtones and the convention had been long established that political matters were never raised at presbytery meetings. Another queried whether it was a proper subject for the meeting as William Black was not a resident of the area, but a week-end cottage tenant. In addition, he was a Plymouth Brother. Nevertheless, the resolution might still have won a majority had it not been for the stolen goods in the outhouse. That fact carried much weight with the laymen even when it was empha- sised that Black was not responsible. One layman summed up the feeling with the remark, "If there were stolen goods anywhere on the premises, the Church must keep out of the matter. It makes no difference who was responsible for them."

I endeavoured to interest the National Council for Civil Liberties in the Black case. At first there was some response and I was able to meet two officials, Jack Dromey and Miss Catherine Scorer, in Belfast on 28th April 1974 during a visit to Northern Ireland which they were making together with Martin Loney, the general secretary. They listened to the Black story and admitted that it had important implications. However, I received the impression that the society was more interested in a scheme for a new RUC complaints procedure and that it was not anticipated that it would be taking up the Black affair in a major way.

Subsequent events bore out my impression. It is a small society and at that time had an annual budget of only £50,000. Nevertheless, it was able to take up various causes from Chilean refugees to the RUC complaints procedure. I could not escape concluding during subsequent weeks that there were certain strong prejudices and preferences within the organisation. It was also rent by internal feuds which culminated in early June in the resignation of Martin Loney, the general secretary.

Amnesty International, too, was unable to help. It pointed out that it is bound by a constitution which limits its work to prisoners of conscience and the abolition of torture and the death penalty.

On the evening of 14th May, 1974 the Ulster Workers' Council began the general strike which spread through Northern Ireland and lasted sixteen days. The special constitutional arrangement which the Westminster government had imposed on the region in the preceding months collapsed like a house of cards. *The Times* commented: *As a constitutional experiment it is finished. It cannot be made to stand up again. The final defection of the protestant community was swift, massive, disciplined and decisive. They will not have it and that is that*[*].

The triumph of the Ulster Workers' Council left it with huge prestige during the remainder of the summer. In early July, I asked its Executive Committee to examine the Black case. One or two members already had some knowledge of it from press reports and Black's fellow employees in Short Brothers.

The Executive Committee invited William Black to meet them and I, too, was asked to attend and speak. The members had a warmth of approach and a human interest in Black and his family which had been less evident among the politicians. Their problem was that they had only one sanction with the British government and that was a general strike. They doubted if the public would respond to a call for a second general strike over what many would see as only the shooting of one man in a period of frequent shootings and violence. If the attempt was made and failed, the organisation would be discredited and no longer able to intervene decisively in Ulster affairs. Also, as with so many of the politicians, some members of the UWC

*The Times, 3rd June, 1974.

Outside St. Anne's Cathedral, Belfast prior to a memorial service for Viscount Brookeborough, former prime minister of Northern Ireland. Various local people absented themselves because of his presence and travelled to Enniskillen to attend an alternative service.
Pacemaker Press, Ltd.

Edward Heath, the first prime minister and (in constitutional theory) head of the secret services during the events of this book, arriving at Aldergrove Airport, Belfast.
Pacemaker Press, Ltd.

Visit to an infantry patrol near the Irish frontier.
Pacemaker Press, Ltd.

Harold Wilson, the second prime minister and (in constitutional theory) head of the secret services during the events of this book. General Sir Frank King, GOC Northern Ireland, is giving a guided tour of Army Headquarters Northern Ireland in April 1974. The army was again to perform the same service for him in the following month except that next time it was a guided tour of the courses of action which were not open to his government as the general strike organised by the Ulster Workers' Council moved to a climax.

Pacemaker Press, Ltd.

James Callaghan, the third prime minister and (in constitutional theory) head of the secret services during the events of this book. Photographed during his first visit to Ulster as prime minister.

Century Newspapers, Ltd.

Margaret Thatcher, the fourth prime minister and (in constitutional theory) head of the secret services during the events of this book. Photographed during a joint press conference with Airey Neave near Aldergrove Airport, Belfast in June 1978. She was leader of the opposition and he was opposition spokesman on Northern Ireland at the time. Neave was in MI9 during three years of World War II and maintained contact with the secret services until assassinated by terrorists on the eve of the general election of May 1979.

Pacemaker Press, Ltd.

Century House, 100 Westminster Bridge Road,
London, SE1. Headquarters of D16.

R.A. McBRIDE

Curzon Street House, Curzon Street,
London, W1. Headquarters of D15.

A cruise missile. One of the new weapons which have made the United Kingdom exceptionally vulnerable to Soviet nuclear attack from the Atlantic.
Popperfoto

Cartoon by JAK of the *Daily Express* (30th July 1977) following press reports that an intelligence organisation had bugged the offices of Harold Wilson, the prime minister.

"If you think that was funny, wait till it gets to the bit where Marcia tells Harold what to do!"

Edward Heath leaves 10 Downing Street on 4th March 1974 to present his resignation to the Queen at Buckingham Palace. In Ulster, every Faulknerite candidate had been defeated despite the backlash caused by the Cromwell Road incident. The successful UUUC MPs had the numbers to have enabled him to remain in office, but were bound by an election pledge not to support him.

Press Association Photos.

did not appreciate the constitutional and other implications raised by the case. Such persons tended to see it simply as a question of money compensation for the injuries which had been inflicted in the shooting.

The Executive Committee discussed the case at several further meetings and decided to re-examine it when Black's solicitor should have had more time to ascertain the prospects of money compensation from the government for the injuries. They did not realise that three years would elapse before Black's injuries would be sufficiently stabilised to enable them to be measured by his doctors or that there are factors in the functioning of the United Kingdom judicial system which would thwart him from securing justice in the courts.

It is understood that the police thoroughly investigated the shooting at Tully-West within the limitations imposed on them. They confirmed that Black was an innocent person who walked into his own cottage on lawful business that Saturday afternoon. They were unable to pursue any line of inquiry which transgressed across the frontiers of authority of the intelligence organisations.

The police report went to the Northern Ireland Director of Public Prosecutions. He declined to make a decision on whether persons responsible for the shooting should be prosecuted and forwarded it to the Attorney General for the United Kingdom. Such a step is unusual and is taken by a director of public prosecutions only when a case has exceptional political or other implications.

I wrote to the Northern Ireland representative of the Attorney General on 28th June 1974, but a reply was not sent to me until August 1st. It read: *The position is that an investigation file relating to the occurrence referred to in your letter has been submitted by the Chief Constable to the Director of Public Prosecutions. Upon the evidence before him the Director has decided that the initiation of criminal proceedings is not warranted.* No mention was made of the special involvement of the Attorney General. Also, Parliament had risen for the summer recess on the previous day. Thus no immediate question could be raised in the House of Commons.

The Attorney General is answerable only to Parliament for his decisions. He is a member of the cabinet and of the ruling political party in Parliament. If he has the support of the prime minister and main political colleagues, he can decide any matter which comes before him as he may think expedient. It is open for him to "take into account the wider interests of the public".

This aspect of the powers of the Attorney General was highlighted in January 1977. The postal workers' trade union publicly announced that it had decided to forbid its members to handle a particular class of mail and that it was aware that the action would be a breach of the law. Samuel Silkin, the Attorney General, refused to intervene to prevent the law from being broken. He subsequently consented to explain his action to the Appeal Court, where three judges presided.* He told them that he was answerable to Parliament alone when he made decisions and that it was his duty to take into account the wider interests of the public. One of the judges, Lord Chief Justice Lawton, then inquired whether this meant that the Attorney General was entitled to consider the political trouble which would be caused by a decision to enforce a particular law. Silkin replied that it was a factor which he was entitled to take into account.† Silkin explained in a press interview that he had refused to enforce the law against the postal workers' trade union because he feared that the action would precipitate a postal strike. In the case of William Black, the political considerations would have been no less difficult to ignore.

The ruling that there should be no prosecutions destroyed the hope that such court proceedings might uncover enough information to stir a public demand for a wider and more thorough inquiry into the background to the conspiracy to murder an innocent man and to frame him with stolen goods.

The RUC men who had conducted the police investigations were fiercely indignant and a senior officer threatened to resign. The file on the case is now lodged at RUC Headquarters, Knock Road, Belfast. A special classification has been placed on it and access forbidden to

---

*The following dialogue took place during Silkin's appearance before the judges:
Lord Justice Lawton: "This court made it as clear as a pikestaff on Saturday that what the union proposed was contrary to the criminal law of the land. What is the court to do if no notice is taken of the declaration?"
Attorney General: ". . . There were countless statements by former attorneys and others, which recognised the principle that the exercise of the Attorney General's discretion could not be challenged in the courts."
Lord Justice Ormrod: "So the only way the exercise of the discretion can be questioned is in parliament and that would turn on what the government of the day thinks about it."
†*The Daily Telegraph,* 19th January 1977.

anyone except the Chief Constable and a small number of his most senior officers.

In May 1977, the Ministry of Defence, although continuing to claim that the shooting had been an unfortunate case of mistaken identity in a legitimate and tense situation, agreed to pay William Black £16,700 in compensation for the injuries he had received. His legal advisers urged him to accept it. The sum was small in relation to what he had suffered, but it was an admission by the state that he was an innocent person and that was what mattered most to the Black family.

The alternative was to wait a further two or three years until a civil case could reach a hearing in the overcrowded Northern Ireland courts and then to endeavour to fight it with the state using against him the formidable privileges and stratagems available to it. Each one of the following would in itself be almost an insuperable barrier to having the real issues of the case examined.

No. 1: The decision by the Attorney General not to prosecute would be construed as a vindication of the legality of the "arrest ambush" at William Black's cottage.

No. 2: The state under "crown privilege" would have the right to withhold crown documents such as the RUC report to the Director of Public Prosecutions and through him to the Attorney General.

No. 3: United Kingdom courts have a convention that judges exclude evidence and refuse to allow the cross-examination of witnesses when the authorities (often on the decision of the intelligence services) claim that reference to it would be "prejudicial to the national interest". An example occurred in the "Angry Brigade Trial" of 1972. The judge, Justice James, explained that "it is the duty of the court to watch the situation and see that certain questions are not asked and, if they are asked, to see that they are not answered".

No. 4: The state can forbid persons to give evidence on subjects specified by it if at any time in their lives they have taken the Official Secrets Oath. This includes a good proportion of the population as, in addition to persons currently employed by the state, many others have been employed by it at some earlier stage in their lives.

9 Acquitted Without Having to Produce a Defence

Major-General Frank Kitson, writing in 1977, laid down a code of basic principles for the guidance of a government fighting terrorism.* Immediately following on the principle that it must establish an effective intelligence system, he placed the further principle that it must provide itself with a legal system adequate for the needs of the moment. By that date the British government had already taken various steps in Ulster to do so.

When "direct rule" was imposed in March 1972, the Special Powers (Northern Ireland) Act and legislation to permit suspects to be interned without trial already gave additional anti-terrorist powers not available in mainland legislation. The problems that juries were liable to arrive at verdicts that were less than helpful and that witnesses and jurors were vulnerable to intimidation were met by the abolition of juries in the criminal courts and the introduction of unorthodox expedients to enable witnesses to remain anonymous. These latter included screens behind which they could be hidden; heavy socks and mocassins to prevent feet from being recognised if seen below the screen; and a "Donald Duck squawk box" instrument which distorted an individual's voice so that it could not be recognised. At the same time, the Detention of Terrorists (Northern Ireland) Order introduced commissioners with legal training to preside over a Detention Appeal Tribunal to which detainees could apply after a period for a review of the justification for their imprisonment.

These new arrangements of the non-jury courts and the Detention Appeal Tribunal were based on the recommendations of an inquiry chaired by Lord Diplock and are known by his name.

Harsh legislation and a streamlined judicial process are normal

*Frank Kitson, *Bunch of Five* (1977), p. 289.

responses when a government is confronted by terrorists. Few will quarrel with the general principle that such steps should have been taken in Ulster. In a totally different category, however, have been the attempts to use the administration of the law for expedients such as unjustified murder charges in order to promote the political interests of the government.

During the second half of 1972, law and order deteriorated badly in Northern Ireland. Assassination and counter-assassination became worse and worse. Between 1st July and 30th November, 112 persons were murdered in "civilian incidents". William Whitelaw, the secretary of state for Northern Ireland, and the Northern Ireland Office administration came under intense pressure from the public.

A joint task force of military and civilian police was formed to patrol assassination black areas around the Irish republican-Roman Catholic enclaves in east Belfast. The step was announced by the secretary of state in person and given maximum publicity. Unfortunately for the credibility of the Northern Ireland administration, murders during December 1972 numbered twenty which was more than double the November figure. Two-thirds of them were Roman Catholics. Politicians of the powerful Irish republican and solidly Roman Catholic SDLP political party were fiercely critical and their co-operation was basic to the government's policies at that time.

The Archbishop of the Roman Catholic Church, the Moderator of the Presbyterian Church, the Archbishop of the Church of Ireland and the President of the Methodist Church asked to meet the secretary of state as a deputation. They did so on 3rd January 1973 and emphasised the public consternation at the government's apparent inability to take effective action against the assassins.

A few hours later that same day, it was announced that three young Protestants, John Orchin, Samuel Richmond and Victor McCready, had been charged with the murders of three Roman Catholics. Three days later (6th January) came a further announcement that four additional young Protestants, David Barr, William Bingham, Charles Martin and Joseph Miller, had been charged with murdering two Roman Catholics and a Protestant married to a Roman Catholic — again in three separate incidents.

The total of seven Protestants charged with murder was credited to the new joint task force and heavily publicised on the government-owned BBC and other news media. The public was impressed and the political and other pressure on the Northern Ireland administration eased.

The public would have been less impressed had it known the facts. The first three lads had been arrested almost three weeks earlier because an unlicensed pistol had been found in a car in which they were travelling. A couple of weeks after the arrests, a lawyer in the Belfast office of the Treasury Solicitor was drawing up charges on the basis of the presence of the pistol when a senior police official ordered him to prepare fresh indictments charging them with murdering three specified Roman Catholics. The lawyer protested that there was no evidence for such charges. When the order was repeated, he refused to obey and later resigned. Charges for two of the murders were subsequently dropped without publicity by the Crown on 26th March 1973. This left charges for one murder and for travelling in the presence of an unlicensed pistol.

The four persons against whom the murder charges had been announced on 6th January 1973 had likewise been travelling in a motor car in which an unlicensed pistol had been found. In addition, in their case the car had been stolen. On 30th March, the Crown admitted that it would not offer evidence on the charges for two of the murders and they were quietly abandoned. On 26th April, it declined to offer evidence on the charges for the remaining third murder and they, too, were dropped without publicity. The lesser charges centred on the unlicensed pistol and stolen car came up for trial on 11th May. One man was imprisoned for three years for possessing the gun and one for one year (suspended for two years) for stealing a car and having no insurance. The remaining two men received sentences of nine months (suspended for two years) for allowing themselves to be carried in a stolen vehicle.

In September 1973, the Insight team of *The Sunday Times* set out the story of the seven arrests and the dropped charges for five murders. It summed up its findings thus: *"It is extremely difficult, often impossible to determine what considerations lie behind the framing of any particular set of charges. But after extensive inquiries in legal circles in Belfast, it is impossible to escape the conclusion that some knowledgeable and experienced lawyers have come to believe, reluctantly, that the impetus behind some of the sectarian murder charges laid in the past nine months has been more political than legal."*

Charges in connection with one remaining murder and travelling in the presence of an unlicensed pistol were still pending against Orchin, Richmond and McCready when *The Sunday Times* published its findings. They had been arrested in December 1972 and, as a result, did not come under the "Diplock" innovations and the more stringent Northern Ireland (Emergency Provisions) Act, both of which were to come into force in the following year. This should have given them several useful advantages, including the right to trial by jury. The authorities, however, had other ideas. All three had been assigned to Long Kesh Prison near Lisburn to await trial. One day they were told that a police officer wished to see them in connection with the charges already preferred. Each replied that he did not wish to see him without consulting his solicitor as the depositions had been taken and it was understood that nothing further was required other than a date to be set for the trial.

The other prisoners in the compound supported their stand as just and reasonable whereupon some fifty warders were assembled and carried Orchin, Richmond and McCready bodily to where a police officer was waiting. He withdrew all charges against them and immediately re-charged them with the same ones. They did not even leave the building.

The date on which they were re-charged was in 1973 and was used as a pretext to deprive them of the right to be tried by a jury. It also threatened to prejudice their trials in other ways. For instance, they became subject to Section 2 and Section 7 of the Northern Ireland (Emergency Provisions) Act in connection with the unlicensed pistol. Under the law prior to that date, the onus was on the prosecution to prove that a person in such circumstances knew, first, of the presence of the pistol and, second, that it was unlicensed. Section 7 reversed the situation and placed the onus of proof on the accused to prove his innocence – a requirement which in most instances would be much more difficult and in some would be impossible.

The date for the trial of Orchin, Richmond and McCready was set eventually for mid-February 1974, sixteen months after their arrests. Sir Robert Lowry, Lord Chief Justice of Northern Ireland, was the judge. The prosecution case against the three (and against four other persons) rested solely on the inconsistency studded testimony of a man convicted some months earlier of four murders and eleven robberies. Sir Robert ruled that it did not have credibility and dismissed the charges without any of the accused having to present a defence.

After the trial Orchin, Richmond and McCready were held in prison for about a month on the charge relating to the unlicensed pistol. They were then released on bail and kept on it until May 1978, a period of over four years (i.e. a total of five-and-a-half years from the date of the original arrests). A long prison sentence is the penalty for an unlicensed firearm and to keep the three men on bail, year after year, with this terrifying threat hanging over them was a most effective way to deter them from exposing the monstrous injustice of their treatment either in the media or with the European Commission of Human Rights.

The above bare statement of the facts tells nothing of the mental agonies suffered by persons wrongly accused of murder and by the members of their families. Sometimes a physical symptom points to what is happening in the mind. For instance, Orchin developed a severe stomach ulcer after he was charged which became increasingly worse during the years on bail until it had to be treated by major surgery. In Long Kesh Prison, fellow prisoners used to save for him part of their daily allowance of milk.

10 In Great Britain Itself

Mrs. Joan Waters* was aged twenty-eight, had golden-red hair and was the daughter of a civil servant. She was a qualified teacher, but chose to work as an accounting secretary with a firm of solicitors instead of in a class-room. John Waters, her husband, was an engineer.

A friend in Joan's office was active in the Womens' Loyalist Action Association and invited her to one of its meetings. It was a group which came together in 1972 in an attempt to focus attention on the severity and inconsistencies of sentences being given in the courts to loyalists charged with politically motivated offences in contrast to those being given to republicans. Sentences were shaped to intimidate loyalists by their severity in the knowledge that the Ulster majority would not raise a finger on behalf of persons convicted for violence. On the other hand, the guiding principle in sentencing republicans was moderation in order not to create new martyrs within the republican minority.

Joan Waters was impressed by the facts presented during the WLAA meeting. She agreed to do what she could to help. She began to visit the families of sentenced persons in order to compile detailed dossiers on the more extreme sentence anomalies. Soon she was recognised by the group as their specialist on facts and figures and formal press officer.

Some of the cases were outstandingly tragic. One lad, belonging to a respected family, had been given a long sentence although he and local residents emphatically maintained that he was not at the scene of the incident for which he was convicted. The most pathetic case was that of a middle-aged man with the mental age of a child of nine. He was sentenced to seven years for throwing a petrol bomb. He had picked up one that was lying in a gutter with a burnt-out fuse. He tossed it into a front garden, laughing like a child and neither doing

*Waters is an assumed name to protect the family from publicity.

nor intending damage. In gaol he refused to try to understand how he came to be there and during the years of his imprisonment spent much time sobbing in his cell as a desperately hurt child sobs. The mental age of his wife was not much older than his. She too refused to accept the justice of the imprisonment. She had a nervous breakdown and her hair fell out. After a time she had a stroke which semi-paralysed her.

The WLAA eventually induced William Whitelaw, the secretary of state for Northern Ireland, to receive a deputation. Joan Waters was included in it and acted as chief spokesman. They pressed on him the anomalies between loyalist and republican sentences. He promised to have certain ones re-examined, but the outcome was that they remained unchanged.

She also took part in one or two television debates which were shown in the English Midland and London areas.

Joan Waters was the oldest of four children. A brother, Derek, two years younger, was closest to her in age. Trailing some years behind were a younger brother and sister.

Derek, as a teenager, was athletic, a non-smoker and a teetotaller. He was uninterested in politics and, like the other members of his family, had little time for sectarian prejudice. On several occasions, he was invited to play for the Roman Catholic Holy Cross football team in charity matches to raise funds for it. He was an outstanding footballer. He played for Northern Ireland once or twice. Sheffield Wednesday recognised his talent and he signed a contract to play for it. In Sheffield he was homesick and missed his girl friend. The team released him and he returned home where he soon married. A few months later, he accepted a contract to play for a Canadian football team.

Derek was a great success as a footballer in Canada until an injury destroyed his kneecap. He was on crutches for three or four months and was just beginning to recover when a stomach malignancy had to be treated by very extensive surgery. He was in hospital for a long time with the doctors far from optimistic that he would recover. He was left in feeble health, unemployed and with a wife, three-year-old daughter and a newly-born one. He and his wife decided to return to Belfast where they secured a house. For a few weeks, he drove a taxi while searching for a permanent appointment. His parents were indignant when they discovered about it and he gave it up through respect for their views. They felt that a low status job of that kind was unfair to the family as a whole and would be unhelpful in his search for a permanent one.

His parents lived in the Balmoral suburb of south Belfast. Both of the younger children were at school. The one who was fifteen attended the Belfast Royal Academy in the north of the city. On Friday evenings, he often attended a disco with school friends in a church hall near to it. Afterwards, his father would collect him by car and bring him home.

The lad was at the disco one Friday evening, three or four weeks after Derek and his wife returned from Canada. His father arrived a little early and sat waiting in the car. His son came out of the building with several of his friends. They were fifteen and sixteen-year-olds. They entered a nearby shop and bought some refreshments. When they came out, he noticed his father waiting. He and a friend separated from the others and began to move towards the car. His father called a greeting.

At that moment, a car drove up and a gunman in it sprayed the boys with a machine-gun. It turned immediately and again passed with the gunman firing at them. The father jumped out of his car and began to run to where his son had thrown himself to the ground. One boy, seeing an adult, rushed towards him with intestines hanging out and screaming "Help me! Help me!" He saw a tall boy slide down the door of the shop and lie still on the pavement. He was seized with a certainty that it was his own son. He moved him a little and saw from his face that it was someone else. He then realised that he had already seen his son some distance from the door and that his conviction that it was him had been totally irrational.

One boy was dead and four were injured of whom one died a year later. It was Derek's introduction to the "troubles". When he left for Canada six years earlier, Northern Ireland had the lowest crime rate in the United Kingdom and no political violence had occurred for a number of years. He and his wife were badly shaken and decided to move out of Ulster so that their children could grow up under normal conditions. A few weeks later, he obtained employment with an engineering firm in Fifeshire about thirty miles from Edinburgh. This was towards the end of June 1973.

Derek's parents were even more overwhelmed by the horror of what had happened. His father had been present and his mother was

92

a sensitive, nervous person. They, too, decided that they could no longer remain in fairness to their young children. His father secured a civil service transfer to a post in Scotland and at the beginning of September moved to a house about three miles from where Derek and his wife had settled.

One evening in the late autumn, Derek entered a bar in a hotel in the town. A man came up and offered to buy him a drink. He said that he had noticed his Northern Irish voice and that he liked the country very much. It was a typical self-introduction. As the evening wore on, he asked Derek if he knew anything about the Ulster Defence Association or anybody in it. He replied that he did not. He asked him if he belonged to the loyalist section of the population and he replied that he did. At that point the subject was dropped.

Two nights later, Derek was having a drink in the same hotel when the same person approached him accompanied by a second man who gave his name as Alexander Atkins.* After a period of normal conversation, they turned to the subject of his loyalist background. Local people later told Derek that the man who had first approached him was a policeman. He was attached to Dysart Police Station and well-known in the district as the "drug squad" detective. He wore the "hippie type clothes then fashionable among teenagers. After the evening when he introduced Atkins, he remained in the background and his place as the latter's companion was taken by a swarthy newcomer.

Alexander Atkins and his swarthy colleague began to accost Derek on various occasions. The former would do most of the talking; the latter said little. They were hefty men in their forties. He had been reduced to seven stone by his ill-health and was some twenty years their junior. They came to his home uninvited once or twice and they would waylay him as he emerged from work at the factory.

One evening Atkins and his colleague were sitting at the factory exit. They insisted that Derek enter their car and drove him to a quiet layby a short distance away. They produced a file which they said was his and took out of it an indistinct, green photograph of someone carrying a parcel. They said that it was of himself and that the parcel contained a gun which had been taken to pieces so that he could

*Alexander Atkins is a substituted name. It has not been ascertained whether the name given by this person was genuine, assumed or even that of someone else.

carry it inconspicuously. They said that the incident had taken place in Belfast and that the photograph had been taken by a night camera. Derek replied that it was untrue and impossible. They added that they were working for the government undercover and that they had enough evidence to "make the charge stick".

They next claimed that he had been responsible for a murder in Belfast which had received considerable publicity. He protested that it was totally impossible and they replied that they had evidence to make certain that he would be convicted.

They told him that his only remedy was to work as a government agent.

The two men produced two further files. One was exceptionally thick and the other empty. The bulky one, they explained, recorded the activities of his sister, Mrs. Joan Waters, and the other belonged to her husband. They refused to allow him to examine his sister's file except to show him that it contained a photograph of her. They threatened that, if he did not co-operate, the Northern Ireland emergency powers of detention would be used to intern her as a dangerous subversive.

Derek was confident that she had never been involved in anything subversive in her life or, for that matter, anything which was not completely dignified and fully reputable. At the same time, he knew that, while he had been living in Canada, she had been an activist for a period with the WLAA and had been outspoken on occasions such as the meeting of the deputation with Whitelaw and the television debates. He suspected that she had been an embarrassment to the authorities and that, in the conditions which then prevailed, what mattered was whether they wished to have such a person interned and not whether she had been subversive. The sheer bulk of his sister's file and the fact that her husband's one was empty registered strongly on him. He knew that his brother-in-law had never been associated with a controversial or political activity at any time and that, if the files were genuine, his one would contain exactly nothing.

Alexander Atkins and his companion eventually told Derek that he had to go to Dundalk to shoot Martin Meehan, an alleged high-ranking member of the Provisional IRA. Instructions were laid out in some detail. He was to go to a hotel where arrangements would be made for him to meet Meehan. In his room at the hotel, he would find a gun and it was emphasised that, after the shooting, he was to replace it in the room as arrangements had been made to dispose of it. Derek refused and they again threatened him that it was the only way to save his sister from being interned and himself from being charged with murder and gunrunning.

Derek felt helpless and told no one. His wife was a tense, sensitive person. So, too, was his mother who, in addition, was in poor health. His father was still badly shaken by the shooting of the schoolboys. Atkins and his colleague had savagely threatened him against telling anyone, but he was influenced more by reluctance to distress the rest of his family as he assumed that they would be as helpless as himself. It seemed futile to go to the police as they appeared to be in the plot. During these weeks, his wife noticed that he ate little, drank too much and suffered abominably with his stomach. He would lie awake for complete nights. An old sword hung on a wall of his house as an ornament. He took it down and kept it beside his bed. He remained at home from work on various days through terror of being waylaid on emerging from the factory. He considered returning to Belfast, but his tormentors anticipated that his mind would turn in that direction. They told him that they were prepared should he attempt to slip back to Ulster. They had an agent, they said, who lived close to where he had lived during the short period after his return from Canada. He would be instructed to pass the word around in militant loyalist circles that he was an informer so that he would be assassinated. They described the person they claimed was the agent in sufficient detail to direct Derek's attention towards a particular individual. He realised that they were unlikely to pinpoint a genuine agent in that way, but their familiarity with the Belfast scene was unnerving.

Derek had an aunt who lived not far from his new Scottish home. Her birthday was on 21st December and he arranged a family dinner party to celebrate it. His aunt, uncle, father and mother were present and it was held in a hotel. At the close of the evening, he left slightly before the others to return home. They saw him leave the room where they were sitting and begin to walk across a bar which lay between it and the entrance to the building. A man intercepted him and began to say something. As they watched, they saw Derek more than once attempt to continue towards the entrance, but each time the man closed up on him again. His aunt recognised him immediately as the well-known local "drug squad" detective. His father rose, walked into the bar and asked his son if he would like a drink. At that the drug detective left.

Derek returned home a desperately worried person. The detective had told him that Alexander Atkins and his companion insisted that he meet them on Boxing Night as they would have definite instructions for him.

On the day before Christmas, a note was sent into Derek at his place of work. It read, "Meet us at 8 o'clock on Boxing Night" and specified a place. The senders of it must have had misgivings as to whether he would obey as they appear to have decided to back it up with physical intimidation. In the evening, Derek went into a bar to have a drink. After a time he went to the toilet. There he was set upon by three hefty roughs. They placed a lavatory chain around his neck and hoisted him off his feet. One placed a knife against the huge scar left by his stomach operation in Canada. They accused him of giving information to the police about a robbery a few weeks earlier at a local company. Derek mistook the name of the company for that of a person and blurted out, "But, who is he? Who is he?"

Suddenly, they let him down and one said, "This guy doesn't know what we are talking about or he would not ask, 'Who is he?'" They than asked what he had done to the police that they had it in for him. At first, he did not understand what they meant. Then he realised that they were referring to their own attack on him. He replied, "I have no trouble with the police. I think that they maybe want trouble with me." His assailants next told him that they had been given three pounds each "to do you up tonight" by the "drug squad" detective with whom he was already unpleasantly familiar.

The experience shattered Derek and for the first time he told his wife and parents the story of his harassments from the first meeting with the drug detective. They were greatly upset, but discussion was cut short as his father had to drive to Glasgow to meet Joan, his sister, and John, her husband, to bring them to Fife to spend the festive season.

In Glasgow, Joan asked her father, "How is Derek?" He replied, "He's all right." Instantly, she recognised from his voice that there was something seriously wrong with her brother. She did not press him further during the journey. They arrived at her parents' house a little before midnight. Derek was in the living room with his wife and two children. He looked very ill. She immediately assumed that the malignancy of the stomach had not been cured and that he was dying. Her mother was incredibly tense. She could not sit down to talk, but kept moving around the room polishing doors and furniture although they already sparkled.

Half-an-hour later, her father drove Derek and his family to their home. Immediately they left, she turned to her mother and asked, "What is wrong?" "Awful, awful trouble," she replied and began to re-tell the story which Derek had told earlier in the evening. Soon her father returned and he continued it in greater detail.

Joan and her husband listened with astonishment. The shock was like a physical thing — like thunder hitting one. The night was spent in deep discussion. Next morning — Christmas morning — Derek and his family returned and all day the only subject was how to rid him of his tormentors. His father suggested going to the Home Office, but then agreed that it would be futile as it was probably implicated. The case of Kenneth Littlejohn had been prominent in the news during the year and they had the impression that he had been working for the Home Office. (Littlejohn claimed that he was working for DI6. The Home Office, however, had been associated with his name because of controversy over certain visits to him in an English prison and unsuccessful legal proceedings to stop his extradition to the Irish Republic.) Joan also hesitated to go to the Home Office as her father was a senior civil servant in line for further promotion and not too far from retirement. She feared that to approach it would simply alert the authorities to a new means of blackmail by threatening her father through his civil service position.

As they talked, they came back more than once to the mystery of the three files which Derek had been shown. Why the thick file on Joan and the heavy emphasis on it? Was there an intention to try to blackmail her in some way as well as Derek?

John and Joan decided that they should meet Alexander Atkins and his colleague in the flesh. They told themselves that they might be frightened off if they knew that Derek was backed up by other members of his family. The note which had been sent into him at the factory had said that he was to meet them at eight o'clock on Boxing Night. They told him to ignore it and to remain at home where they would join him for the evening.

At ten o'clock there was a sharp knock at the door. Joan opened it, endeavouring to appear calm. Two burly men were on the doorstep. One said, "Can we speak to Derek?" She replied, "No, you cannot speak to him. He is in the living room, but he is not going out with you." They replied, "Oh, but we were to go for drinks with Derek tonight." Joan retorted, "Well, as far as I am aware the licensing hours in Scotland are until 10.30 at night. That does not leave you much time for drinking. Besides, if Derek continues to drink, at best he probably has a year left to live and at worst a matter of months." This was not altogether an exaggeration as he had lost much of his stomach in his operation and was supposed to be on a rigid diet. They laughed and between them said with insistence in their voices, "So you are the boss. But can we speak to him." The dialogue continued:

"No, as I said, you cannot speak to him. You've been a bad influence. I take it you are his drinking partners. This is fine for you. You are two healthy, strapping men. My brother is an extremely ill person. No, he is not joining you to drink and please don't come back again because he will not ever be joining you to drink again."

"Well, just let us talk to him for a few moments," said one of them.

"No, you will not. By the way, what is your name."

"Oh, Derek knows my name."

"Since you are Derek's friends — or rather since you don't care very much for his health and welfare I will not call you his friends — but surely I ought to know your name!"

"My name is Alexander."

"Well, Mr. Alexander, I can assure you that Derek will not be drinking with you again. In fact, he will not be seeing you again."

"Tell him Alexander is here."

"No, Mr. Alexander, I will not."

"It is not Alexander."

"Oh, you are not Mr. Alexander!"

"It is Alexander Atkins."

"Well, I will not forget that name."

"I will not forget yours."

"That would be strange if you did not forget mine. You do not know mine."

"Oh, I know more about you than you think."

At that point, John joined Joan at the door. He, too, took up the theme that it was unfair to encourage a person, who could be dying with each drink he took, to take more. Finally, both men left appearing very exasperated.

John and Joan Waters had hoped that, once they realised that

Derek had the support of other members of his family, they would leave him alone. The confrontation convinced them that, on the contrary, they were so dogmatic and sure of themselves that it was obvious that they had no intention of being deterred. They returned to Joan's parents' house and about four o'clock in the morning decided on two steps. First, she would find a local solicitor and recount the events to him and, second, both would return to Belfast to obtain advice and help.

They decided that the undercover plotters would be most afraid of publicity and political pressure and that their best hope would be to find an influential member of parliament who would believe their story. They were acutely conscious of how unbelievable it was and felt that an Ulster MP would be more likely to credit it than one in Scotland.

In the meantime, a further development had taken place at Derek's home. His sister and brother-in-law had left about 2.00 a.m. A few minutes after they drove away there was a knock at the front door. He and his wife had just gone to bed. He assumed that they had forgotten something and had returned. He came downstairs and found Alexander Atkins and the second man back again on the doorstep. They told him to meet them two nights later and threatened frightful consequences if he should fail to appear. Their chief was coming specifically from London to see him, they said, and had ordered them to make certain he was present.

Joan went into Kirkcaldy to find a solicitor next morning. She passed two closed solicitors' offices on the main street. A third was open and one of the partners, an elderly man, saw her at once. She recounted the harassments and blackmail threats by Atkins and his undercover colleague. She explained that she wanted someone outside her family to know about them in case anything should happen to her before she would be able to raise the issue with someone with influence in Northern Ireland. The solicitor made notes and promised to do all that he could to help if contacted.

At five o'clock next morning, John and Joan Waters returned to Northern Ireland via the Stranraer to Larne ship route. From her home, Joan telephoned William Craig, a party leader in the Northern Ireland Assembly and former minister of Home Affairs in the disbanded parliament of Northern Ireland. His name was the first to come to her mind and his telephone number was in the directory. She told him that it was a life and death matter and could she speak to him? He said that unfortunately she could not. He was going out and would be engaged for the following few days. She next tried to telephone Dr. Ian Paisley, the MP for North Antrim at Westminster and a member of the Northern Ireland Assembly, but was unable to locate him.

She was uncertain of who to try to contact next. She felt it would have to be an MP or someone of similar standing in order that her story would at least be believed. She later explained, "I did not think that anyone was going to believe us as a family. The story was so mad that your brother was being told to shoot Martin Meehan and that I was going to be interned for doing nothing."

The Waters drove into Belfast. On the Shankhill Road they saw by accident a person whom Joan had talked with during the WLAA campaign for legal justice. She asked if he could suggest how she could contact an MP. He replied that a member of the Northern Ireland Assembly was due in the district and suggested that she wait. A few minutes later, Miss Jean Coulter arrived. She listened attentively to the story and recommended the Waters to see Ernest Baird, a fellow-member of the Northern Ireland Assembly.

They drove at once to Baird's home which was in the Dundonald suburb of Belfast. He and his wife were at home. He seemed at first to be hyper-critical — if not disbelieving. She began to feel that she was wasting her time and that he probably thought that she was mad. Eventually, he mentioned the present writer and suggested that I should be brought in on the matter as I had already knowledge of one or two other cases. The Waters agreed and he telephoned me. Forty minutes later, I arrived. John had just left and I heard the story from Joan.

On the following day, Sunday, 29th December, Ernest Baird, Joan Waters and myself re-met at the Baird home. It was realised that our first aim should be to secure more tangible evidence and, if possible, further witnesses. It was decided that Joan should telephone Alexander Atkins at a number which he had given to Derek and which had been discovered to be that of the police station at Dysart. A tape recorder was attached to the telephone. The rest was left entirely to Joan's initiative.

Atkins answered the call. Joan was conscious of the long-distance noises on the telephone. She had gone to school in Scotland and in order to lull suspicion said that she was in Glasgow visiting an old school friend.

She said that Derek had told her the whole story. She appealed that he be left alone. She hinted that she could be of more help to them than her brother, provided that they left him alone in his present state of health. Atkins arranged with her that she and her brother would meet him and his superior from London in the Commodore Hotel near Edinburgh at seven o'clock on the following evening.

The next problem was who should go to the hotel to act as a witness. It had to be someone who would not be recognised easily by undercover men familiar with Ulster. By good fortune, Jean Coulter was already booked to travel to Glasgow the following day and very courageously agreed to go to the hotel with a male friend.

Next morning, the Waters left for Scotland via Larne and Stranraer. They missed the train connection in Glasgow which meant that they could not be at the hotel by seven o'clock. Joan telephoned the hotel. She told Alexander Atkins that she had missed the train after leaving her Glasgow school friend. She said that she would travel by the next one and should be at the hotel about eight clock. He was angry. He said that he had his boss with him and that they would not wait longer than eight.

Jean Coulter and her friend had arrived early and were sitting quietly at a table with a good view of the room when, about half-past-eight, Joan and Derek entered the hotel, having left John outside in the taxi. Atkins and the other man who had been with him during the doorstep confrontation on Boxing Night were waiting. They invited them to sit at a table and were joined by an unusually tall, thin man who was extraordinarily blonde for his age which was thirty to thirty-five. He had the stance of a soldier. They said that the "chief" was upstairs in a bedroom. They referred to him as "David" and emphasised that he had to catch a plane back to London at midnight. They said that he wanted to talk to Joan. Atkins was sent to the bar for drinks which would suggest that he had the lowest standing or rank.

After a brief interval Alexander Atkins left and returned with "David". He was in his forties and his manner and speech clearly indicated that he belonged to a much higher social class than Atkins and his colleagues. He wore casual country tweeds and checked shirt which was unusual on Old Year's Night. At the same time, he looked comfortable and not out of place in them. His speech, manner and inbred courtesy reminded Joan of the 13th Earl of Antrim. The latter was the president of the National Trust in Northern Ireland and she had met him when helping with its work.

Jean Coulter and her friend watched the group in conversation and were impressed by what appeared from across the room to be the relaxed self-control of Joan and Derek. One of the men she recognised as someone she had seen on the prosecution side in a Belfast court during trials for terrorist offences. At one point, Joan rose from the table and went to the ladies' room. Jean Coulter joined her there and they had a brief conversation. A little later "David" went to the telephone to call the airport. The telephone was within earshot of Jean Coulter's table. She heard him say that he was still flying as planned, but would be departing somewhat later than originally intended. He was thus of sufficiently high rank to have an aircraft at his disposal.

"David" asked Joan if she would infiltrate the loyalist paramilitary organisations to find out where they hid their arms or ammunition. She said she would provided they left her brother alone as he was so very ill.

At that point John abruptly joined the group and sat listening quietly. Joan asked whether her brother would be charged with murder if she did not work for them. She was assured that he would be. She asked whether it could be made to stick as he had been told. Atkins interrupted and said that they certainly could make it stick.

A few minutes later "David" said that they would go to the bedroom where they could talk in privacy. The group instinctively rose to their feet, but John said in a firm voice, "You are not taking my wife up the stairs. Don't try to and don't move from here. You are big, burly men and I am small, but I will cause a lot of noise and draw attention to us all before I go down." "David" and his companions were obviously frightened by the threat and appeared glad to sit down again quietly. He suggested that Joan should meet him in Belfast. He mentioned four possible hotels. They were in the suburbs and she replied that she would prefer the Royal Avenue Hotel in the centre of the city. He said that he would telephone her on the following Thursday.

Joan, John and Derek rose to leave. The others were tense. For a moment or two Joan and Atkins were engaged in a separate conversation from the rest of the group. She felt that he was beginning to smell a rat. She said, "I have taken a great risk in coming to see you tonight." He retorted that it was nothing to the risk he had taken.

Joan, John and Derek travelled into Edinburgh by their taxi and out of Fife by train. It was a minute to midnight when Joan and John reached her parents' house as the bells were beginning to ring out the old year. Derek would have reached his house some minutes later.

Within an hour, Derek's wife telephoned Joan. She was hysterical. She said Derek had been arrested. Joan asked if the police had had a warrant and she replied, "Yes." Joan immediately telephoned Dysart Police Station, the police headquarters for Fife and asked where was her brother. The police assured her they were certain that no warrant had been issued for his arrest and that they did not even know his name. She next rang the solicitor with whom she had called in Kilkcaldy and who was having a New Year party at the time. He, too, checked with the police and rang back to confirm that Derek had not been arrested and that he felt she must have made a mistake.

A little later, Derek knocked at the front door. He was in shirt sleeves, shaking all over and greatly upset. After he had reached home, two men in police uniforms had appeared at the door, waved a piece of paper which they said was a warrant for his arrest. They bundled him into a car and drove him to a car park at the rear of Dysart Police Headquarters and afterwards to an isolated road. At one stage, one seized him by the neck and nearly chocked him. Finally, they said slowly to him, "You do not know Alexander Atkins. You do not know David. You were never in the hotel tonight. You spoke to no one and tell your sister the same." They then bundled him out of the car and left him on the road. The place was fairly close to his parents' home and possibly had been chosen for that reason. He soon recognised the locality and walked to it.

Joan Waters immediately telephoned Dysart Police Station. Unlike the earlier occasions, it was claimed that no one knew of an Alexander Atkins. She asked for the duty sergeant. He appeared genuinely not to know of Atkins and to be trying to be helpful. She said that it did not matter whether or not he knew Alexander Atkins and instructed him to take down a message for him. The message read that she had been in the hotel that night; that she had met David; that a tape had been taken of the conversation; that if he thought he could arrest her brother and charge him with murder, he should now try; that, if he thought he could intern her whilst completely innocent, he should now try; that several persons had listened to the conversation in the hotel that night and that one was an Ulster MP.

Next morning, she telephoned Ernest Baird and gave him a short account of developments. He contacted the Scottish police and insisted that the Waters should be given police protection until their return to Northern Ireland. His approach was successful. On the train to Stranraer and on the steamer to Larne two men and a woman shadowed their every movement. On the train to Belfast, they were no longer present. In addition, Joan's uncle and aunt travelled with them in the hope of giving some protection by their presence.

The attack on Derek by the roughs who had been paid £3 each was worrying lest it should be repeated. John thought it might be useful to try to locate them and to warn them off. A club notorious in the area as a hang-out for the criminally inclined was suggested as a place where someone might know of them or their whereabouts. Before the return to Northern Ireland, John and Derek went to it. On opening the door, Derek saw two of them drinking at a table. John walked across to them. He was shaking in his shoes, but said as calmly as he could, "You roughed up a man from Belfast a few nights ago." They answered, "Yes, but it was a mistake." John then continued, "If any of the police again approach you or any of your colleagues-in-crime just tell them that this thing is bigger than any of you." The blunt statement and Ulster accent made an immediate impact. For a moment neither spoke. One of them asked John if he would like a drink. He replied, "No, I don't drink." At that both rose, ignoring their unfinished drinks, and left the club. John's aim had been to frighten them so that they would not again attack Derek. He was himself much surprised at his apparent impact.

Derek did not again see Alexander Atkins or his swarthy companion. Nor, was he again attacked by roughs. Joan Waters, too, was left in peace apart from the following two minor incidents which may have been attempts to impress upon her that she had not moved beyond the reach of the long arm of the undercover services.

A few days after she returned to work, "David" telephoned her office. The switchboard operator asked his name and he replied, "Just tell her that David rang." She said, "Hold a minute and I will put you through to her." He replied, "No, I don't want to speak to her. Just tell her that David rang."

Early in the new year, Joan Waters went into hospital and spent five months in it. Afterwards, she stopped with her mother-in-law. One afternoon, two men came to the door of the house and demanded to see her. She was in the bedroom at the time and in an advanced state of pregnancy. She came two-thirds of the way down the stairs and confronted the men as they stood in the hallway. She asked them for identification. They said that they were police and flashed white cards. She knew that the police do not have white cards, but did not press them further on the issue. She said that she did not need the police; that she was just out of hospital and had no knowledge of anything requiring police attention. She could see that they were startled and embarrassed by her condition. In fact, she felt that they were deterred by it as they left quickly with no attempt at explanation. She immediately reported the incident to the RUC by telephone. The police made inquiries and telephoned back. They reported that they knew of no matter involving her in any way and asked for a description of the white identification cards. The RUC officer confirmed that they were not police ones. He added that the army used white cards and that the RUC would keep watch on her house as it was all very mysterious. The police did so for several days, but there was no further development.

11 Guy Fawkes Style Electioneering?

When public opinion is central to the fortunes of a government, unscrupulous expedients to manipulate it are to be expected. It has always been like that. One of the most successful was the operation to which the hit man, Guy Fawkes, gave his name in 1605.* The target was public opinion. Neither the buildings of Parliament nor the members were in serious danger from the amount of gunpowder to be used. Of course, the three, original, amateur conspirators had other ideas. They initiated the plot in order to rid England of James I and his régime. The Earl of Salisbury, director of government intelligence (and chief minister of the realm), infiltrated and masterminded it as a timely and much-needed device to make permanent the rule of the same monarch and régime. He knew that a conspiracy (exposed with the maximum publicity) to murder the king and Parliament in one horrific holocaust would cause public opinion to recoil into solid support for the less than popular James I and himself. When the plotters decided to abandon their scheme after failing in an attempt to dig a tunnel under the House of Lords, no-one was more concerned than Salisbury. He arranged as quickly as possible for the vault under the House of Lords to be vacated by its tenant and the news that it was available for renting to be passed to the associates of Guy Fawkes. They fell for the stratagem and the plot was resumed.

In the twentieth century, public opinion has an added importance because, when expressed through elections, it can decide the lifespans

*Another modern feature of the Guy Fawkes operation is that, as with many covert agents, he believed that he was being directed on behalf of the cause to which he himself subscribed, but in reality was being "controlled" by its enemies. There are communists, for example, who believe that they are agents of the KGB, but who have been recruited and are "controlled" by the CIA or, on the other hand, non-communists who believe that they are employed by the CIA when their master is the KGB. (This feature of undercover work will be mentioned again in a later chapter in connection with Ulster and especially the Ulster Freedom Fighters.)

of democratic governments. If it can be manipulated, the dividends can be high. In certain elections, they will appear to be particularly high and the expedients to sway public opinion are likely to be correspondingly determined and extreme.* One such election was the United Kingdom general election of February 1974.

A period when a killer volcano threatens to erupt and in the end does not is a non-event to subsequent generations. To the men and women who wait in its shadow with the ground rumbling under them and the volcanic ash hiding the sun, it is a terrifying reality which may drive them to the most desperate expedients. The British establishment passed through a non-event of that kind in the weeks leading up to February 1974. The economy had been in serious trouble during 1972 and 1973. Edward Heath's Conservative government adopted stringent regulations to restrict increases in wages. This, in turn, led to direct confrontation between it and the coalminers in the latter part of 1973. On 12th November, the National Union of Mineworkers announced a ban on overtime work and the nation's reserves of coal began to deplete rapidly. On 13th December, the government restricted industry throughout the country to three working days per week to conserve fuel. Capitulation to the wage demand of the miners, it was believed, would be followed by an avalanche of wage claims from workers in other industries with the result that the pound, already precarious, would collapse on the international money market.

The arrangements for running the country in an extreme national emergency, such as a nuclear attack, were alerted. These assume that centralised, parliamentary government will cease and that regional administrations under military and civil service commissioners will endeavour to operate essential services. The persons assigned to act as regional commissioners were placed on standby and the secret bunkers from which they would control their regions were prepared for occupation. Emergency generators were distributed with water supplies and the pumping of sewerage the first priorities. Eventually,

---

*For example, the break-in at the Watergate Building had an election motive. Nor was it an accident that during the eleven years prior to 1976, 32% of covert operations approved for the CIA by the Committee of Forty were to support selected parties and individuals with money in foreign elections *(CIA: The Pike Report* (Spokesman edition, 1977), p. 190).

in January, Heath decided to go to the country in a general election on the theme, "Who rules Britain?"

The public was apprehensive at the shortage of heat and light and the inconveniences of the three day working week. However, for those in the higher echelons of government it was a period of seemingly near apocalypse. Many believed that the country was teetering on the precipice of political anarchy and economic collapse. A recollection of John Davies, the minister for Europe in Heath's cabinet, indicated the mood, "We were at home in Cheshire, and I said to my wife and children that we should have a nice time, because I deeply believed then that it was the last Christmas of its kind that we would enjoy."*

A number of persons who were involved in the crisis, or were well-informed observers, later joined the militantly anti-trade union National Association for Freedom. Among them were Vice-Admiral Sir Louis Le Bailey, director-general of military intelligence, and the counter-insurgency experts, Sir Robert Thompson and Field Marshal Sir Gerald Templer. Colonel David Stirling was so alarmed at what he believed was the dubious ability of the government to cope with a major strike affecting essential services that he turned to the possibility of forming a private force of military and other experts to assist the civil authorities. Sir Walter Walker, the retired NATO commander-in-chief, was equally perturbed and formed the less specialised Civil Assistance which, he reported, attracted 100,000 volunteers.

It has been claimed that criminals, sportsmen and senior government officials are the most conservative groups in every country. Of the senior government officials, none can be more conservative than the members of the Foreign Office, the officers of the armed forces and the officials of the intelligence services. In addition, in February 1974, these interlocking groups had special reasons for wanting a Conservative government returned apart from the fear of a miners' victory leading to anarchy and national bankruptcy.

The officials of the Foreign Office had a fanaticism about United Kingdom membership of the EEC such as has seldom been seen since the early crusades. Joe Haines, from his vantage point as Harold Wilson's press secretary, reckoned that so strong and so determined

*Quoted in "The Fall of Heath" by S. Fay and H. Young, *The Sunday Times*, 22nd February 1979.

was their resolve to make the country a member that no government, regardless of party, could have resisted it indefinitely.* The present writer, too, can testify to the fanaticism from discussions at that time with diplomats in London and overseas. When Edward Heath and the Conservatives took the country into membership, the Foreign Office officials regarded it as their very own special triumph. In February 1974, they feared acutely that a Labour victory would reverse their achievement. A powerful section of the Labour Party was demanding that Britain withdraw. Only a year earlier, Wilson himself had denounced the legislation which made it a member. "In ninety-three legislative words," he said, "the safeguards gained after centuries of constitutional struggle, even bloody civil wars, were swept aside by a provision that said simply that hereafter anything enacted by the EEC automatically became British law, annulling any laws which were inconsistent without debate. We have sold, with hardly a murmur from the media, our constitutional birthright for a mess of highly problematical economic pottage."

On the eve of the election, Wilson pledged that, if the Labour Party won, his new government would have "a fundamental re-negotiation" of the terms of membership. The Foreign Office officials knew that fundamentally improved terms were not possible because the other member countries could not concede a privileged position to one member only. This meant that Wilson would have to accept from the re-negotiation the same conditions as Heath had accepted, with perhaps a few minor, cosmetic modifications, or else withdraw the United Kingdom out of the EEC. In the event, Wilson opted for the cosmetic exercise, but no one could foretell this in February 1974.†

The Foreign Office and even more the armed services and intelligence organisations were alarmed at a commitment in the Labour Party election manifesto to reduce spending on defence.

A strong lobby within the Labour Party was urging more open government and greater access to official information on the lines of the Freedom of Information Act which has since been implemented in the United States. The Foreign Office, Ministry of Defence and intelligence services were resolute in their opposition to relaxation of the

---

*Joe Haines, *The Politics of Power* (Coronet edition, 1977), p. 71.
†The main modification secured in Wilson's re-negotiation was the "correction mechanism" formula in the rules for calculating a member country's contribution to the EEC budget. The formula has not yet been used once.

security rules. The Labour manifesto did not refer to the issue, but that did not mean that a Labour government would not legislate on it. Later in the year, the manifesto for an October election did contain an undertaking that a new act would place the onus on government departments to show cause why information should not be disclosed.

The Foreign Office and the Ministry of Defence were acutely aware that the Republic of South Africa is the sole stable country in Africa; that its government is opposed to the increasing presence of the USSR and China in Africa and that it controls the sea route to the Indian Ocean where the USSR has mounted a powerful naval challenge. Also, the British intelligence services co-operate closely with South Africa's BOSS. Each year, the Labour Party at its annual conference had pledged itself to boycott South Africa as a protest against apartheid. Harold Wilson himself had emphasised publicly that he would ban the export to it of all arms except the minimum necessary for self-defence against foreign aggression.

Some months after Wilson resigned from being prime minister, he admitted to two journalists that he believed there was a faction in DI5 sympathetic to the South African and Rhodesian authorities.* He also said that he was convinced that South African agents and others concerned with intelligence gathering were responsible for more than a dozen burglaries at the houses and offices of himself and his professional advisers. His claim about South African involvement was subsequently ridiculed in the press and elsewhere in a way reminiscent of the scorn poured for so many years on the suggestion that British intelligence might have had a link with the Zinoviev letter.† That Wilson should have turned to South Africa as a prime suspect was not unreasonable. It spends heavily on its undercover services and Britain is the country whose policies most vitally affect it. American concern as to who rules Iran or Guatemala, for example, is modest compared with South African interest in who rules the United Kingdom. Nor is Wilson likely to have forgotten an earlier incident in which a young lady in the cabinet office had to be charged and was convicted of supplying documents to a South African intelligence agent.

*_The Observer_, 17th July 1977. See also B. Penrose and R. Courtiour, _The Pencourt File_ (1978), Chapter 2.
†See footnote, page 1 13, for a short account of the Zinoviev episode.

In the same interview with the two journalists, Wilson made the further point that he believed that a faction in DI5 had pursued a vendetta against himself and his close colleagues. A whispering campaign by it that there was a communist cell linked with his cabinet and involving himself and his personal secretary, Lady Falkender, had led him to call in Sir Michael Hanley, director-general of DI5, in the summer of 1975. The latter had confirmed that a disaffected faction with extreme right-wing views existed in the service.

The remarks to the journalists were published in *The Observer* on 17th July 1977. Later in the same month, the *Daily Express* carried reports by its defence correspondent, Chapman Pincher, that Wilson's offices had been bugged by security men in both 10 Downing Street and the House of Commons. James Callaghan, who had replaced Wilson as prime minister, issued an official denial and Mrs. Margaret Thatcher, the leader of the opposition, put out a brief supporting statement that she shared his confidence in DI5. Pincher replied that a denial by the intelligence services about bugging or other secret operation carries no weight because denial is part of their stock-in-trade. He also pointed out that he had been careful to avoid stating that DI5 was the agency responsible.

On 28th August, *The Observer* printed a short statement by Sir Harold Wilson in which he expanded a little on his earlier remarks. He said: *My impression is that what has been going on over a period of years has come from, or been fed by, a small mafia group of MI5 who have contacts outside in one or two sections of the press, and a few self-appointed private enterprise security agents.*

It is my strong impression that it is probably a very small MI5 mafia who have been out of the service for some time, who still continue the vendetta for no doubt extremely right-wing purposes of their own.

I'm equally confident that the higher direction of MI5 and those operating today do not have anything to do with this, nor have they done so at any time.

An article in the same issue explained that *The Observer* accepted assurances obtained at three different levels from the "security authorities" that they had no evidence that Sir Harold or his private secretary, Lady Falkender, had been a target for KGB blackmail or had been "a plant". It then raised the possibility that "there is indeed a faction within MI5 which is gunning for the former prime minister (and by implication the whole Labour leadership)." It then continued: *Mr. Callaghan's statement is not the end of the story. Material now with* The Observer — *which we are still checking* — *suggests that there may well have been a group hostile to Sir Harold Wilson (and hostile to leaders of the Liberal Party) extending far beyond a 'faction of MI5'.*

"Whether Sir Harold himself appreciated the full ramifications of the matter is doubtful.

Four days before *The Observer* published this statement by Wilson, Chapman Pincher wrote in the *Daily Express* that he had a copy of a DI6 report, detailing the heavy surveillance of Harold Wilson prior to the general election of February 1974. It was several pages long and marked "Top Secret for Addressee Only". Next day, he gave more information. The document was a progress report during an inquiry into possible communist affiliations of colleagues and friends of Wilson. The details, Pincher wrote, "reveal political overtones suggesting that certain intelligence men were strongly opposed to the re-election of Sir Harold Wilson as prime minister".

The document expressed great concern that Wilson had been strongly pro-Israel when prime minister from 1964-70 and that his return to office would sour relations with the Arabs at a time when the international oil crisis was acute. It referred to his close friendships with prominent Jewish businessmen, some of whom had commercial links with iron curtain countries. It expressed fears that Wilson as prime minister would increase trade with the USSR which would allow the Soviets to infiltrate more KGB agents into the United Kingdom under diplomatic cover.

The last apprehension may have been as much influenced by professional considerations as patriotic ones. The more KGB agents in the country, the more men the intelligence services have to deploy to watch and counter their activities. The Conservative government of Edward Heath had expelled one hundred and five KGB agents in 1971 who were operating under diplomatic cover and there was reluctance to have the old situation restored.

Also, the feared return of large numbers of KGB agents may not have been the only operational reason to influence the intelligence men to fear the election of a Labour government under the premiership of Harold Wilson. A British undercover agent in one of David Cornwell's [John le Carré's] novels is so exasperated by platitudes by a superior that he exploded within himself that it was like working for a bloody clergyman.* There could have been a similar reaction to the prospect of a Wilson administration and especially with the kind of rough-neck covert operations that were in progress in Ulster.

Political parties can no more escape from their pasts than can individuals. The British Labour Party was formed by Keir Hardie, a self-educated Scottish miner of high ideals and stout integrity. Many of its earlier leaders were lay preachers who entered politics in order to apply their religious ideals in practical ways. It was the party's ideals of social justice which eventually brought it a measure of middle-class support. Bernard Shaw, the Webbs and their small circle led the way and it should not be forgotten that the Fabian Society, which they founded, is today stronger than ever, no less idealistic and no less a major influence in the councils of the party. Sir Harold Wilson himself was in the mainstream of the party traditions. He grew up in a Free Church home in Huddersfield with grace before meals and friends in for hymn singing on Sunday evenings after the service in the Baptist church; he was a Fabian of long standing; a co-founder of War on Want; and his wife was a daughter of a Congregational minister. James Callaghan, who succeeded him as prime ministe₁, ᵥas brought up a Baptist. On Sunday, he attended Sunday school twice and church service twice and during the remainder of the day was allowed to read only the Bible and Children's Encyclopedia.

Dick Crossman was deputy-director of British psychological warfare in the Second World War and knew the murky, ruthless world of intelligence organisations from inside. At an early stage of the Rhodesian crisis, he was a member of Harold Wilson's cabinet. In his diary, he wrote that he had frequently tried to cross-examine Wilson on his plans for overthrowing the government of Ian Smith. He added, "I get the impression that he considers the choice for Britain to lie between conventional military action or conventional diplomatic action, and that he denies the possibility of a third course in between. This is, of course, ludicrous. There are only 250,000 whites in Rhodesia and we have I presume an SIS [DI6], and SOE† and other organisations of paramilitary war. And yet I am pretty sure that Harold and his military advisers have never considered the use of

*John le Carré, *The Spy Who Came in from the Cold* (1963), p. 20.
†Abbreviation for Special Operations Executive, the organisation established in 1940 to conduct covert operations and foment insurrection in countries occupied by Germany and Japan.

black propaganda or subversive organisations to put pressure on Smith."*

There was an earlier occasion when the same elements in high places were fearful about the outcome of an election. It was in 1924 and the Labour prime minister, Ramsay MacDonald, was the bogeyman. As fifty years later, the Foreign Office and armed services were among the most strongly affected. Again, as later, the intelligence set-up had its own special reasons for alarm. It was anticipated that a new Labour government under MacDonald would close down MI 1c (as DI6 was then called) in the interest of economy and aspirations of international brotherhood.

The response was a forgery purporting to be a letter from Gregori Zinoviev, president of the Third International in Moscow, to the British Communist Party, urging it to promote revolution and to foment mutiny in the armed forces.† The document appeared in the press shortly before polling day and swung many votes against MacDonald.

The February 1974 general election contained one incident‡

*Richard Crossman, *The Diaries of a Cabinet Minister* (1975), vol. I, p. 379.

†Some of the mysteries of the Zinoviev letter still remain, but much of the story has now been set out by L. Chester, S. Fay and H. Young in *The Zinoviev Letter*. An agent of MI 1c [DI6], Captain Sidney Reilly, a Russian by birth, probably set events moving, but is unlikely to have masterminded the plot. The forgery was undertaken by Alexis Bellegarde, a White Russian emigré who, later in the second world war, worked as a British intelligence agent inside the Abwehr, the German counter-espionage organisation. Polish intelligence, too, was implicated. In London, intrigues and manoeuvres of incredible complexity were undertaken to give the document the appearance of complete authenticity and to ensure that it was published at the most devastating moment. The main people involved were Admiral Sir Hugh Sinclair, the Head of MI 1c; Colonel Vernon Kell, Director of MI5; Vice-Admiral Sir Reginald Hall, former Director of Naval Intelligence and former MP and Principal Agent of the Conservative Central Office; Lt.-Col. Frederick Browning, former second-in-command of MI 1c and friend of Thomas Marlowe, editor of the conservative *Daily Mail*; C. D. im Thurn, a war-time agent of MI5; Sir Eyre Crowe, Permanent Secretary, Foreign Office, and G. C. Gregory, Head, Northern Department, Foreign Office. (The Polish prime minister mentioned to the speaker of his House of Deputies that the last named had been "helpful in exploiting the forgery".) Sir Eyre Crowe sent the protest note to the Soviet ambassador in well-timed haste and despite the fact that Ramsay MacDonald, who was electioneering in Wales, had withheld his initial from the draft. Nor was Arthur Ponsonby, MacDonald's junior minister of Foreign Affairs, consulted although he was available in London.

‡For an account see Joe Haines, *The Politics of Power* (Coronet edition, 1977), pp. 193-196.

reminiscent of the Zinoviev letter episode. A few days before the poll, an attempt was made to interest *The Guardian* in a story that Harold Wilson was involved in land speculation. Such a story would have been heavily damaging to the electoral prospects of the Labour Party as it was pledged to end such speculation. Wilson telephoned the editor who accepted his denial. The attempt then appears to have been transferred to the *Daily Mail*. Wilson's solicitor and adviser, Lord Goodman, was called in. He was also chairman of the Newspaper Publishers Association and pointed out to the proprietor of the *Daily Mail* the danger of damaging democracy through a last minute election stunt story. The result was that the story was set aside for the time being.

There is no evidence to indicate who was responsible for the attempt to have the alleged land deal story published. Assumptions based on the analogy of the Zinoviev letter could be totally wrong.

On the other hand, an incident which occurred in Ulster during the same February 1974 general election left so much circumstantial evidence, suggesting undercover involvement, that a judicial commission absolutely must be used to establish whether or not this was so. It was an explosion which destroyed 6 Cromwell Road, Belfast, the headquarters of the Alliance Party of Northern Ireland.

Forecasts predicted that the overall election result would be close. Opinion polls suggested a Conservative win, but they had been wrong too often in the past to inspire confidence. The issue, "Who rules Britain?", began to lose momentum part-way through the campaign and the prospects of Labour correspondingly picked up. When the count was over, the Conservatives had 296 seats and Labour 300. Heath immediately proposed a coalition to the 14 Liberals who had been returned. They rejected it, but he refused to admit defeat. He was only four seats fewer than Wilson and the Ulster loyalists could perhaps be brought into the equation. In the previous parliament there had been 8 Official Ulster Unionists who had accepted the Conservative whip and considered themselves part of his party. Heath was sufficiently encouraged to delay surrendering the seals of office and to have two further cabinet meetings. He was disappointed. Of his 8 previous Ulster supporters, 4 had gone down in defeat, 1 did not re-stand and 3 were marching under new orders which forbade them to give support as in the past.

The February 1974 election in Ulster thus decided that the Labour

Party and not the Conservative Party would form the government at Westminster and that Harold Wilson and not Edward Heath would be the new prime minister. This outcome, in turn, gave the Labour Party the double advantages of being able to choose the date of the next election and of going into it with the prestige of being the government. It used both to good effect and at a further general election, held in October of the same year, won 42 more seats than its Conservative opponent. It was enabled to continue in office until May 1979 and in the recriminations of defeat the Conservative Party polarised into the Thatcher and Heath factions, the implications of which are still only partly worked out on the political scene.

Northern Ireland returns a total of 12 MPs to Westminster. On three occasions all 12 have been Unionist, but over the years the usual figure has been 10 Unionist. In the outgoing parliament in February 1974, it was 9 and consisted of 8 Official Unionists and 1 Democratic Unionist. For some time before that election, it had been recognised that, in the event of a close overall United Kingdom result, the Ulster MPs could hold the balance in the House of Commons. Much therefore depended on which brand of them would be returned and whether, as in the past, they would align themselves with the Conservative Party and accept its whip.

A little earlier, the Westite Official Unionists, Vanguard Unionists and Democratic Unionists had formed the United Ulster Unionist Council to oppose the pro-government Faulknerite Official Unionists. Most of the Official Unionist members at Westminster had remained close to the Faulknerites. One had even held an appointment under Heath as minister of state for Employment. The Ulster public was critical and unhappy at the way they had been passive and ineffective as Heath's government had set up a "power sharing" administration complete with Irish republican ministers and had arranged a semi-condominium with the Irish Republic in the Sunningdale Agreement and Council of Ireland scheme. On the other hand, the outgoing men had been returned in the previous election by large majorities and established MPs are difficult to oust.

The UUUC coalition informed each of the 8 Official Unionist members from the dissolved parliament that he had either to align himself with it or fight for his seat. 4 chose to fight; 1 did not re-stand and 3 linked up with it in constituencies where UUUC support was strong. Even among the 3 men who aligned with the UUUC, there was reluctance to identify too closely with it for fear of losing a stratum of middle-class voters more conscious of social status than constitutional complexities. The reluctance was even stronger in their party organisations and the UUUC had to impose firm pressure to ensure that "UUUC" appeared on their election literature and posters. In South Antrim, the constituency of the present writer, no satisfaction was received on the matter until an exasperated meeting of my own constituency party presented the Westite Official Unionists with an ultimatum that either "UUUC" appear on the literature and posters of their candidate or it would present its own rival one.

The UUUC candidates consented to work together as a group at Westminster. I pressed that such an undertaking would be meaningless if they were free to take the Conservative whip in common with Faulknerite unionists. (At that time even the most optimistic in the UUUC camp assumed that some of the latter would be returned.) At first there was reluctance to jeopardise the concessions already gained by pushing for yet another. The Official Unionists within the UUUC argued stubbornly that the most effective place from which to influence events at Westminster was inside the Conservative Party. In the end, the point of view which I urged prevailed. All UUUC candidates undertook to respond solely to their own parliamentary whip if elected. There was particular resistance within the camp of the Official Unionist candidate in South Antrim and, not until the final pre-nomination meeting of coalition party leaders in the Seagoe Hotel, Portadown, was it confirmed that the point had been conceded even in that constituency.

The position was thus clear and unambiguous from nomination day onwards. Successful Faulknerite unionists would continue to act in the new parliament as members of the Conservative Party. Successful UUUC candidates, in contrast, would form their own party and act independently and possibly often in opposition to it. As events were to demonstrate, **eleven parliamentary seats or a difference of twenty-two votes in a parliamentary division were at stake.**

The UUUC campaign went well. It had undertaken, a few weeks earlier, a massive drive across the region for the signing of a petition to Parliament appealing for the removal of the "power-sharing" constitution. The exercise had made the public familiar with the coalition and had given the local branches of the three parties experience in working together for a common purpose. The Faulkner administration, complete with its Irish republican members, had assumed office at the end of the previous month and the sense of humiliation and indignation among the public meant easy UUUC canvassing. As the days sped past, we knew that the tide was running strong for the coalition and growing stronger. Then on Tuesday morning, 26th February – two days before polling – came the Cromwell Road incident. It did not stop the UUUC candidates from winning every seat in Northern Ireland, with one exception. It did, however, have a violent, adverse impact on their votes. A further Westminster general election took place in October of that year. By then the Faulkner administration had been out of existence for some months and hostility to it no longer rallied the public. The total UUUC vote should have fallen in the less tense conditions. Instead, it rose by a further 6.6%. At least part of the explanation is the setback in February caused by the explosion which destroyed the head-quarters of the Alliance Party in Cromwell Road, Belfast.

The Alliance Party was small. It had only three candidates and their prospects varied from slight to nil. It aroused no strong antag-onism in any section of the population. At worst, it was regarded as consisting of sanctimonious, middle-class persons who mouthed government clichés about "power-sharing" and said that they would be equally satisfied to live under London or Dublin. There was no fierce detestation of it such as loyalist unionists had for Faulknerite unionists or Sinn Féin republicans for SDLP republicans. The Provisional IRA consistently ignored it even in its verbal propaganda.

Cromwell Road is a quiet street of three-storey, Victorian brick houses. It is off Botanic Avenue, a busier thoroughfare with shops. Number 6 was the Alliance Party headquarters. Beside it was an alleyway which provided rear entrances to a row of Botanic Avenue shops. The nearest rear entrance belonged to a home bakery. At seven o'clock on the morning of 26th February two men and two women were busy with the morning's baking. The electric light was burning and mixers and other equipment were making a steady hum. The door into the alleyway was open, giving a clear view into the bakery. A vehicle was heard in the alleyway, followed by the foot-steps of either two or three men walking past the open door. The persons in the bakery assumed that they were the milkmen making the morning delivery and paid no attention. One of them left a couple of minutes later to buy a newspaper. A motor car was parked in the alleyway about three metres from the bakery door and alongside the Alliance building end wall. He walked past it and turned the corner into Cromwell Road. Seconds later 200 lb of high explosive detonated in the car. The people working in the bakery escaped alive only because its wall collapsed outward into the alleyway. Windows were shattered over a wide area and a number of persons had to be treated for injuries from flying glass and shock. The Alliance Party headquarters was totally wrecked. The building, however, was empty as it was so early in the morning.

The Ulster public, in the main, accepted that the bomb was the work of loyalist extremists. The Alliance Party had a slightly Roman Catholic image with the man in the street. The leader of the party belonged to a Roman Catholic family and in the council and Northern Ireland Assembly elections of the previous year, Roman Catholics had frequently voted for it when a republican candidate was not standing.

The public had also come to accept a rule of thumb that the Provisional IRA gave a warning when they placed a bomb and loyalists rarely gave one. The persons responsible for the Cromwell Road bomb gave neither a telephoned nor shouted warning.

The Provisional IRA usually endeavoured to give a warning of some kind. Experience had taught them that nothing alienated support within their districts more swiftly than bombs which killed or injured Roman Catholics and that nothing reduced the inflow of money from Irish American sympathisers more drastically. It had further taught them that bomb casualties in Protestant districts frequently included a substantial proportion of Roman Catholics. An example was "Bloody Friday", 21st July 1972, when the Provisional IRA exploded twenty-two bombs in Belfast with slight or no warnings and killed 16 people and injured 120 others. Many Roman Catholics were among the victims and the inflow of Irish American money is said to have slumped by two-thirds almost immediately. As it happened, the occupants of two upstairs flats in 4 Cromwell Road were Roman Catholics. They escaped solely because of the strength of the end wall of the building.

Loyalist extremist groups which planted bombs, on the other hand, often gave no warning. They were invariably amateurs, usually ill-organised and indifferent to public opinion. Their targets were frequently public houses used as gathering places by the Provisional IRA and the chance of killing co-religionists was small.

The motor car which contained the bomb had been stolen in York Street which is frequented by both political communities. The place of theft of the car is often a pointer to the political allegiance of the bombers. On this occasion, it was no help.

Although the public as a whole accepted that loyalist extremists had destroyed the Alliance Party headquarters, a number of local people, including some caught in the blast of the explosion, doubted it from the beginning. They insisted that neither loyalists nor republicans would have left 200 lb of explosive within a few feet of men and women working contentedly in the bakery kitchen and suggested that it was more like the work of outside agents, acting under strict and impersonal orders. The bombers must have seen the persons in the well-lighted room through the open door and realised that they were almost certain to die in the explosion. Nor could panic be the explanation. The footsteps which were heard passing in the alleyway were of men walking — not running in panic.

The bomb weighed 200 lb. Only the two main loyalist urban paramilitary organisations were able occasionally to produce a bomb of that size. Either would have regarded it as a special achievement and in either the semi-democratic command structure would have ensured that a number of men would have participated in the decision where to detonate it. It is not believable that a Protestant residential street would have been selected nor is there any instance of such an occurrence on any other occasion.

Also, the bomb consisted of best quality commercial explosive — a substance which loyalist bomb makers seldom had in quantity. Most of their larger bombs were made of agricultural fertiliser "mix" and similar substitutes.

The size of the bomb was exactly right to wreck the Alliance Party headquarters without bringing down additional buildings such as No. 4 in which several families lived in flats. It was placed a little further forward along the wall of the building than would have been selected by a novice and apparently with a knowledge of the positions of the interior walls. There was a professionalism and explosive expertise about the operation totally alien to the loyalist slap-dash, amateur bombers.

The Alliance Party headquarters explosion was forty-eight hours before polling was to commence. Radio, television and the evening newspaper carried reports of it that day and the morning newspapers carried them next day. The anti-UUUC backlash among voters, although difficult to measure, was formidable. No proof is available that the incident was designed to produce such a backlash nor that it was masterminded by an element within the government's under-cover set-up. On the other hand, if there were as many unanswered question marks ranged against an individual, he would be under arrest and behind bars with bail refused. When the hoped-for judicial inquiry into the activities of the United Kingdom intelligence organ-isations is conceded, high on the agenda must be an investigation of this incident. It might even result in information which, in turn, could help to elucidate why army undercover men were stealing the three vehicles that night a few months earlier near William Black's house at the junction of Black's Road and Tildarg.

12 Court of the Secret Informer

Saturday, 25th May 1974, was the eleventh day of the general strike called by the Ulster Workers' Council. Andrew Beattie arrived around 9.00 a.m. at Central Strike Headquarters. It was in the Vanguard Unionist Party Central Office, 9 Hawthornden Road, Belfast. Some strike leaders were already there and others kept arriving at intervals. They chatted informally until the Constitutional Stoppage Central Co-ordinating Committee began its daily session at 10.00 a.m. It consisted of the Central Council of the Ulster Workers' Council together with representatives of the loyalist parties and paramilitary organisations.

Harry Murry (UWC) was chairman and Jim Smyth (UWC) secretary. William Craig, a former minister of Home Affairs, represented the Vanguard Unionist Party; Harry West, MP, the Official Unionist Party; and Dr. Ian Paisley, MP, the Democratic Unionist Party (each was leader of his respective party). Among the representatives of the paramilitary organisations, the best known was Lieut.-Colonel E. H. Brush, CB, DSO, OBE, the commander of the Down Orange Welfare Volunteers. He was Deputy Lieutenant for Co. Down and was subsequently a representative for South Down in the Northern Ireland Constitutional Convention of the following year. Andrew Beattie was present as the South-East Antrim political and welfare representative of the Ulster Defence Association.

The big issue that morning was whether to release feeding stuff from the mills for distribution to the farms. There was a strong case against favouring one section of the community (i.e. the farmers), but it was known that animals and poultry were hungry. In the end the humanitarian arguments won and instructions were issued for the release of a limited amount.

Apart from an interval for lunch, the meeting continued until 3.30 p.m. and then adjourned until 7.00 p.m. to allow representatives to report to their parties and organisations.

Reports had come in before the Central Co-ordinating Committee adjourned that the British government was about to take control of the refinery at Sydenham and the distribution of petrol and oil throughout Northern Ireland. A report, too, came through from London that the cabinet had decided to arrest the strike leaders and to place the region under martial law. Harold Wilson, the prime minister, had stated earlier in the day that he would give a television broadcast to the nation at 10.15 p.m. in the evening. The assumption grew that his purpose was to announce martial law for Northern Ireland.

The present writer was co-ordinator of the UUUC "Advice and Relief Centres" of which several hundred had been set up across the country. They were the framework through which the region was being administered. They issued travel passes and petrol permits for essential services, circulated strike regulations as they were formulated, encouraged mass rallies and cavalcades and resolved an infinite variety of local problems as they arose. Around mid-afternoon, I had a report from Ballymena that the large police station in the town had been ordered to clear its cells of ordinary prisoners in preparation for a large number of arrests. Shortly afterwards, more generalised reports came in from Co. Down that mass arrests of strike organisers were imminent. In the later afternoon, Andrew Gregg, deputy co-ordinator of "UUUC Advice and Relief Centres", and I returned to Central Strike Headquarters and collected a portable typewriter and some other items of equipment useful for continuing the strike should we have to go into hiding. I next made preparations for sleeping away from home that evening.

Andrew Beattie returned to Newtownabbey in south-east Antrim and reported on the decisions of the Constitutional Stoppage Central Co-ordinating Committee to a joint meeting of the local paramilitary organisations. Afterwards, he went home to have dinner and a wash and shave before returning to Central Strike Headquarters at 7.00 p.m. At the latter, he found the building deserted except for two strikers on guard-duty. They explained that the meeting was cancelled and everyone dispersed as it had been confirmed that the government was about to arrest all strike leaders. A few minutes later, Andy Tyrie, Supreme Commander, UDA, arrived for the cancelled meeting. He decided to accompany Beattie back to Newtownabbey. The driver of the car was unfamiliar with that part of Belfast. He turned right at the foot of Hawthornden Road instead of left. He realised his mistake when he was stopped by the gates of Parliament Buildings at Stormont and turned back. A police landrover followed the car to the gates and for about a mile after it turned. Beattie and Tyrie were not much concerned. It was not trying too hard to follow and they knew that there was much sympathy for the strike inside the police force.

They went to a hall where they would meet a cross-section of men from the various paramilitary organisations. A television set had been set up in it and, at 10.15 p.m., they watched Harold Wilson make his speech. It was cautious and non-commital and sounded unlike a man resolved on martial law and a mass arrest of strike leaders. The present writer, who in another district also watched him speak, promptly set aside the plan to sleep away from home that night.

Beattie went to Ardeene Social Club in Rathcoole after Wilson's speech and chatted with local residents. Eventually, someone advised him to go home and have some sleep. He took the advice and turned in about 2.00 a.m.

The army came at 3.45 a.m. There was knocking on the front door. Andrew Beattie came down and opened it. Twelve soldiers at least were in his small front garden and on the footpath. Others were at the back of his house. In the background along the street were numerous other soldiers and many vehicles.

A young soldier said that he had a warrant to search the house. He was wearing camouflage dress and no rank insignia was visible. Beattie invited him into the living room. He entered accompanied by four others. He asked permission to bring his family downstairs. It was granted and his wife and four children came down in pyjamas and dressing-gowns.

Two soldiers were detailed to search the lower part of the house and two the upper. Beattie asked to accompany the two who were to search upstairs. He had heard stories of security forces planting illegal objects during searches of houses and hoped that his presence might help to safeguard against it.

The soldiers searched the house superficially. They appeared to be checking only if there were any additional persons in it. Upstairs, they looked in the roofspace, but otherwise did not search. In the living room they did not even look under the cushions. A woman soldier was present, presumably to reassure any women who might be in the household.

Andrew Beattie was secretary-treasurer of the Eastway Social Club. The club account books were in the house and over £2,000 in cash. He drew the attention of the soldier-in-charge and explained about his position in the club. He accepted the explanation without question. He did not check through the money. He looked into the box and then immediately closed and left it.

The soldiers withdrew from the living room and went to the front of the house. After a couple of minutes, one of them returned and placed a hand on Beattie's shoulder and said that he was arresting him under Section 10 and Schedule 1 of the Northern Ireland (Emergency Provisions) Act.

He was taken immediately to an armoured personnel carrier or pig as these vehicles are nicknamed. Five minutes later, he was joined by a UDA officer who had just been arrested. The vehicle was then driven to the flat of another UDA officer. It was searched, but he was not at home.

Beattie and the other arrestee were driven to the army base on Church Road, Newtownabbey. They were placed in a large room with about thirty men. All sat on the concrete floor. Twelve of the men were paramilitary officers in the area centred on Rathcoole, Newtown. bbey. The remainder were men who had been arrested at Ardeene Hall in Rathcoole.

Local UDA vigilantees used Ardeene Hall nightly as their base for patrol and watch duties in the district. The army authorities appear to have been afraid that they would intervene to prevent the arrest of the paramilitary officers and mounted a special operation by 43 Royal Marine Commando to arrest them also. The marines chatted with the vigilantees for a time and exchanged cigarettes with them. Suddenly, an officer blew a whistle and the vigilantees were overpowered, arrested and brought to the army base on Church Road. In the morning, they were released. None of them were paramilitary officers.

After about two hours sitting on the concrete floor, the prisoners were taken, one by one, into a room to be interviewed by an Englishman in plain clothes. He was thirty-five to forty and it was assumed that he was an army intelligence officer.

Beattie sat facing him across the table during his interview. The room was rather dark. He asked him his name and address and rank in the UDA. He replied that he was a captain in the Social Welfare wing. He asked about several crimes of violence that had happened in south-east Antrim and Beattie told him that he knew nothing about any of them. He then turned to the general strike and asked him about his role in it. He answered that he was a UDA political and welfare representative on the Central Co-ordinating Committee. He asked about proceedings at Central Strike Headquarters and lingered for some time on the subject although he received no information. He gave the impression that he was well informed about it. At the end of the conversation, he again asked a question or two about crimes in south-east Antrim, but Beattie once more told him that he could throw no light on them.

The interrogation over, Beattie was given a rapid medical examination by an army doctor, and his photograph taken. A little later, he was placed with three others in a landrover which drove to Castlereagh Police Holding Centre, Ladas Drive, Belfast.

The police at Castlereagh allocated a cell to each man and gave them a good meal. It was the first food that any had had since arrested. Beattie slept for the rest of the day. He had had little sleep from the commencement of the strike and was dog-tired. At night, the police served tea and toast. They also gave out their own cigarettes and were exceptionally considerate. They told the men in custody that they would be released soon and appeared to believe it.

Next day was Monday. Two RUC officers in plain clothes interviewed the men, one by one, in the morning. They asked for information in a general way about various obvious crimes that had taken place in south-east Antrim. They did not stress any particular one. They were easy interviews and lasted about ten minutes. In fact, the interviews were so casual that everyone was reassured that they would be released as soon as the general strike eased.

Andrew Beattie was allowed a visit by his wife for a few minutes around half-past one and for the first time he learned that no strike organisers had been arrested other than in the Rathcoole district. This astonished him. He was not surprised that the government had declined to arrest members of parliament such as Dr. Ian Paisley and Harry West or other elected representatives such as members of the Northern Ireland Assembly. He could also understand that a Labour government led by Harold Wilson might be reluctant to arrest Jim Smyth or Harry Murray because of their support among the workers and their trade union links. But, the paramilitary leaders were in a less-privileged position and, if arrests were to be made, they were obvious targets. However, to limit them to twelve officers in the Rathcoole district made no sense. He himself was the only one among them to be on the Constitutional Stoppage Central Co-ordinating Committee and although that part of south-east Antrim was militantly behind the strike, it had no particular strategic importance.

His wife was again allowed to visit him about the same time on the following (or third) day of custody. She brought sandwiches and a bottle of milk. A policeman assured her that she had no need to worry as her husband would soon be home as would the others. Reports were circulating that Brian Faulkner, the head of the Westminster government supported Northern Ireland Executive, was about to resign and that his departure would signal the end of the strike. (The resignation was announced about 2.30 p.m., but Beattie did not hear about it until later.)

A policeman came to Beattie's cell after teatime and said that he had a visitor. He took him to a room in which was H. W. Hall, a solicitor. Beattie exclaimed, "When are we going home?" Hall replied that there were a lot of wagons outside and that it looked as though some men were to go to Long Kesh Detention Camp. He explained that he had fought tooth and nail to be allowed to see the men in custody since the time of the arrests. The authorities had eventually allowed him in, but only to see a spokesman. He had selected Andrew Beattie as the spokesman as he already knew him. He did not know who was to be detained or whether any were to be released.

Beattie was taken back to the cell and shortly afterwards brought down to the main police office where the other men who had been arrested were being assembled. His personal belongings were produced and checked out. He was handcuffed to another prisoner and placed in an army, armoured personnel carrier. It was the first time that he had been handcuffed.

The men were unloaded in the reception area at Long Kesh Detention Camp and placed in cubicles. Everywhere was in darkness as the strike was still in progress and the electric power was off. There had been no preparation to receive them. Names were noted down and there was a long wait before blankets could be located. About 1.30 a.m. they were taken to Compound 14. It was the only one for loyalist detainees and was already full. All the men in it were being held "on suspicion" under the Northern Ireland (Emergency Powers)

Act. None had been charged before a court.

Next day the Constitutional Stoppage Central Co-ordinating Committee discontinued the general strike. (The term used was "suspended" in order to remind the British Government that it could be resumed if it were to give cause.) The men from the Rathcoole district waited for the order to come for their release, but nothing happened. They were exasperated and mystified. They assumed that their arrests had been a political move and began to suspect that their continued detention had equally a political motive.

The men were correct that their arrests had been a political decision. This chapter begins with an account of events on Saturday, 25th May. During the early part of that day, orders were given to the army to arrest strike organisers over much of Ulster. As the hours went past, senior army commanders and others persuaded Whitehall that the step would make the region ungovernable and create a situation in which the government would be soundly worsted.* The orders were countermanded and the speech for which Harold Wilson had alerted the nation was an innocuous anti-climax.

The soldiers who had been detailed to make the arrests in the Rathcoole district together with a handful of other arrests in a section of Belfast were accidentally omitted when the new instructions were sent out. They were 1st Battalion, Light Infantry Regiment and 43 Royal Marine Commando. They carried through with the original orders.

The news media learned of the arrests next morning and over a number of days outraged protests went up from loyalist spokesmen, including leaders of loyalist political parties and Andrew Beattie's colleagues on the Constitutional Stoppage Central Co-ordinating Committee. The authorities reacted swiftly with a smear counter-attack. An army spokesman pointed out to journalists that the men were being held under anti-terrorist legislation and added that they had already been interrogated and had been "singing like birds", a phrase from the criminal underworld implying that they had confessed to crimes.

---

*It is interesting that Lord Wigg, a former professional soldier and Wilson's Co-ordinator of Intelligence, 1964-67, even baulked at the comparatively modest scheme for the army to take over the Sydenham oil refinery and to man twenty-one petrol-filling stations. He told the Lords, "He [the prime minister] has entered into an unlimited military commitment for political reasons with limited resources."

The police had been excluded from prior knowledge of the arrests, but quickly built up an accurate picture. One useful source of information was 43 Royal Marine Commando which had made the arrests at Ardeene Social Club. Its officers shared quarters with the police in North Queen's Street Police Station, Belfast.

The police were angry. They had not been consulted and they knew that they would be caught in the middle if, as for a time seemed probable, there should be violent local protests. They also knew that the arrested men were respectable and law-abiding and they were highly indignant when they heard that an official spokesman had smeared them with the suggestion of criminal activities. Journalists who telephoned the divisional police were told bluntly that the men had not even been interviewed at the time the army spokesman had made his statement. Several plain-clothes detectives went further and telephoned a commentator on commercially-owned Ulster Television and asked to be quoted as anonymous detectives in the police division responsible for Rathcoole* who knew that no evidence whatsoever existed against the men arrested.

The cancellation of the plan for the mass arrest of strike leaders across Ulster doomed the Northern Ireland Executive to a speedy demise. The Irish republican SDLP and other groups which had had members in it turned on the Wilson government with the utmost ferocity for being weak, cowardly and treacherous. Outside Northern Ireland political forces in the Irish Republic and the Irish lobby in Wilson's own Labour Party were little less restrained. Suddenly, the loyalist outcry over the arrests in the Rathcoole district was the government's best friend. It was not weak, cowardly or treacherous, it told its assailants and for proof pointed to the arrests and the fact that it was not releasing any of the men.

The loyalist leaders who pressed for the release of the arrested officers were handicapped by a coolness just then among the public at the name Rathcoole. Early in the general strike, the Constitutional Stoppage Central Co-ordinating Committee had instructed that pubs, clubs and all places for the sale of alcohol were to remain closed. Thirty-three bored and idle men from Rathcoole and nearby Carrickfergus took two minibuses and a taxi and drove to north Antrim for a

*It was D Division which was responsible for north Belfast and part of south-east Antrim.

pub crawl in districts where the writ of the Central Co-ordinating Committee was not observed. In the evening, a man from the group shot dead two brothers at their own public house in the townland of Tannaghmore. The police arrested all of the group before they reached home and they, the army authorities and NIO knew that the paramilitary organisations were not involved in any way. The public, which did not have the inside information of the police, could be less sure. It knew that the incident had been the only serious act of indiscipline during the strike and that Wilson had used it in his speech to taunt and smear the Ulster people.

The Northern Ireland (Emergency Provisions) Act laid down that a person arrested on suspicion could be held without further formality for up to twenty-one days. Beyond that period, he had to be issued with a holding order and eventually served with allegations of his suspected terrorist activities which he could contest before a commissioner in a special "Diplock" Detained Persons' Tribunal.

Five of the men arrested in the Rathcoole district were released within twenty-one days and two more after a much longer period, but without "allegations" having been made to justify their detention. The remainder spent the summer waiting to be released or to receive "allegations" which would give them something definite to contest. Time passed slowly and the men worried about their families and jobs. Long Kesh was like a prisoner-of-war camp. The men lived together in a compound or — to use their term — a cage. Food was delivered to the gate and they distributed it among themselves.

The tentative explanation came to be accepted by the men that they were victims of what they called "the Northern Ireland Office's numbers game". This was the theory that it kept a Long Kesh compound filled with loyalists as a propaganda exercise to impress observers outside Ulster that it was acting impartially towards both the British loyalist and the Irish republican community.

Andrew Beattie was given parole from 7th to 10th August. His wife was feeling the strain and the family doctor had recommended it. Also, his youngest daughter's birthday was on the 8th.

On 5th September 1974 came the first indication that something new and more sinister than the "numbers game" was afoot. The secretary of state for Northern Ireland appeared on television to read a special apologia for detention without trial. The public was weary of the pros and cons of the topic, but, when the statement made specific allegations, interest was intense. It claimed that those detained "have been involved in terrorism — the use of violence, including murder, intimidation, arson and the use of explosives" and asserted that among them were persons who, but for the intimidation of witnesses, would have been charged with:

(1) The "Bloody Friday" atrocity of 21st July 1972 in which Provisional IRA bombs had killed sixteen people and injured one hundred and twenty others.

(2) A shooting in Rathcoole on 31st January 1974 in which two Roman Catholic workmen were killed and three others injured.

(3) A shooting at Abbey Meat Packers, Ltd., near Rathcoole, on 11th February 1974 in which a sixteen-year-old boy and an eighteen-year-old girl were killed and four others injured.

The last atrocity had been claimed at the time by the Ulster Freedom Fighters with the explanation that it was in retaliation for a bomb which the Provisional IRA had exploded in an army bus in England seven days earlier, killing twelve men, women and children.

Andrew Beattie's wife saw the secretary of state read the statement on television. She and the wife of another detained paramilitary officer took a taxi shortly afterwards. It was crowded and the other passengers had also watched the broadcast. They accepted the claims without question and assumed, equally without question, that the detained paramilitary men from the Rathcoole district had been responsible for both of the specified shooting atrocities. "They don't detain them for nothing!" was the refrain. The two women dismounted from the taxi as soon as possible. They were shocked and greatly distressed.

Of the twelve men arrested in the original swoop in the Rathcoole district, five continued to be detained in Long Kesh. They, too, saw the secretary of state read the statement. They bitterly resented the unfounded claims, but after a time pushed it from their minds as no more than another instance of government ruthlessness in propaganda. They were thus still thinking in terms of the "numbers game" when, about a month later, they at last received "allegations" as required under the Northern Ireland (Emergency Provisions) Act.

They astounded and horrified them. Each man was accused of one or more serious crimes. Andrew Beattie's "allegations" were, first, that he had been a member of a gang which had murdered the teenage boy and girl at Abbey Meat Packers, Ltd. in the previous

February and, second, that he had hijacked vehicles for road blocks during the UWC general strike. There could hardly be a more serious accusation than these particular killings and they had been given renewed publicity by the secretary of state's broadcast of only four weeks earlier.

The five paramilitary officers from the Rathcoole district had each an unblemished record as a law-abiding citizen. One or two had quite responsible positions in their employment. Beattie was a senior foreman and had been twenty years with his company. All were freed eventually by the "Diplock" Detained Persons' Tribunals through failure of the prosecution to produce convincing evidence that they were other than innocent.

It is difficult not to conclude that the motive for the "allegations" was the political self-interest of the government. It had announced an elected convention to recommend new constitutional arrangements to replace the ones overthrown by the UWC general strike. The elections for it were promised for the following year and already by the time of the secretary of state's television broadcast in early September both the NIO and the Ulster political parties were evolving respective plans. In the loyalist camp an intense controversy on strategy was in progress and was to continue through the following months. (It led to the partial withdrawal of the present writer from my political party and was a factor in my decision in the following year to join with others in setting up a new political party, the British Ulster Dominion Party.) One section of loyalists correctly forecast that the proposed constitutional convention was an exercise to buy time and that the Westminster government would ignore its recommendations as cynically as it had ignored earlier constitutionally expressed wishes of the loyalist majority. The electoral campaigning in the constituencies, they said, had to be accompanied by a strengthened UWC and mended fences with the paramilitary organisations. They urged that if the loyalist political parties were to go into the convention without having in reserve the weapon of the general strike, they would be as naked and helpless as Aneurin Bevan, the post-war foreign secretary, had said Britian would be in international councils if she were unilaterally to discard her nuclear weapons.

None knew the force of such reasoning better than the NIO which had been humbled by the general strike of the previous May. But, it also knew that no politician in the run-up to an election would allow himself to be associated in any way with organisations or groups tainted with crime or violence. Here, ready to hand, was the means by which political parties could be isolated from the physical force (including the UWC with its trade union links) wings of the loyalist army and brought naked into the constitutional convention.

It was the urban UDA with its mass membership, which, during the general strike, had dominated the greater part of Belfast, the political and industrial capital. Sections of the Belfast battalions were contaminated by both crime and violence. Nevertheless, the organisation as a whole continued to have a large measure of credibility. This was partly because of respect for Andy Tyrie, the intelligent supreme commander, but even more to the existence of battalions outside Belfast that were well disciplined with dedicated officers and that were free of crime. Such battalions had the additional valve that they made liaison practicable between the UDA and the law and order sensitive rural paramilitary organisations and kept open a bridge of respectability into UDA circles over which even pre-election politicians could come and go.

The decision to accuse with serious crimes the Rathcoole UDA officers held in Long Kesh can be seen as part of the NIO's strategy for forestalling a general strike confrontation with the combined physical force and political wings of loyalism in the context of the coming constitutional convention. A wedge was to be driven between the political parties and the UDA and between the rural paramilitaries and the UDA.

At the same time, the additional possibility is not excluded that some of the crimes may have been chosen for the "allegations" because individuals in high places had vested interests in having them pinned on persons other than the real culprits. There is no reason to assume, for instance, that the attempted assassination of William Black in January of that year was totally unique.

Andrew Beattie received his "allegations" in the first few days of October. About two weeks later, on Thursday, 24th October, he was informed that he would appear before the "Diplock" tribunal on Wednesday, 30th. He was further informed that the main charge against him was amended to what in reality was a new charge. It was no longer that he had been a member of the murder gang, but that he had presided over a meeting of UDA officers in order to plan it. The lesser charge of hijacking remained unaltered.

Patrick Donnelly was Andrew Beattie's solicitor and Anthony Cinnamond his barrister. They had only three working days in which to prepare the defence against the new charge. Much of the work of the previous fortnight securing evidence to counter the original charge was suddenly irrelevant.

The hearing was held in a portacabin building in the grounds of Long Kesh Detention Camp. The room was square, but curtains and a carpet helped to conceal the prefabricated austerity. The commissioner was Judge Ireland who was on a temporary transfer from Scotland. To his right was a heavy curtain behind which prosecution witnesses could be concealed. Defence witnesses were kept in a separate room from the court. They were permitted into it only when giving evidence and not more than one at a time. No press or member of the public was allowed to be present.

Andrew Beattie and his wife grew up in Oldpark, Belfast, and as a young married couple settled in Rathcoole. Intimidation by the IRA sent most Protestants and a number of moderate Roman Catholics fleeing from the district at an early stage of the Ulster political crisis. For a time many of these refugee families were housed in five halls belonging to three Presbyterian, a Methodist and an Anglican church in the Rathcoole area. Andrew Beattie knew some of them personally and was drawn into the work of finding new homes and dealing with the problems of the young, sick and old. (On one occasion he helped in conjunction with a Dutch charitable organisation to arrange a holiday in the Netherlands for some of the children.) A little later when local people formed themselves into vigilantes and eventually into a battalion of the UDA, he was asked to take charge of the extensive social work sponsored by it in the district.

Beattie's outstanding record as a dedicated social worker stood him in good stead at the "Diplock" tribunal and partly explained the presence of a total of twenty-four persons who came to testify on his behalf. It was the highest number at any hearing up to that time. They were:

Glenn Barr (VUP), Jim Craig (DUP), Vincent McCloskey (SDLP) and Peter McLachlan (UPNI), four members of the Northern Ireland Assembly who belonged to four different political parties.
Chief Inspector Kyle and Inspector Jardine. The former was in charge of the investigations into the shooting at Abbey Meat

Packers, Ltd. and the latter was one of the police officers assisting him.

Rev. Robert Allen, minister of Rathcoole Presbyterian Church.

Thomas Seymour, mayor of Larne.

Harry Murray, chairman of the Ulster Workers' Council and Constitutional Stoppage Central Co-ordinating Committee.

Councillor Alex McGowan, whose son chanced to be driving past Abbey Meat Packers at the time of the shooting and was severely injured.

Councillor C. W. Stringer, who lived in Rathcoole.

Thomas Braniff, supervisor at the department in Gallaher, Ltd., in which Beattie was a senior foreman.

Mrs. N. Nelson of the Newtownabbey Society for Handicapped Children. She had come to know and respect Beattie through his social work.

Mrs. Fenton, chairwoman, Eastway Old Age Pensioners Club, Rathcoole.

Mrs. Betty Brown, now a social worker with the United Kingdom Prison Service.

Andy Tyrie, Supreme Commander, UDA.

E. W. H. Christie of Lincoln's Inn, London, who knew from high level contacts the story of the countermanded order for the arrest of the leaders of the general strike.

Seven other individuals, not related to his family, who had come to have a high regard for Beattie over the years — among them were three or four Roman Catholics, including a man whom he had helped to find a new house after he and his wife had been intimidated out of their home by the Provisional IRA.

After two days, Beattie's trial was adjourned for eighteen days and then resumed for a further three days. This was a total of five days of hearing and was the longest period spent on one case by a "Diplock" tribunal. The adjournment was because Judge Ireland had commitments in Scotland.

The lesser charge of hijacking vehicles to form roadblocks during the general strike collapsed when the soldier called as a witness could give only vague and imprecise descriptions.

The prosecution's only witness on the main charge that Beattie had convened and presided over a meeting of UDA officers to plan the murders was an anonymous Special Branch detective who claimed to be reporting evidence of a paid, anonymous informer. He said that the latter was a member of Beattie's UDA company and that the meeting had been attended by four other UDA officers whcm he named.

The four named officers had been arrested at the same time as Beattie and had already appeared before "Diplock" tribunals and been released. During their hearings, the prosecution had made no reference of any kind to suggest that the authorities had information to connect them with the murders or the alleged meeting to plan it.

The Special Branch man remained hidden behind the screen for prosecution witnesses, but did not wear the heavy socks and mocassins or use the voice distorter. He thus appeared to assume that Beattie and those among his witnesses who were from south-east Antrim would not recognise him. Presumably, he was from outside that area.

Beattie's defence barrister, Anthony Cinnamond, called Chief Inspector Kyle who was in charge of investigations into the murders at Abbey Meat Packers, Ltd. and Inspector Jardine who was assisting him. They testified that they had supervised one hundred and seven interviews in connection with them and examined several hundred telephone calls from the public and that not once had Beattie been mentioned.

It was pointed out to the Special Branch man behind the screen that the police team investigating the murders had no knowledge of his information and he was asked why he had not passed it to them. He replied that he had given it verbally to a police sergeant, but that he must have forgotten about it. When pressed why he, a trained detective, had not committed such important information to writing, he had no answer.

Beattie was a captain in the social welfare wing of the UDA. The Special Branch detective was asked whether he thought it probable that a more junior officer in the social welfare wing would call such a meeting and at it preside over ones of much more senior rank from the military wing. Again, he did not reply.

There were three other mysteries to which the prosecution had no answer. The army intelligence officer who had asked Beattie on the morning of his arrest for information on crimes in south-east Antrim had not even mentioned the one of which he was now accused. Why was this? Nor had he been interviewed by any policeman or other official whatsoever during the five months of his stay in Long Kesh Detention Camp. Was this a normal or reasonable way of conducting murder investigations? And then, too, he had been allowed three days of parole some weeks earlier. Was this a likely concession to someone whom the authorities believed had committed such horrific killings?

E. W. H. Christie, an English barrister, testified that an order to arrest the strike leaders throughout Northern Ireland had been countermanded, but that the new instructions did not reach the troops who were to make the arrests in the Rathcoole district and a small section of Belfast. Further, he offered to provide Judge Ireland with irrefutable proof from his personal contacts at the highest level in London.

Anthony Cinnamond reserved one particularly effective item of information to the end of the cross-examination. He turned to the Special Branch detective behind the screen and asked whether the prosecution knew that a man was awaiting trial in Crumlin Road Prison, Belfast, because the murder weapon used at Abbey Meat Packers, Ltd. had been found in his house. The reply was "No." He then gave the man's name and address, the date of his arrest and details of the weapon (a Schmeisser), including its serial number.*

The prosecution was allowed to sum up its evidence in secret hearing as part of it had been given in camera. Cinnamond was greatly disquieted by the move as it deprived him of guidelines on which to base his reply. However, on the resumption of full hearing, Judge Ireland instructed that Beattie be released immediately.

Four days later, Patrick Donnelly, his solicitor, wrote to him from a hospital bed: "What a tremendous thrill to hear of your release! . . . Yours is one case I will always remember not for the large number of witnesses, but for the meeting of a man who right from the first impressed his lawyers with his innocence − a conviction that grew and grew the more that one went into the case and met the many people who knew Andy Beattie so well."

---

*The police discovered that the gun had been used in a total of ten murders, including the two at Abbey Meat Packers, Ltd. The man who was awaiting trial in Crumlin Road Prison was subsequently charged with being the person responsible for the house in which the gun was found. He was eliminated from suspicion of having been involved in the killings.

13 Something Which We Can Hardly Mismanage

Counter-insurgency and its attendant covert and intelligence aspects have had an inordinate degree of latitude and influence on policy in Ulster partly because the Westminster cabinet and parliament are incredibly ignorant of the region and have been well content if the English politicians and Whitehall civil servants who administer it from the Northern Ireland Office at Stormont Castle succeeded in preventing its problems from impinging on the affairs of the mainland.

A Labour government under Harold Wilson was in office until June 1970 which was the vital, formative phase of the Ulster crisis. Richard Crossman's *Diaries of a Cabinet Minister* (vol. III) give an insight into its attitudes. A cabinet committee, including the prime minister, existed on Northern Ireland. Crossman joined it on 29th April 1969. In his diary, he records Denis Healy's description of it prior to his arrival. "You have no idea," said Healey, "what it was like before you came into the committee. The prime minister was always demanding active intervention early on, with this crazy desire to go there and take things over, that we should side with the Roman Catholics and the Civil Rights movement against the government and the Royal Ulster Constabulary, though we know nothing at all about it."

Crossman urged that the government begin to build up political intelligence about Northern Ireland. James Callaghan, the home secretary, said that the idea was absurd and that the Northern Ireland government would dislike it. Healey backed Crossman and pointed out that they would be "blind men leading the blind if they had to go in there knowing nothing about the place". In a later diary entry on 17th August, Crossman noted that the Ulster situation was awful and depressing, but, "Nevertheless, from the point of view of the government it has its advantages. It has deflected attention from our own deficiencies and the mess of the pound. We have now got into something which we can hardly mismanage."

Crossman's own special contribution to the debate on Ulster completes the impression of a new version of the Mad Hatter's tea party. He suggested that Ulster Roman Catholics should be encouraged to emigrate to England, Australia or elsewhere. It would be much cheaper, he added, than promoting policies to create new industries in the region.

The same blind complacency has equally prevailed in the ruling circles of the Conservative Party. If the abolition of the B Specials and the other limited interventions had brought such plaudits on the mainland and from Irish republicans, how much more would result from the abolition of the government and parliament of Northern Ireland! Also, if they were swept away, the stage would be clear for the introduction of new arrangements "to solve" the Ulster problem. Why not be the statesman to take the step? In March 1972, Edward Heath, prime minister of a Conservative government, succumbed to the temptation. He demanded that the Northern Ireland government surrender its authority over all aspects of law and order, including powers of legislation, police and courts. It refused as it knew that it could not do so and survive at home. Heath and his colleagues next abolished the parliament and constitution of Northern Ireland in defiance of all Commonwealth constitutional precedent and despite the fact that the action was a unilateral tearing up of an international treaty registered at the League of Nations.

In addition to the ignorance and naiveté at Westminster has been the assumption that the region is expendable in the wider context of Westminster politics. Whether the party in office has been Conservative or Labour, the first consideration has been that Ulster policies must never injure electoral prospects. Better that soldiers or policemen or civilians be murdered and maimed in that corner of the United Kingdom and millions of pounds of property be destroyed than that votes be lost in mainland constituencies. Better to buy time with covert operations and the steady working of violence, crime and racketeering than to risk vote-endangering controversy.

Neither party would stomach the firm legislation and other measures needed to stamp out IRA terrorism while working within the law. Both were too sensitive about the middle-of-the-road, liberal, humanitarian public. From that social stratum come the brains of the

Labour Party and its middle-class infrastructure. They are equally a force in the Conservative Party and provide a high proportion of the leaders of public opinion in the media and elsewhere. For a time, soldiers in Ulster were denied the protection of armoured personnel carriers because pictures of them on television and in the press would remind people of the Russian tanks which overran Czechoslovakia. The army command long pressed for a local "home guard" such as had been the rule in Malaya, Kenya and other terrorist situations. It would have freed numerous troops from guard and patrol work. The refusal was stubborn and continuous. Outside Ulster, the proposed force might be regarded as a return of the B Specials. The pressure from London was continually for low profile military and police activity in the interest of a good propaganda picture in the mainland constituencies. **Unfortunately, the obverse of that coin is intensified covert activity.**

Everyday is election day in politics and few governments have been more aware of it than the Westminster ones since the beginning of the "Ulster troubles". In 1969 the Wilson government was worried about the general election which it was to call in June 1970 and lose. Heath formed the new one with an overall majority of only thirty. During his period of office by-elections came near to eroding it. The next general election was in February 1974 and placed Wilson back in office, but with a minority in the House of Commons. A further general election in October of the same year gave him a majority of three. By the time Wilson resigned the premiership in April 1976 and was replaced by James Callaghan, by-election defeats had reduced Labour to an overall minority party. Thus, during these years, the overriding concern of the government in office was parliamentary survival and electoral prospects. Ulster was never more than a facet of it.

The ill-informed and uninvolved are easy victims to simplistic solutions. The Northern Ireland government had had a bad press for years as have had all weak and well-meaning governments in a classical revolutionary situation whether they were Stuart, Bourbon, Romanov or more modern. The cabinet ministers, parliamentarians and civil servants in London knew it only from its press image and inability to assert itself against mounting agitation. They were persons who had been brain-washed by years of experience of dis-engaging from colonies and saw Northern Ireland as another external colony from which Great Britain was destined to disengage in order to hand it back to the natives whom they assumed were the republican Irish of the island as a whole. When Edward Heath destroyed the government and parliament of Northern Ireland, he sent William Whitelaw to the region with such a mission. Four months earlier, Harold Wilson, leader of the opposition Labour Party, had proposed a scheme for the unification of Ireland within fifteen years. A little later, he met the leaders of the Provisional IRA in Dublin and assured them that he would be delighted if he could cut it down to ten or eight years. Heath did not indicate a time scale for unification, but appears to have seen it materialising even sooner than Wilson.

The general consensus between the leaders of the Conservative and Labour parties made easy the initial reckless imposition of "direct rule" from Westminster and at every subsequent stage has provided the basis for a bipartisan policy under which the party in opposition has supported the measures taken in Ulster by the one in office. The policy has stifled realistic thinking and become a conspiracy whereby happenings such as the attempt to assassinate William Black was carried out under a Conservative government and the decision by the Attorney General to have no one prosecuted was taken under a Labour one.

The special conditions at Westminster are one part of the explanation of the relatively free rein given to counter-insurgency and covert activity. The other part is to be found in Ulster.

In the land of the blind the one-eyed man is king. The English politicians and Whitehall civil servants sent to govern Northern Ireland were quick to grasp that Provisional IRA violence had to be contained by physical force or their administration would collapse in chaos with probably some of their own number murdered in the process. They had no short-term solution to the bomber and assassin and they knew it. In contrast, the counter-insurgency specialists had never been better prepared with schemes and theories. Experience based on anti-terrorist operations in half-a-dozen countries from post-war Malaya to more recent Vietnam gave them confidence and authority. The region's new political masters turned to them in a desperate hope that their expertise would make good their own helplessness. They gave them much latitude in day-to-day operations and allowed them to mould law and order policies according to counter-insurgency theories.* The next step was to realise and accept that the expertise and advice of the counter-insurgency specialists could be used for a more ambitious purpose than the discomfiture of terrorists — that it could be employed to destabilise the region and in the process to destroy the organisations and popular support of inconvenient, legitimate political opponents of the government.

Mao Tse Tung compared guerrillas to fish that swim in the water of a sympathetic population. Modern counter-insurgency practice concentrates on ways by which the water can be poisoned so that the fish shrivel and die. Terrorism is a two-edged sword. A terrorist organisation, such as the Provisional IRA, can cause a government much inconvenience and heavy expenditure, but, if the struggle is prolonged, the violence will cause a backlash in the host population. This was largely why the terrorist organisations of the 1960s and 1970s collapsed, including the Tupamaros in Latin America and FLQ in Quebec.

Counter-insurgency theory accepts this fact as basic and concentrates on ways to expedite the process by making terrorists appear even more violent, callous and irresponsible than they are. In Ulster the application of the theory has been taken a stage further and much effort has been spent, in addition, on ways to discredit and alienate non-terrorist opponents of the government from their host populations. The indictment of this book is not only that the authorities have permitted certain specific excesses of which examples are described, but that they have deliberately promoted and condoned violence, crime and racketeering in order to alienate both their terrorist and political opponents from their natural sympathisers. It has been a clinically planned destabilising and brutalising of the population, year after year, for both military and political ends.

Edward Heath disbanded the government and parliament of Northern Ireland in March 1972 and created a new post of secretary of state for Northern Ireland. He gave it to William Whitelaw, his

*The primacy given to military opinion and judgement even extended to the Foreign Office and led it to transfer the Irish desk from the Western European Department to a new Irish Republic Department under the control of the under-secretary responsible for defence matters and liaison with the armed services. Another manifestation was the appointment in 1976 of the DI6 specialist, Christopher Ewart-Biggs, to be British ambassador in Dublin.

leader of the House of Commons, and despatched him to Stormont Castle to administer the region. The local press referred to him as the Supremo. The comparison with General Douglas MacArthur at the height of his Far Eastern career was apt. There was a similar concentration of power in the hands of one person and a similar relaxation of constitutional restraints and accountability in the exercise of it. The Ulster majority was humiliated and alarmed, but its immediate emotions were channelled into a two-day general strike and peaceful protest rallies, one of which attracted 100,000 people.

Four minor English politicians were placed in control of the seven ministries of the otherthrown Northern Ireland government. English civil servants and other English appointees were brought in to fill policy-making and sensitive positions. Most of them were concentrated in Whitelaw's headquarters and secretariate, the Northern Ireland Office at Stormont Castle. For a period, many of them were housed in the Culloden Hotel amid rural surroundings in Co. Down. Later, some fifty superior houses were purchased for them and expensively furnished. Most were in the Cultra to Helen's Bay area of the north Co. Down coast, a district referred to locally as Belfast's Beverley Hills. With them came a small retinue of mainland filing clerks, bodyguards, etc. for whom well-furnished houses and flats were also purchased.

William Whitelaw was perhaps the most experienced manipulator in British politics in this century. He had been Conservative Party whip and leader of the House of Commons. More important, he was the man who manipulated the United Kingdom into the European Common Market against the strong inclinations of a very large section of the population. He was the manager of the entire domestic campaign for entry. Geoffrey Rippon, who was in charge of negotiations, reported to Whitelaw more often than to Heath, the prime minister. The most formidible public relations exercise of modern times was launched and Whitelaw was the controlling spider at the centre of the network.

Public relations firms were engaged across the United Kingdom. Press and television men were invited to breakfast or lunch with Whitelaw in a steady stream. Front organisations were used such as European Movement, United Europe Association, Campaign for Europe, Trade Union Committee for Europe, and European Educational Research Trust. Large sums of money were diverted to them.

Academics at the universities, such as Uwe Kitzinger of Oxford, were involved.*

On Whitelaw's arrival in Northern Ireland, he began a similar far-flung operation to manipulate the Ulster public. Transfers and new appointments were made from the mainland to BBC Northern Ireland so that it became almost as firmly a government instrument as, for instance, the army's information office in Lisburn.† The

*See *Diplomacy and Persuasion: How Britain Joined the Common Market* by Uwe W. Kitzinger for an account of William Whitelaw's management of the campaign for United Kingdom entry into the EEC.

†Lord Reith, the first director-general of the BBC, strove to create a broadcasting authority which would be independent of the government of the day. The pretence that it is so has survived until the present, but the reality was killed dead in the opening stage of World War II when the government of Neville Chamberlain dismissed the BBC Board of Governors with the exceptions of a former Conservative mayor and the managing director of Baring Brothers. (Among those dismissed were H. A. L. Fisher, the historian, and Margery Fry, the penal reformer.) It remained dead during the cold war years and is still dead.

An entry in Richard Crossman's diaries in September 1969 (*The Diaries of a Cabinet Minister,* vol. iii) indicated how the wartime master and servant relationship remained unchanged. It referred to a development in Ulster and the occasion was a cabinet meeting presided over by Harold Wilson, the prime minister. The entry read: "He [James Callaghan, the home secretary] was most alarmed by the Catholic and Protestant radio broadcasts whipping people up . . . Jim said, 'I wanted to jam these stations but I found to my amazement that there was some BBC objection.' Harold said, 'Well, we'll have that knocked aside.'"

Crossman commented, "The moment we have a problem, as in Northern Ireland, Harold, Jim and the rest of Cabinet say, 'What is all this nonsense of the BBC being so choosey and intellectual?' and out goes a civil liberty straightaway." He should have realised that the BBC had been integrated into the intelligence and covert operations business long enough to know that its first concern must be to cultivate the image of an unbiased institution totally free from a political master. An undignified jamming vendetta with insignificant, anti-government pirate radio stations would not contribute to that end. Without the right kind of credibility, it cannot help the government in a serious crisis. Nor is Ulster the only place where the Crossman diaries acknowledge government intervention into BBC policies. Another entry describes how a minister was detailed at a cabinet meeting to see Sir Hugh Greene, the director-general, to arrange for it to co-operate in a new government move in the Rhodesian crisis.

The BBC was used against the Ulster Workers' Council in the initial stage of the first general strike of May 1974. (It dismissed the farmers' first pro-strike cavalcade as a local protest over the cost of cattle food.) The public began to compare its reporting with what it read in the press and to tune in increasingly to RTÉ in the Irish Republic. A decision was taken that BBC credibility was more important than open partisan support for the government and it fell into line with its media competitors.

correspondents and editors of Fleet Street were courted as assidu-
ously and tactfully as earlier during EEC entry with the result that the
Whitelaw regimé had almost invariably a sympathetic and co-
operative press on the mainland. He had the additional fortune that
the *Belfast Telegraph*, the daily newspaper with the largest circula-
tion in Ulster, was strongly pro-government and anti-Ulster majority.
It was one of the London based Thompson chain and was the only
evening newspaper. On one occasion in early 1973, the Vanguard
Unionist Movement issued an important statement. *The Times*
[London] gave it fourteen column inches; *Guardian* [London], eight
inches; *The Irish Times* [Dublin], twenty-four inches; *Sunday News*
[Belfast], forty-four inches; and *Belfast Telegraph,* nil.

The mice in the fable had the problem of how to bell the cat. The
existence of Ulster's British majority posed a similar difficulty
although it was not fully recognised at Westminster until the general
strike organised by the Ulster Workers' Council in May 1974.
Wilson treated the majority with caution prior to his defeat at the
polls in June 1970. Heath was apprehensive about it as he forced the
Stormont government to resign and ended the parliament of Northern
Ireland. But, as the great loyalist protest rallies faded out and a
section of the Official Unionist Party showed signs of succumbing to
the bait of office in a new Northern Ireland Assembly, he became
confident that the main danger was past and that there would be no
"loyalist backlash". On a visit to Northern Ireland, he was brash
enough to taunt the region that it was a burden on the Westminster
exchequer and could be cut off without a penny.

However, even persons as brash as Heath had to recognise
continually that the majority was uneasy and dangerous and much
effort was expended in monitoring it and in camouflaging the government's Irish unification objective from the man-in-the-street who,
initially, was almost incapable of believing that a British government
was endeavouring to cede its own subjects to a foreign power.

The Whitelaw and subsequent "direct rule" administrations
depended heavily on the friendly co-operation of the British majority
in Ulster. The houses of the Whitehall civil servants were on the safe
(and comfortable) north shore of Co. Down. Persons in close contact
with them at work or at their houses were drawn from the majority
population for "security reasons". One or two English senior officials
engaged a housekeeper. They were impressed by her intelligent

appreciation of political matters and took to consulting her on political problems that confronted them at work. Months later, they were to discover that she was the aunt of an Ulster Unionist MP at Westminster. During the UWC general strike of May 1974, a key employee in the secretary of state's personal kitchen at Stormont Castle had to be fetched to work by helicopter from her home in south-east Antrim. On one occasion, loyalist strike pickets asked the pilot on touchdown for his UWC essential service pass. He answered that he had not realised that, as a pilot of an aircraft, he needed one. At that point, the passenger-to-be produced her UWC pass and, on her assurance delivered in Ulster speech that the flight was indeed an essential service, it was accepted as valid for both herself and the pilot.

English civilian and army personnel found it natural to consort with the Ulster majority when off duty. An attempt was made to introduce a non-fraternisation policy, but with limited success. A young, newly-arrived Guards officer asked for permission to spend his first weekend at the home of a retired service officer in Co. Down whose son had been bestman at his wedding. Within two weeks he was transferred to Hong Kong without an explanation.

The army was made dominant in matters of law and order. The Royal Ulster Constabulary acted under army instructions in anti-terrorist and related matters. They also had to share ordinary police duties with Royal Military Police in order to give the latter civilian experience and to condition the public to being policed by them. Metropolitan and other English detectives were seconded to Northern Ireland and a number of English recruits were enrolled into the RUC.

Promotions and appointments within the RUC were made on political attitudes and submissiveness to the regimé. Resignations through frustration became commonplace. The proportion of Roman Catholics in the most senior posts rose to 25%, but in the force as a whole the proportion dropped from 11% to 4%. Among those who turned to other occupations were Roman Catholic career policemen whose families had been associated with the RUC and its prede-cessor, the RIC, for two and three generations. Preparations were made to re-equip the force with green uniforms. A report spread that it was the first step towards establishing a joint all-Ireland police force with the Irish Republic. Protests came from the men and the Northern Ireland Office assured them that the change of colour was solely because the black dye previously used was no longer manufactured. A small batch of uniforms in the new colour was issued. The men refused to wear them. The attempt was abandoned and no more was heard of the alleged dye problem.*

A police reserve was recruited as a partial replacement for the disbanded B Specials. They were assigned to police stations with slight training to undertake chores for the regular police and caused an all-round dilution of competence. Unlike the B Specials they had no officers or NCOs of their own.

Some of the Metropolitan and other English detectives on transfer from the mainland shocked the straight-laced policemen of the RUC by their slick shortcuts. One was the planting of bullets on IRA suspects. The latter were incensed at what they regarded as hitting below the belt and retaliated with vicious shootings at policemen regardless of whether they were the men responsible. Such planting activities would surprise less today. Sir Robert Mark's campaign to root out corruption in the Metropolitan Police is well known.† Less publicised, but equally significant has been evidence of corrupt practices in police forces outside of London. An example on English provincial home ground of the type of short-cut activity imported into Ulster was the planting of drugs by policemen in Liverpool which was exposed by Radio Merseyside in 1971 only a few months before the imposition of "direct rule". A policewoman in Liverpool stated that in certain police stations, particularly in the city centre, brutality and drug planting took place regularly. She added, "After hearing the word 'agriculture' used on a number of occasions, I asked what it meant. The reply was 'planting', but you can leave that to us."‡

The RUC was excluded from policy making on security and even most administrative decisions of consequence. Too often, it was

*Police uniforms are blue in the Irish Republic, but what the RUC men feared was a joint all-Ireland force such as was envisaged shortly afterwards in the Sunningdale Agreement. After the collapse of that Agreement the RUC accepted the reintroduction of a bottle green uniform which had been withdrawn a few years earlier.

†Shortly after Sir Robert became Commissioner, he told a meeting of representatives of the Metropolitan CID that "they represented what had been the most routinely corrupt organisation in London". Some fifty detectives were suspended during his first few months in office and few of them returned to duty. Sir Robert Mark, *In The Office of Chief Constable* (1978), pp. 130-131.

‡For a concise account see Derek Humphrey and Gus John, *Police Power and Black People* (1972), pp. 18-19.

remembered only when some chore required to be done as on the night when William Black arrested the men on the covert operation and someone was wanted to allay with a concocted story any suspicions which might be forming in the mind of Seán McNamee. This situation continued until a phased transfer of the administration of security from the army back to the police began in 1976. During those years, the main influence of the police force on policy and security decisions was that, by its existence, it set bounds to what was practicable. Covert operations, for instance, had to be concealed as far as possible from the police as well as the public.

On at least one occasion, this negative or limiting influence was decisive on a top policy matter. The "Feakle" Agreement of early 1975 between the Wilson government and the Provisional IRA promised the latter free movement for its members without arrest for previous crimes and the right to carry concealed hand-guns for self-defence. The chief constable of Northern Ireland seconded from the Metropolitan Police by the Westminster government prior to "direct rule" had returned to London and until the following year the RUC was administered by Ulstermen. They informed the NIO that the force would not recognise any such understanding by the government with criminal terrorists and would continue to arrest and charge without exception for previous crimes and the carrying of weapons unauthorised by the police themselves.

14 Alienate the Host Populations

Shortly after Edward Heath became prime minister in 1970, the United Kingdom government began to build up an intelligence system in Ulster independent of the RUC. An index was begun which today includes information on some 65% of the adult population. After a time, the data was stored in a computer at army headquarters, Lisburn.* Army intelligence supervised most of the information gathering and army technicians handled much of the technical work.

About a year later and some six months before Heath closed down the government and parliament of Northern Ireland, army technicians began systematic telephone tapping or landline intercept as it was euphemistically termed. Later, when the Northern Ireland Office was established, it relied heavily on it for the information on which it based security and political activities. No one was sacrosanct. Even as recent as 1978, senior police officials in the office of the Chief Constable suspected that their private lines were tapped.

A complete floor in a central telephone complex in Belfast was taken over by army technicians. It was converted into a monitoring centre with numerous listening consoles and bays of multi-track tape

*The computer has four main sections. The first, known as P section, has names, addresses, ages, descriptions, occupations, habits, relatives, vehicles used, recorded movements and persons in whose company previously seen. A second computer section is an elaborate street directory designed partly to help with the speedy identification of suspects. It has the names, occupations, computer reference codes and political preferences of the occupants of each house together with a distinguishing mark for it such as colour of door, type of blinds or pattern of wallpaper in a selected room. Sometimes the names of dogs are even recorded. The third computer section has the registration numbers, makes and colours of motor vehicles, religions of owners and recommendations as to degree of suspicion appropriate in a road-check. The fourth computer section is the Vehicle Check Point Index or record of every time a vehicle has been encountered by the security forces in a road-check or elsewhere. Security forces engaged in search, road-check or other operations tap the information by radio.

recorders. Permanent taps were soldered into the telephone lines of selected individuals and organisations at intermediate distribution frames — a place where civilian technicians were unlikely to discover them. Telephones in the republican Andersonstown district of Belfast are centred in the exchange at Balmoral. At one time, would-be subscribers had to be refused telephones because outgoing cables were overloaded with intelligence telephone taps.

In addition to the permanent taps, the monitors have been able to tap a conversation on any telephone within a few seconds by means of the TKO device. The latter is normally intended for an operator in a central exchange to tell a subscriber engaged in a conversation on an automatic exchange that he has an incoming trunk call.

Anne McHardy, a correspondent of *The Guardian*, has confirmed that the Belfast telephone of her newspaper has been tapped. The proof came in December 1977 when an indiscreet civil servant in the Northern Ireland secretary of state's team divulged the details of private conversations that he had listened to "on the tapes". She commented, "His disclosure showed clearly that whoever was doing the physical tapping, the government had access to the end result."*

The intelligence men also have used infinity bugs and other devices by which telephones can be converted into microphones to relay conversation in the rooms in which they are placed. Concealed miniature radios and microphones which use wires other than telephone have been other bugging expedients. More recently, they have been supplemented by the galium arsenide laser instrument with opto-electrical linkage for picking up conversation at a distance from the vibrations in window panes. It is reported to have been used for surveillance of the United Unionist Action Council strike head-quarters in May 1977 together with an infinity bug in a newly-installed telephone in a committee room.

The opening of mail was as extensive and systematically organ-ised as telephone tapping. Letters addressed to the present writer have been opened from time to time from at least 1973 to the present. For a long period, they were opened by the same intelligence case officer as opened correspondence between William Black and the European Commission of Human Rights at Strasbourg. His distinguishing mark was an inept smear of glue left on enclosures.

The Guardian, 11th July 1978.

When the Heath administration first began to expand its intelligence activities in Ulster, it operated a number of agents, complete with English accents, before it built up an indigenous network. One ran a shoe shop on the Shankhill Road in Belfast where he sold cut-price footwear until the local people chased him. Another joined the Finaghy Branch of the Vanguard Unionist Movement in Belfast — an innocuous group by any standard. He was accompanied by a woman whom he introduced as his wife. She was elected secretary. A member of the branch had served with army intelligence in World War II. He became suspicious and denounced them at a branch meeting. Within hours, they had vacated the flat which they were occupying and were not seen again. The members of the branch were indignant that the government should have planted two spies among them. Later, when they discovered that the couple were not married, they were more than indignant — they were scandalised.

An agent who can provide information is useful. One that, in addition, can influence or control the target organisation, group or individual is even better. A further refinement is for government intelligence to use agents to form a special organisation in which they occupy the controlling positions. For example, American intelligence is believed to have been responsible for setting up Alpha 66, the most violent and unpredictable of the Cuban, anti-Castro exile organisations. A strong belief exists in Ulster that British intelligence was responsible for the emergence of the secret Ulster Freedom Fighters in the late summer of 1973. It is said that initially it consisted of a small number of ex-convicts brought together and controlled by British intelligence. These, in turn recruited and controlled others who believed that they were members of a genuine loyalist secret organisation.

The truth of this belief cannot be tested at present. However, three factors threw suspicion on the UFF. From the beginning, it claimed credit for outrages in widely separated places in Ulster. Secret organisations in competition with other secret organisations require time to grow and do not emerge with countrywide capabilities. Second, its members appeared immune from detection regardless of the outrage. Third, it gave as justification for some of its outrages that they were in retaliation for attacks on the army. Not that such claims were decisive. Such attacks provoked strong local indignation and on several occasions the UVF and UDA had issued similar justifications after attacks on republicans.

British intelligence has been able to secure numerous local informers and agents through blackmail, bribery and straight payments. Blackmail has always loomed large in intelligence work, but never more so than today. It is the easiest way to secure and retain informers and agents and its other uses are legion. Nowhere is it easier to blackmail than in the criminal underworld and the grey areas of conduct that surround it. For that reason alone, the official connivance at and encouragement of conditions for mafias and racketeering has paid the Northern Ireland Office handsome dividents in both republican and loyalist districts.

A minor episode gives a glimpse of the ethics involved. DI5 in conjunction with army intelligence and the Special Branch set up two brothels and a "massage parlour" in the Malone Road and Antrim Road districts of Belfast to obtain material with which to blackmail clients into becoming informers or agents. A London vice king was brought in to make the arrangements. The girls were required to take the Official Secrets oath. They were young and presentable and paid £500 per week. Conversations with clients were tape-recorded and remote controlled 35 millimetre Olympus cameras took photographs in the bedrooms. In August 1972, the Provisional IRA discovered what was happening and fired shots into one of the buildings. The establishments were closed immediately and some time later the main details appeared in the Dublin press. It was a type of operation relatively common in international intelligence work. For instance, the CIA at one stage ran a brothel in Paris in conjunction with the French intelligence organisation, SDECE, with the purpose of obtaining blackmail material for use against eastern block diplomats and similar people.*

Various bomb explosions and violent incidents, including assassinations have been attributed to British undercover. The most widely attributed bomb explosions occurred in Dublin in the Irish Republic. It was on 1st December 1970. The Irish government had introduced a bill to provide stiffer penalties for terrorists. There was doubt whether it would pass. The debate on a second reading was in progress when news circulated along the lobbies that bombs in

*Miles Copeland, *The Real Spy World* (1974), p. 153.

central Dublin had killed two people and injured eighty-three. A few hours later, it passed by seventy votes to twenty-three.

The dramatic effectiveness of the timing of the bombs lead to wide suspicion that they had been planted by British agents. Almost twelve months afterwards, on 11th November 1973, the British government issued an official denial. Some days later, Patrick Cooney, the Irish minister of Justice, in response to a Dublin newspaper report denied that the Irish Special Branch had a dossier, implicating British agents from the Special Air Service in the bombings. The denial was less than helpful to London as it excluded only one specific army unit.

"Dirty tricks" gave good results when used against the IRAs. They gave even better against the paramilitary organisations and political groupings of the majority British population which is as instinctively law-abiding as that of any other part of the United Kingdom and probably even quicker to disassociate itself from senseless or politically motivated violence.

Unchecked IRA shootings and bombings and fears that steps were afoot to transfer Northern Ireland to the Irish Republic caused the majority population to erupt into a one day strike on 7th February 1973. In Belfast, where five civilians died from violence, there was considerable evidence of *agents provocateur*. Their handiwork also appeared in other areas. In the evening, the present writer drove to Saintfield in Co. Down by way of Lisburn, the town with the large army base and Northern Ireland army headquarters. At the round-about outside the town, I saw the entrance to the M2 motorway to Belfast blocked by three overturned motor cars, including one which was burning fiercely. The IRA did not operate in the area and I subsequently learned that the local paramilitary commanders were confident that their members were not responsible.

In the months that preceded the general election to the short-lived Northern Ireland Assembly set up by Whitelaw, a number of explosions occurred in church and other emotive buildings in quiet parts of the country with no terrorist problem. As the police privately noted at the time, most of them showed substantial expertise and one in particular was carried out with the skill to be found only among persons such as highly trained army saboteurs.

British undercover agents are suspect in a number of assassinations. One is the murder of Tommy Herron, the vice-chairman of the Ulster Defence Association, who was kidnapped and shot. It is known that the RUC has accumulated considerable evidence which would be of great interest to an impartial inquiry.

The murder, it is suspected, was intended to foment open conflict in Belfast between the Ulster Defence Association and the rival Ulster Volunteer Force as relations between them were strained at the time. The standing of each organisation with its host population in Belfast was far from good and such an outcome would have greatly worsened it. In practice, the sole result was an outbreak of fisticuffs between the UDA and UVF prisoners in Long Kesh prison.

One development was the Military Reconnaissance Force, or MRF. It consisted of small units which patrolled in mufti in civilian cars. Its purpose was fourfold. (1) To restrain the Provisional IRA by a mobile army presence and to prevent them from completely taking over republican districts through the absence of uniformed soldiers and police. (2) To have at least one mobile force thoroughly familiar with these districts and available for immediate reaction to terrorist moves. (3) To collect information and to keep the districts under constant surveillance. (4) To undertake special covert operations.

It has been suggested that the ambush on William Black at his cottage was the work of an MRF unit which had been placed under the charge of the SAS specialist from Hereford. For a time, the Northern Ireland army press office denied that such a force existed. Such information as is known about it transpired during court proceedings following the shooting and wounding of three taxi drivers by an MRF squad on 22nd June 1972.

The incident occurred at the Bunbeg bus terminus on the Glen Road, Andersonstown. The three taxi men were cut down by machine-gun fire from a passing civilian car. Shortly afterwards, the Northern Ireland army press office issued the statement: *About eighteen shots have been fired in an incident in which security forces were not involved. When a patrol of the Second Field Regiment, the Royal Artillery, arrived at the scene they found nothing. Our men were not involved in this shooting at all.*

Unknown to the army press office, the RUC had stopped the car, from which the shots had come, at a roadside vehicle search a short distance from the scene. They found two soldiers in civilian clothes in it and a Thompson sub-machine gun. They said that they were members of the MRF and that the Thompson had been issued to them by the RUC's own Special Branch at Castlereagh, Belfast. The latter denied that it had issued any such weapon and the policemen, backed by courageous superiors, charged the man who fired the shots with attempted murder and both men with illegal possession of the weapon.

The army press office reacted with the further press statement: *Shortly after midday a mobile patrol wearing plain clothes and on surveillance duty was travelling eastwards on the Glen Road. A group of men standing at a bus turn-about opened fire on the patrol and a number of bullets passed through the rear window, narrowly missing a soldier. The patrol immediately fired back, and the men were seen to fall.*

The soldiers charged by the police were Captain James A. McGregor, who was on secondment to the MRF from the Parachute Regiment, and Sergeant Clive G. Williams, who was on secondment from the Royal Military Police.

The charge for being in unlawful possession of the Thompson was the first to come to court. It was dropped as both men were soldiers under orders and carrying the weapon as part of their duties. This left Williams alone to face the attempted murder charge, which eventually was tried in Belfast on 27th and 28th June 1973.

Williams described the Military Reconnnaissance Force at the trial. It had a strength of forty men at the time of the shooting and carried out surveillance work in areas where uniformed troops could not move freely. It was sub-divided into units of fifteen men and they worked in squads consisting of one vehicle and from two to four men. The vehicles were civilian cars owned by the army. Each unit had its own armoury. He, himself, commanded a unit and its armoury included two Thompson sub-machine guns.

The most startling and controversial aspect of the shooting had been the use of a Thompson sub-machine gun. It is an American gun and has been the main weapon of the Official IRA. They have had a substantial number dating back to the abortive anti-British campaign of the 1950s. The Provisional IRA have also used it on a few occasions. The British army has never been issued with it.

The noise of a Thompson when fired is unmistakable and its large .45 calibre bullet is easy to identify after a shooting. If *agent provocateurs* had been endeavouring to make trouble between Official and Provisional IRA, it would have been the ideal weapon to use. Also, a truce between the Provisionals and British authorities was due to begin in a few hours. It would, again, have been the ideal weapon if the shooting had been an attempt to make trouble between hawks and doves within the Provisionals.

Williams explained in the court that the MRF had just had a new intake of NCOs. On the morning of the shooting at Bunbeg bus terminal, he had accompanied them to a firing range at Kinnegar to familiarise them with weapons used by the terrorists. He had taken the Thompson with him for a practical demonstration and afterwards had not had an opportunity to exchange it for the army's normal issue Sterling gun.

Williams gave the following description of the shooting. He had two of the new NCOs with him in the car. He made two crossings through Andersonstown to familiarise them with the work which they would have to do. Another squad belonging to his unit was also patrolling in a car in the area. They radioed that, at the Bunbeg bus turn-about and taxi stand on the Glen Road, they had seen a man with a revolver accompanied by two other men, one of whom was looking at the nearby mountain through binoculars. He ordered the second squad to make another pass along the Glen Road. They did so and radioed to confirm their original report.

He decided to see for himself; took the Thompson out of a holdall under the back seat; loaded it; and began the approach to the bus turn-about. There he saw a dark green car near the entrance with a light blue one behind it. The driver's door was open and kneeling behind it was the man looking through binoculars. In front of the door was another man holding a pistol. A third man was standing on the far side of the car.

Williams said that he glanced away and suddenly heard several single shots. He looked around and saw that the third man was now lying over the roof of the light blue car and firing at them with what he took to be an M1 carbine. As he seized the Thompson and dived for a rear door window, he heard shattering as a bullet came through the back window. He saw two other bullets strike the road behind the car. He discharged eight or ten bullets in three bursts of fire. He saw the man with the binoculars fall back holding his chest; the man in front slump over the bonnet and the man with the rifle disappear. His back window was starred where the bullet had entered so he knocked out part of the pane to give clear vision as he feared the car might be followed by other gunmen.

Williams was asked why he had not taken his squad back to recover the weapons. He replied that his unit had orders never to become involved in any follow-up action, but to leave that to regular, uniformed troops.

A taxi driver, who was with his parked vehicle at the bus turnabout, told the court that he saw the three other taxi men talking together. One was looking through binoculars at the mountain. He heard a burst of gunfire and saw a car disappearing down the Glen Road. He said that he saw no one at the bus turn-about with a weapon and heard no shooting other than from the passing car.

The jury withdrew for two hours and returned with a majority verdict of "not guilty".

In the previous chapter it was emphasised that the authorities deliberately promoted and condoned violence, crime and racketeering in order to alienate both terrorist and legitimate political opponents of the government from their natural sympathisers. This is more ambitious and outrageous than its use for day-to-day covert operational functions such as securing and controlling well-placed informers and agents. The pattern was most conspicuous in the loyalist working-class urban districts from not long after the imposition of "direct rule" until the second general strike of May 1977.

In them, the police were not shot at by gunmen as in the home districts of the Provisional IRA. On the contrary, they were not only welcome, but received deputations from residents from time to time imploring them "to take the gangsters off our backs". They were however, the districts where the loyalist paramilitary organisations were strong and where the more uncompromising political parties had much support.

Gangsters and racketeers gained a hold on sections of the urban paramilitary organisations quite early. At all times, the BBC and official propaganda has been industrious at smearing them with crime and violence. The smear campaign was also extended to political and other organisations associated with the majority cause. When deputations, for instance, from loyalist organisations and political groups met Whitelaw, the Northern Ireland Office would afterwards issue a press statement that such and such topics had been discussed and that he had emphasised the evils of violence and gangsterism. The only occasion that the present writer met him was as a member of a deputation to appeal for troop protection for Protestant homes that were being stoned and shot into by the Provisional IRA. At the close of the interview, I said forcibly that, if a press statement were to be released, on no account must it contain the usual smear phrases. Whitelaw turned red, said nothing, but for once they were absent.

The Ulster Defence Association, the main loyalist urban paramilitary organisation, was initially a coming-together of law-abiding vigilantes in Belfast and certain provincial towns. In the first months of Whitelaw rule, strong-arm cliques began to assert themselves in Belfast. A violent, ruthless man (released from prison early) gained control of a section and placed it at loggerheads with another section. The more moderate, responsible men and women began to leave in ones and twos and then in a landslide. With them went most of the ex-servicemen who had contributed much to the discipline and parade-ground smartness. The people who were left behind were unable to prevent the drift into "tit for tat" terrorist vendettas with the IRAs which in turn led to ever larger numbers of their members being imprisoned. On the other hand, in the provincial towns outside of Belfast and in areas such as Newtownabbey the UDA has had a comparatively clear record from crime and racketeering. In at least one such area where it did eventually intrude, the original "rotten apple" is believed to have been a government agent.

The history of the rural paramilitary organisations is a contrast to that of the Belfast UDA and the other urban ones. The Down Orange Welfare and Ulster Service Corps (both rural and small town) have not had a single member imprisoned for a terrorist offence nor has the rural section of the Orange Volunteers. Also, it has been admitted by at least one officer in military intelligence that government undercover has had practically no success in penetrating them with agents. Their discipline is friendly, but strict and crime and rackets are unknown in their ranks. Their strength has been that recruits came to them already vetted and character-tested through membership of a church or Orange lodge.

It was the ordinary police who prevented a complete collapse of law and order in the loyalist urban districts of Belfast. Despite limitations on their deployment, they kept making arrests. But, it was the low-grade criminal, often teenagers, who were caught. The "godfathers" and syndicates in the background remained untouched. Further, they still remained untouched even after the second Ulster general strike of May 1977 forced the NIO to crack down on gunmen, bombers and violent criminals. An exception was the closure in loyalist and republican districts of the main illegal drinking shebeens in the summer of 1977 and there is doubt about the motive behind it. They are important to the Provisional IRA as a source of revenue. It was threatening to resume bombing on the mainland and it is suspected that the closures were linked with indirect negotiations to induce them to change their intention.

The absence of police from the republican districts, until a cautious and limited return in 1977, left a vacuum which was filled by the Provisional IRA. They monopolised the more profitable rackets. Originally, the main ones were "protection" of public houses, shops and businesses; Provisional controlled legal and illegal drinking clubs, pirate taxi fleets, hold-ups and blackmail. The Belfast bus company was induced to allow the taxi fleets a monopoly of certain routes by the device of burning its buses when they appeared on them. A London based international construction company closed down all its operations in Northern Ireland rather than pay the protection money required.

Contract bombing of buildings has been an excellent source of income for the Provisional IRA. Some of the contracts have been straight business deals whereby the Provisionals and the property owners split the profit from the government compensation. On other occasions, the Provisionals have been hired by property speculators who wished to buy the bombed site cheaply or to reduce the value of adjacent property preparatory to buying it cheaply. More often, the Provisionals intimidated the owners of bombed buildings into sharing with them part of the compensation. In 1971, the Criminal Injuries to Property Compensation Act (Northern Ireland) enabled the government to refuse to pay compensation for bomb damage if the owners had not taken satisfactory security precautions. The Provisionals replied by appointing a "security officer" to each brigade to inspect buildings to be bombed for compensation and to arrange with the owners that the security arrangements be brought up to the standards specified in the government regulations. Some six million pounds of taxpayers' money, it is thought, was syphoned to the Provisional IRA through compensation claims for bombed buildings prior to 1976. In the latter year more stringent regulations reduced the flow, but has not ended it.

The business undertakings of the Provisional IRA and other racketeers require substantial book-keeping and written records. Al Capone need not be the only gangster to be caught out on his tax returns. Also, standards of integrity have fallen dramatically in other fields. For instance, certain building permissions granted by the Department of Planning have been associated with inexplicable circumstances. In one case, police admitted that they cried out for investigation, but explained that they could not undertake it as they had no men with the expertise needed. When Roy Mason arrived in 1976 to take up his duties as secretary of state for Northern Ireland, the present writer met him as part of a deputation from my political party. We urged on him that the RUC must be given a "fraud squad" as quickly as possible. His adviser on police matters dismissed the idea with vigour. It was normal, he insisted, that police forces in an area of the United Kingdom such as Northern Ireland, call upon outside "fraud squads" such as those of the Metropolitan Police.

It was one more indication that the government had its own vested interest in allowing Ulster to stew indefinitely in its crime and racketeer misery.

Not until recent months has a small "fraud squad" of limited expertise been formed within the RUC and it has still to be asked to investigate something with potential political repercussions.

One of the government's liaisons with racketeering is partially documented. A Provisional IRA bombing campaign was in progress on the mainland during the latter part of 1974. Two explosions in Birmingham killed twenty-two people and injured one hundred and eighty-one. At Westminster alarm grew that a strong backlash against IRA violence would "destabilise" English politics. Christmas brought an eleven day truce partially negotiated at Feakle. It was extended, but the Provisionals continued to make noises about renewing the violence. One of their demands was for a phased release of internees. The government agreed to it, but the Provisionals were not satisfied. In desperation, it searched around for additional incentives. On 13th January 1975, Stan Orme, MP, deputy to the Northern Ireland secretary of state, met representatives of the internees and undertook "to make work available" for released ones in the Andersonstown district. It took the form of contracts for three firms to renovate residences belonging to the Northern Ireland Housing Executive, the state corporation responsible for public-owned housing. Officials within the Housing Executive protested, but to no avail. One of its senior men recorded in a memo that an official of the Northern Ireland office emphasised to him that the Housing Executive had to do everything possible to prevent unemployment because of the political situation. He had protested that it did not have the money and had been told that "the Minister would not wear a statement that funds were exhausted". The Housing Executive stood its ground and refused to transfer money earmarked for other projects. Officials within the Northern Ireland Office then arranged for money to be secured for the scheme from the Department of Environment.

The Northern Ireland Housing Executive's standing orders that contracts must be advertised and be subject to tender were ignored. The Provisional IRA named the Andersonstown Co-Operative* and two private building construction firms and it was agreed that the work would be in the Provisional-controlled Maynard Estate. The police had been long withdrawn from the district and army patrols ventured into it only occasionally. Employees of the private firms selected would be helpless to resist Provisional dictates.

The contracts were open-ended. Payment was either on time plus $112\frac{1}{2}$% and materials plus 25% or on day work plus 35%. Workers on the sites prolonged their tasks indefinitely; building materials vanished; workmen claimed for overtime which had neither been worked nor authorised; and non-existent workers were kept on the payroll by the workers. Costs rose quickly until renovations were averaging £15,996 per flat.

The ceasefire ended on 25th August. The firms engaged in the renovation scheme were called to a meeting with officials at Stormont and their contracts terminated on 11th and 12th September as part of retalitory moves against the Provisionals.

In September 1975, Mrs. Jill Knight, MP for Edgbaston, Birmingham, learned about the Maynard contracts and raised the matter with the secretary of state for Northern Ireland, setting out the main facts. She urged an inquiry, but as she explained some months later, "This was brusquely and rudely refused by Mr. Merlyn Rees,

27th May 1972. Loyalist urban vigilantees begin to form themselves into the Ulster Defence Association. Note the mixture of
mufti and military garments. *Pacemaker Press, Ltd.*

28th June 1972. The UDA is four weeks older. Note the standardisation in uniform
and parade-ground efficiency. A short time later, government agents, violence and
racketeers had caused an exodus of the more responsible men and women, including
most of the middle-class and ex-servicemen. *Pacemaker Press, Ltd.*

Fifeshire Constabulary Headquarters, Dysart. It was used as a base by the government undercover agent, Alexander Atkins.

D. Ireland, Kirkcaldy.

The people of Belfast in a spontaneous victory celebration at the end of the general strike organised by the Ulster Workers' Council.

Pacemaker Press, Ltd

The violence, crime and racketeering are allowed to continue. Firemen search the rubble of the Golden Pheasant for the bodies of two brothers. Many Ulster pubs, inns and clubs have been destroyed in order to divert their business to illegal drinking establishments.   *Century Newspapers, Ltd.*

Burned out vehicles dumped on waste ground at York Street, Belfast in early 1976. Each had been used in a bombing, robbery or other criminal activity and set on fire to remove fingerprints.   *Century Newspapers, Ltd.*

Betty Williams and Mairead Corrigan of the Peace People read the movement's pledge to a 30,000 strong rally in the loyalist Shankhill area of Belfast on 30th August 1976.

Century Newspapers, Ltd.

A Peace People march in the Irish republican Falls Road area of Belfast on 25th October 1976.   *Century Newspapers, Ltd.*

Farmers block the Newtownards Road route into Belfast during the UUAC general strike of May 1977.

Pacemaker Press Ltd.

Hercules transport aircraft of the Royal Air Force. During the UUAC general strike, these aircraft were touching down every few minutes at Aldergrove Airport in the largest air and sea movement of troops undertaken by the British government since the Suez operation twenty-one years earlier.

Air Portraits.

An interrogation room at Castlereagh Police Holding Centre.
Pacemaker Press, Ltd.

A corridor and cells in Castlereagh Police Holding Centre.
Pacemaker Press, Ltd.

the then Secretary of State, on the grounds that my allegations were untrue."* In November 1975, Dr. Ian Paisley, MP, published classified figures from within the Northern Ireland Housing Executive for part of the work at Maynard.

The Northern Ireland Office would normally have ignored the moves by Jill Knight and Ian Paisely knowing that matters affecting a public corporation, such as the Housing Executive, could not be raised in Parliament and that, in lethargic Ulster, the matter would soon be forgotten. The fly in the ointment was that money had been switched from the Department of the Environment which is accountable to Parliament. Arrangements were made for explanations of the transfer to be demanded by the influential Public Accounts Committee of the House of Commons. Chief Inspector West and District Detective Sergeant Treadcole of the "fraud squad" of the West Midland Police were seconded to the RUC to make a report on the Maynard scheme. The explanation given for the impor-tation of two comparatively low-rank police officers was that the RUC lacked the expertise in accountancy needed for an investigation of that kind.

The report of the West Midland led team ran to ninety-eight pages. It confirmed that £2.9 million had been spent in the Maynard renovations and that one million of the sum had gone astray. It was assumed that most of it went to the Provisionals and a smaller amount to the Official IRA.

On 12th June 1977, twenty-one months after the Maynard contracts were terminated, Ian Paisley announced publicly that he had information about additional irregularities in Northern Ireland Housing Executive contracts which he would reveal in due course. About midnight four days later, the headquarter building of the Housing Executive burst into flames and was badly damaged. The police reported that a number of fires — believed to be malicious — had ignited simultaneously on the fourth floor. The office housing the records relating to contracts was on the fourth floor and

*A commission of inquiry was subsequently conceded in 1978, but without powers to compel witnesses to appear nor to require them to give evidence on oath. Also, the terms of reference excluded events such as the destruction by fire in 1977 of records relating to contracts. When its report was published in July 1979, Jill Knight, Dr. Ian Paisley and others dismissed it in scathing terms. The commission of inquiry spent £224,000 in preparing its report.

was totally destroyed. The building was one of the most closely protected in Ulster and the staff employed in it had been doubly vetted for security.

Racketeering and syndicate crime have been invaluable to the government in that the persons and organisations involved develop the characteristics of legitimate business men. They have employees, profits, overheads and customers to be supplied on a regular basis. Their political interests, if any, evaporate and, like business men elsewhere, they are concerned most of all to have the *status quo* maintained and to grant, where useful, co-operation to the authorities. For instance, during the hurried preparations for the second Ulster general strike of May 1977, the loudest protests within the Belfast urban paramilitary organisations came from such persons.

The government has another not dissimilar pressure point in the fact that the IRAs and the loyalist urban paramilitary organisations with members in detention or prison contribute to the upkeep of their families. The financial burden has been heavy and much energy and organisation has had to be diverted from politically motivated activities to illegal or legal fund raising.

15 Backlash

A government which condones and orchestrates crime, racketeering and violence as a means of alienating and isolating terrorist or political opponents from their host populations will, in the long run, pay the price of alienating itself from the general public. The latter may not realise in a coherent way what is afoot, but it knows that the duty of a government is to provide law and order and senses that it is not deploying its resources to do so.

The first grassroot backlash in the Ulster public came within the Irish republican districts. Mrs. Anne Maguire was walking in Andersonstown, Belfast, with her four children, including a baby of four months, in August 1976. A Provisional IRA "get-away" car was fired on by a soldier and the driver injured. It swerved off the road; killed three of the children; and badly injured Anne Maguire. She had a sister, Miss Mairead Corrigan, who, overwhelmed by the tragedy, began to knock on doors in Andersonstown, asking people to join with her in making a stand against the violence and destruction of life and human values. Thus began the Peace Movement which continued through the remainder of the year with marches and hymn-singing rallies and which led to the award in 1977 of the Nobel Peace Prize to Mairead Corrigan and her co-founder, Mrs. Betty Williams. It was basically a Roman Catholic movement with substantial Protestant support and sympathy.

The backlash within the majority population took a different path. In early summer, three unionist parties and several other organisations, including one or two paramilitary, came together in the United Unionist Action Council. Some of the political personalities saw it as a new political pressure point on the Westminster government. All recognised, however, that it would be the ground-swell against terrorism and crime which would give the new body its momentum. No less significant, a new, highly disciplined vigilante organisation, the Ulster Service Corps, sprang up in rural areas where Provisional IRA units were active.

The killings, maimings, destruction of property, crime and racketeering continued through the autumn and winter. Often the activists were fifteen and sixteen years old and parents lived with the fear that their own children could become involved. Some of the atrocities were unbelievably revolting. A Provisional IRA gang, for instance, laid an ambush for a part-time member of the Ulster Defence Regiment on a country road in County Antrim. He was driving a lorry and accelerated away, escaping with minor injuries. The gang then went to his home and shot his aged mother.

Farmers in Provisional IRA harassed districts were selling their land and transferring to Scotland so frequently that Scottish estate agents began to advertise farms in the Ulster press.

A large proportion of Ulster people are of Scottish descent and, as in Scotland, Presbyterianism is the main Protestant faith. The ministers and other officials of the Presbyterian Church in Ireland, in common with those of its sister churches, the Church of Scotland and the Free Churches in England and Wales, are ultra-cautious in making political pronouncements. At their elbows stand the ghosts of the fallen in the first world war, reminding them of that earlier occasion when so many ministers preached uncritical political guidance from their pulpits. Interventions by them during the Ulster crisis had been limited, in the main, to generalities about building bridges across Christian divisions and holding out hands of friendship. It was thus a new phenomenon when, during the winter and early spring of 1976, outspoken resolutions on law and order began to arrive at the Presbyterian central office in Belfast from congregations and presbyteries across the country.

Dr. Jack Weir, moderator of the Presbyterian Church in Ireland, met Roy Mason, the secretary of state for Northern Ireland, on 31st March and presented him with a memorandum drafted in judicious, forceful terms. It explained that the basic complaint expressed in the formal church resolutions was that "the government was failing in its fundamental duty of providing security of life and property to those going about their lawful business." And again, "people are more conscious of the widening circle of violence, involving more and more the decent, public-spirited people of the province and not just riotous bullies who may be creating the violence themselves."

The army had been partly withdrawn following the agreement and truce made between the Wilson government and the Provisional IRA in negotiations associated with Feakle in the Irish Republic in the winter of 1974-75. Further withdrawals took place after Callaghan succeeded Wilson as prime minister. Prior to Feakle, army battalions were able to spend only five months outside Northern Ireland between tours of duty. By the time Callaghan took over, the average interval had been increased to a little over two years. On 17th December 1976, the secretary of state for Northern Ireland told the House of Commons that there were 14,500 troops in Ulster. He was not believed.

As pointed out in an earlier chapter, security was placed in the hands of the army as part of the innovations of the Whitelaw administration. A phased return of responsibility from the army to the civilian police was begun in 1976 and had been completed for most of the region by early 1977. RUC officers decided when troops were to be called in and how they were to be used. Only in the more militant republican districts did the army continue to be the overlord force in law and order matters. The new arrangement enabled the police to gain an excellent idea of the total troop strength. They placed it at 7,000 in early 1977 and were far from happy at the knowledge. They saw themselves, untrained in guerrilla warfare and with inadequate equipment, being pitted against the armour-piercing bullets and landmines of the Provisional IRA while the remaining troops stayed in the background, protected, it was assumed, by a secret understanding between the NIO and the Provisionals. In March, Alan Wright, chairman of the Northern Ireland Police Federation, protested in a public speech, "The government says there are 14,500 troops here, but I do not believe it." He added, "You can drive the length and breadth of the province without seeing a single soldier. In some police divisions I know there are no soldiers."

A further official assurance was given on the total number of troops, but the public preferred to believe its own eyes. There was also another factor making for scepticism. Statements by officials, including some made by ministers in Parliament, have been used too often to mislead in connection with Ulster affairs. Not that Ulster has been alone in being so treated. The same device has been used in various areas of government activity where the British public is ignorant or indifferent. The Rhodesian sanctions-breaking saga is not as unique as many suppose.*

The United Unionist Action Council, which had been set up in the early summer of 1976, had a slow and troubled start. The Official Unionist Party withdrew in order to have inter-party talks with the Irish republican Social Democratic and Labour Party — talks to which the other loyalist parties objected strenuously. The Ulster Workers' Council remained outside the UUAC, but like an honest sheepdog endeavoured to herd parties and organisations into it. It made clear that, once a unified, credible coming-together had been achieved, it, too, would join.

Early 1978 brought a change in momentum and purpose. A public concensus began to form, especially in rural areas, that something had to be done to force the Westminster government to act against the killing and crime. The UUAC was looked to as the natural vehicle for action. As it responded to the grassroot demand, its political objectives were largely forgotten. The Ulster Workers' Council joined as did the remaining paramilitary organisations. The exceptions were the UVF, Red Hand Commando and UFF (if such a paramilitary organisation exists). Each of these had been proscribed in law.

The UUAC decided that its only effective recourse was a general strike. It was by now April and intense discussion went into selecting a date. It was agreed that the choice was between May-June or the autumn. The political parties were unhappy about May as the local council elections were due on 18th May. Certain branches of the Ulster Workers' Council wished for more time to prepare their particular factory or section of industry. One argument overrode all others

*A clear-cut example was the assurance repeated at intervals during the Nigerian Civil War that Britain was supplying only 15% by value of Federal Nigeria's arms purchases. After the war, the official trade statistics of Nigeria revealed that the figures for British arms supplies for the two full years of the war were 79.19% in 1968 and 97.36% in 1969. Suzanne Cronje examined this episode in Chapter 3, *The World and Nigeria: The Diplomatic History of the Biafran War, 1967-70.* (The figures exclude a quantity of second-hand aircraft and artillery supplied by the USSR. They were obtained in exchange for cocoa and were not entered in the Nigerian trade statistics.) Another example was the assurance in parliament in 1977 that no government body was shipping goods to the Uganda of General Idi Amin. It was placed in proper perspective shortly afterwards by *Tribune* when it published photocopies of cargo manifests which detailed Uganda bound merchandise together with the government bodies shipping it.

in the end. The country demanded that the killing be stopped at once. It would not understand delay until the autumn. The strike was called for 2nd May.

The strike began well. The petrol tanker road crews responded to a man and the dockers in Belfast and Larne equally well. Many of the smaller shops, factories and workshops closed at once. Queues began to form outside the strike headquarters for travel passes.

The Callaghan government replied with the largest airlift and sea movement of troops since the Suez operation twenty-one years earlier. Giant Hercules transport aircraft were touching down at Aldergrove Airport every few minutes. Some of the vehicles accompanying the troops were direct from the factory with wood and fibreglass sections still unpainted. The world press thronged into Belfast. It was exactly the over-reaction for which the strike organisers had hoped.

The electrical power workers, however, did not respond in the forthright way they had done in the general strike of May 1974. The largest generating station was at Ballylumford near Larne, County Antrim. A second station at Coolkeeragh, County Londonderry, had to be discounted as the work force had altered from 60% loyalist to 60% Irish republican since the 1974 general strike. The two remaining stations were small and in Belfast. They undertook to close down immediately Ballylumford took action.

Ballylumford had had a long, bitter industrial dispute a few months earlier and the scars were raw and unhealed. During it, the workers had seen the managers run the station without their help and knew that they could again run it. No less important, the choice of 2nd May had left no time to consult them beforehand and they resented what appeared to be an arbitrary order.

If the electric power could be cut, industry everywhere would be brought to a standstill. A complication was that it had to be reduced in a complicated, controlled manner or the electricity grid throughout Ulster would be burned out and would require a long time to replace after the strike would be over. No less important, once the electric power could be turned down, the State became responsible for supporting all workers and their dependents for the duration of the strike. Under the United Kingdom national insurance scheme strikers are disqualified for unemployment payments, but workers sent home because there is no electricity receive them. Also, employers who close their premises because there is no electricity cannot be accused of a lockout and are no longer responsible for wages.

The Ballylumford workers eventually invited Jim Smyth of the Ulster Workers' Council, Dr. Ian Paisley of the Democratic Unionist Party and Ernest Baird of the United Ulster Unionist Party to meet them. Their spokesman said that the men were prepared to close down the generating plant immediately, but it would mean that the grid would go and that factories and hospitals would be without power for an indefinite time. They emphasised that they were unable to operate a reduced load such as the UUAC urged. Could they please have instructions? The strike was in its second week. It had almost certainly achieved its objective of jolting the Westminster government into strong action against the Provisional IRA. The spokesmen were asked to thank the men, but to tell them that a shutdown which destroyed the grid would be too disastrous for the country.

The Northern Ireland BBC fought back with a ferocity that was frightening to anyone with theories about impartiality by state-owned broadcasting bodies. It concentrated on talking the public back to work by exaggerated claims of the numbers of people at work. On one occasion, it asserted that 50% of the 8,000 workforce of the Harland and Wolff shipyard had clocked in when there were only twenty-five motor cars in the workers' car park.

The press had been hostile at the beginning of the 1974 general strike, but swung over to a more balanced view once the electric power went off and the country came to a halt. It was equally hostile at the beginning of the 1977 one, but when no dramatic evidence of success materialised, such as the lights going out across Belfast, it continued hostile. The most frustrating aspect of the press reporting was the almost universal failure to accept that the objective was to force the government to act against the terrorists and criminals. The strike was launched with a press conference. At it each speaker emphasised this fundamental point. Jim Smyth of the Ulster Workers' Council emphasised and re-emphasised it with particular skill and persistence. The Northern Ireland Office pushed the line that the strike was an attempted coup by Paisley and most of the media accepted it uncritically despite the fact that the Democratic Unionist Party, of which he was leader, was only one of three political parties in the UUAC and that the Ulster Workers' Council, which carried most of the industrial muscle, was beholden to no political party or personality.* Three exceptions to the stereotyped reporting were Anne McHardy and Derek Brown of *The Guardian* and Mary Holland of the *Observer*. The latter exposed the BBC's numbers fraud.

After a few days, the strike began to slip in Belfast and to gain momentum in rural areas where farmers (including a small number of Roman Catholic farmers) laid on huge tractor cavalcades. The Statistics Branch of the Northern Ireland Department of Commerce has since confirmed that the slump in industrial production was similar to that of the earlier strike in 1974. By the beginning of the second week, the organisers knew that the strike had achieved a substantial measure of success, but were much concerned that the media reports suggested the contrary. The intention had been a fairly short, impressive strike which ended on a note of strength and with the obvious ability to resume at a later date should the government drag its feet on terrorism and law and order. No one had reckoned on a strike which was not a clear success or a clear failure. One or other would have been easy to end. As it was, the temptation was to continue in order to demonstrate success through staying power.

On Tuesday, 10th May, came disaster beyond remedying. A part-time member of the UDR who was the son of a representative on the UUAC was killed when a bomb exploded at a petrol filling station where he and his wife were making a purachase and, in a further incident, a bus driver was shot dead at the wheel of his vehicle. The firm and repeated instruction of the strike organisers was that passive resistance alone was to be used. In one instance after some teenagers had burned a milk float, it was spelled out with the additional phrase "the same as was used by Mahatma Gandhi in India".

Government agents were suspected, but it was also realised that a freelance group could have been responsible for the killings. Most of the men and women who formed the UUAC had strong religious and ethical convictions. Each morning the strike council opened business by someone offering a prayer. Usually it was a member of a political

*The three political parties were Democratic Unionist Party, United Ulster Unionist Party and British Ulster Dominion Party. The last named had been critical of co-ordination and political preparation in the UUAC and had joined it only on the morning that the strike went into effect.

party; occasionally of a paramilitary organisation. On a few occasions, there was also a short reading of scripture. Such persons were shattered by the killings. The blackleg buses disappeared off the streets and other vehicles which had been beginning to return to the roads. But, in the UUAC there was unanimity that it did not wish to preside over that kind of success. The strike was continued for another four days, partly to show that it had not been panicked by the killings into throwing up its responsibilities and partly to ensure that persons on unemployment insurance and social benefits received payment for a full week.

16 Crushing the Provisional IRA on the Cheap

The general strike of May 1977 had lasted practically a fortnight. The British government had been forced to undertake a massive air and sea movement of troops. The Northern Ireland Office was shaken to its foundations and accepted that it had to curtail drastically the activities of the Provisional IRA and be seen to move against the more violent gangsters in loyalist urban districts. On 9th June, Roy Mason, secretary of state for Northern Ireland, announced increased penalties for terrorists. "I must frankly admit the fact," he remarked, "that to the people of Northern Ireland it does not seem that the battle against terrorism is being won fast enough." The maximum penalty for conspiracy to murder was increased from ten years to life; for causing explosions from twenty years to life; and membership of proscribed organisations from five years to ten.

Only a week after the strike, a clean-up of the more open violence had begun in the worst harassed loyalist districts. Over a number of days, eleven men belonging to a gang were arrested who subsequently were convicted of nineteen horrific murders.*

Provisional terrorism was a more formidable problem. The stiffer penalties announced by Mason were of limited value by themselves. The large troop reinforcements brought in during the strike were withdrawn. Russia and Cuba were expanding their activities in Africa at the time and the generals were demanding every man as a counterweight in Europe against the Warsaw Pact armies. It is understood, too, that the Provisional IRA had warned that it would resume

---

*The gang came to be known as the Shankhill Butchers. Their killings had followed a pattern over many months. Shortly after a Provisional IRA murder, men from the gang would overpower an isolated Roman Catholic in a street at night and brutally put him to death. **During the trials, the prosecution admitted that it had not been possible to charge the man whom the gang believed had masterminded their activities.**

bombing in England if the army were not reduced to its pre-strike strength in Ulster.

The Northern Ireland Office resolved the dilemma by a decision to crush the Provisionals on the cheap by re-introducing the interrogation "in depth" techniques (the hooding and noise were excluded) used on IRA suspects in 1971 and subsequently condemned by both the European Commission and Court of Human Rights. The fact that the United Kingdom had given assurances at home and at Strasbourg never again to use them appears to have caused no qualms. It was accepted that Amnesty International would investigate and draw up an adverse report. It is a private body with no power other than to embarrass. The British press, it could be hoped, would play down its finding in a "responsible" way as it has done with those of the European Commission of Human Rights in 1976* and the European Court of Human Rights in 1977. Some of the new cases, no doubt, would be taken to Strasbourg, but, as with the earlier ones, the United Kingdon could delay proceedings for at least six years by which time the Ulster crisis might be half-remembered history.

The condemned techniques had already been used in experimental interrogations in the month or two prior to the UUAC general strike and had demonstrated how effective they were in inducing confessions. A special team of over forty plain-clothes, interrogation detectives was formed. Most were assigned to Castlereagh Police Holding Centre in Belfast (38 cells and 21 interrogation rooms) and the remainder to Gough Police Holding Centre in Armagh (24 cells and 9 interview rooms). It was the first time that anything of that kind had happened in the long history of the RUC and its predecessor, the RIC. The arrest and interrogation of the IRA suspects in 1971 had been a military operation with only one or two RUC men of low rank involved in a supporting role and under army direction.

The "in depth" interrogation techniques began to produce rapid results. The special "emergency" legislation allowed the police to detain a person for interrogation for three days or, on an order from

*For example, *The Times* bereated the Irish government for "all this raking over of the recent past" when it decided to proceed with the brutality cases to the European Court of Human Rights after the Commission gave its findings. It wrote, "The citizens of Northern Ireland would have been equally well served in the vindication of their rights — perhaps better served — by a friendly settlement reached by the two governments helped by the good offices of the Commission" *(The Times, 3rd September 1976).*

the secretary of state for Northern Ireland, for seven days. Three days were usually enough to secure a signed confession. Some confessed to crimes going back three or four years. It is morally certain that a number of persons signed confessions to crimes of which they were innocent.

94% of all persons charged with offences in the anti-terrorist, non-jury courts in Belfast during the remainder of the year were convicted. This compares with 70% for persons charged with normal crimes in the United Kingdom as a whole. 80% of the convictions were made on signed confessions either with no corroborative evidence or with almost none.* People who glibly hold that the United Kingdom judiciary is a guardian of the rights of the citizen should ponder over these figures. J. A. G. Griffith, Professor of Public Law, University of London, may have been near the mark when he wrote, "In both capitalist and communist societies, the judiciary has naturally served the prevailing political and economic forces. Politically, judges are parasitic."†

Soon two-thirds of the activists of the Provisional IRA in Ulster were reported to be in prison either awaiting trial or convicted. Only its senior, policy-making members (i.e. thirteen members of the Executive, seven of the Army Council and certain others) appeared to be immune from arrest. One of the more charitable of various explanations which circulated was that the officials of the Northern Ireland Office preferred not to arrest those particular persons lest new men with more original and enterprising minds should take their places.

A team from Amnesty International visited Ulster at the end of November 1977 to investigate the Castlereagh activities. It was unable to interview persons in prison awaiting trial or convicted. Nevertheless, its report, published in June 1978, confirmed that there was serious maltreatment and that it was by persons other than the uniformed members of the RUC. It demanded a public and impartial inquiry. The government refused to concede one and counter-attacked with assertions that the Police Complaints Board and civil

---

*These figures are the result of research by members of the faculty of Law, Queen's University of Belfast.
†J. A. G. Griffith, *The Politics of the Judiciary* (1976), p. 215.

courts are open to anyone with a genuine experience of improper treatment. Ignored was the consideration that interrogators of prisoners do not come forward as witnesses against themselves before police boards or civil courts.

The Northern Ireland Office knew that a point had been reached where the overwhelming majority of the population, including Roman Catholics in the districts which the Provisional IRA claimed to protect, was so hostile to it that few cared as to what methods were used to wipe it out. An indication of the changed mood was an acceptance of the SAS as a valuable weapon against the Provisionals. As noted in an earlier chapter, the Irish republican population had been hyper-sensitive about that body of men with its ruthless reputation. Mason in his previous post as minister of Defence, had given assurances that no SAS were in Ulster. In contrast, when he was forced to admit, in early June 1977, that the troops concentrated in response to the UUAC general strike were to be withdrawn as soon as possible, he endeavoured to reassure the public with the remark, "More is being done in the field of SAS-type activities than is realised and this will now be intensified."

The Amnesty International report embarrassed the government more on the mainland and abroad than in Ulster and could not be completely ignored. A three man committee of inquiry was set up, consisting of a judge, a former chief constable and a medical specialist. All three were English and the judge, Harry Bennett, gave his name to the committee as he was chairman. It was instructed to recommend improvements in procedures used by the police when holding suspects in custody in Northern Ireland. It was forbidden to interfere in individual cases which were "to continue to be addressed to the Chief Constable and the Police Complaints Board". No power was given to conduct investigations on its own and it had to advertise in the local press for information to be brought to it. With limitations so precisely and clearly defined, the exercise promised to be innocuous. It did not work out that way. The committee gave a guarantee of strict confidence to certain RUC officers of substantial rank and they in return gave forceful accounts of the interrogation usages and the helplessness of the regular police to intervene. Police surgeons, too, gave valuable evidence. It was not accidental that the report of the committee later included the remark, "It is difficult to see what private or public purpose is served by the exaction of untrue confessions, and it is a danger to be constantly guarded against."*

The internal police evidence and surgeons' confirmations enabled the committee to draw up a report more positive than anyone had originally anticipated. It stated that "medical evidence revealed cases in which injuries, whatever the precise cause, were not self-inflicted and were sustained in police custody". It acknowledged the difficulties of the police in a terrorist campaign: complimented the RUC on its restraint and professional integrity and pointed out that the number of detectives who had resorted to physical violence appeared to be small in relation to the total force.

On 11th March 1979, Dr. Robert Irwin, a police surgeon, stated in an Independent Television programme shown throughout the United Kingdom that he had examined some one hundred and fifty persons who had received physical injuries during interrogation, including bruises, damaged joints and several ruptured ear drums. There was widespread disquiet in the media and elsewhere. Civilian and police press officers attached to RUC Headquarters, Belfast retailed various smear stories against Irwin, including a claim that he was bitter and vindictive against the police because they had failed to arrest a soldier who, it was alleged, three years earlier had raped his wife.† Gerry Fitt of the SDLP and Dr. Ian Paisley of the DUP supported Irwin in the House of Commons and the controversy over Castlereagh interrogation methods appeared set to escalate into an embarrassing crisis for the Westminster government.

The outcome, instead, was an illustration of how a report of a committee of inquiry can be used to disarm and neutralise public and parliamentary agitation, regardless of the nature of its findings. The publication date of the Bennett Report was brought forward. As is normal in such documents, the wording was restrained and tactful

---

*One purpose which, in theory, can be served by the exaction of untrue confessions is to pin on innocent persons crimes for which the government's own undercover services were responsible. It is not known whether this aspect was discussed with the Bennett Committee.

†In the House of Commons, Roy Mason did not deny that the smear stories had been put out, but remarked that he would be "ashamed and angry" if they had been spread by his own office. Anne McHardy confirmed in *The Guardian* that, "A number of journalists, including senior reporters representing Dublin papers, had all been told one or other of the stories about Dr. Irwin" (*The Guardian,* 17th March 1979).

and the authorities were able to quote from it selectively in the knowledge that few would ever read it. In the Commons, on a Friday when only a handful of MPs are ever present, the secretary of state for Northern Ireland spoke deferentially about it and on behalf of Jim Callaghan's Labour government singled out two of its recommendations which, he promised, would be implemented as soon as possible. These were that interrogation rooms in police holding centres should be monitored by silent, closed-circuit television and that a prisoner should be given the right to be visited by a solicitor every forty-eight hours until either released or charged.

Nothing had been done when, six weeks later, a general election placed in office a Conservative government with Margaret Thatcher as prime minister. Eventually, in July 1979, a new secretary of state for Northern Ireland pronounced on the Bennett Report on behalf of her government. The proposal for monitoring by silent, closed-circuit television cameras, he said, would be implemented as recommended, but the one to allow a prisoner the right to consult a solicitor every forty-eight hours would be curtailed to the extent that "where it is thought necessary" a senior police officer would be present.

The concessions impressed the public, but were worthless without a new policy decision at the same political level as the original one to re-introduce interrogation-in-depth techniques. Screams from a nearby interrogation block have been heard loud and clear at the desk of the duty sergeant at Castlereagh without causing anyone to intervene to stop the maltreatment. If screams do not cause a single person to react, what hope is there that a small, silent television screen in a bank of twenty-one such screens will be more effective? The right to be visited by a solicitor after each forty-eight hours is also less satisfactory than might seem even if there were no question of the probable presence of a policeman. Most confessions at the police holding centres have been signed during the first two days of custody. In addition, there is no protection against the old device of refusing admission to a solicitor (or doctor) and asserting afterwards that the prisoner did not ask for him or even that he had refused to see him.

17 A Castlereagh Interrogation

When the present writer decided to include in this book a detailed account of an interrogation at Castlereagh Police Holding Centre, I had a number of cases from which to choose. The Northern Ireland (Emergency Powers) Act allows a suspect to be held in custody for up to three days and the Prevention of Terrorism Act for up to two days or, with an order signed by the Northern Ireland Secretary of State, for up to seven days. Persons interrogated under the latter seven day holding order have usually had the more shocking physical mal-treatment. For instance, Joseph Hunter is believed to have been urinating blood when finally he signed a confession of murder on the sixth day. An outside doctor was not permitted to see him for some time afterwards despite an appeal to the National Council of Civil Liberties in London to use its influence. Or there is the case of Desmond Thompson, one of the few persons who resisted for the full seven days all pressures to sign a confession. When a lawyer was subsequently allowed access to him, he shrank away, expecting to be mal-treated and was so dazed and confused as to be unable either to understand that he was a lawyer or to answer the simplest questions.

The temptation was strong to select the most horriffic account from those available in order to shock readers into realising the gravity of what is happening. In the end, I decided that that would not be the best way of doing it. A reader shocked by physical brutality will remember and condemns, but he may fail to grasp that the interrogation system as operated in the police holding centres, since the UUAC general strike of May 1977, does not need the physical agonies of the medieval torture chamber to reduce a prisoner to a state where he is likely to sign a confession to a most serious crime even when innocent. No less effective are ruthless, un-scrupulous questioning; physical exhaustion; lack of sleep in over-heated cells; depression through loss of body salts in perspiration in overheated cells; impaired judgement from easy availability of drugs; inability to eat because of nervous tension and occasionally refusal to drink liquids for fear of being drugged.

The account which I have selected is that of Samuel Eaton, a man of remarkable moral fibre, who resolutely resisted for three days all pressures to sign a false confession. I am telling it in detail as the minutae of his experience make more understandable the intolerable strain he was under and his subsequent condition. He was aged twenty-nine; lived in Rathcoole, Newtownabbey, Co. Antrim, with his wife and four young children and was employed by the Northern Ireland Electricity Service.

A reader may ask himself, after each incident recounted, questions such as, "Could I have withstood being prodded in the stomach like that?" or, "Could I have withstood so many push-ups?" and each time answer, "Yes", with confidence. He may even feel that Eaton's ordeal could have been much worse. After all, he had no nails drawn with red hot pinchers! Such readers are making the mistake of seeing the three days of interrogation as a race track where each obstacle is surmounted and immediately left behind and forgotten. A more realistic parallel is the journey of the camel on whose back package after package is laid until, crazed in mind and with muscles pained beyond endurance, one more package or even one more straw causes it to collapse in the dust. Five other men, sturdy in body and robust in mind, were interrogated at the same time as Eaton and likewise released without being charged with any offence. Each of them appears to have been as shattered and disorientated as he and to have differed mainly in that they were able to return to work more quickly. Again, in common with Eaton, they had for a time an overwhelming terror of being re-arrested. For that reason, one lived away from home with relatives for the first fortnight after his release.

The fact of being accused of a crime such as murder or attempted murder is a traumatic experience which leaves mind and body in a state of profound shock. The prospect of spending a great part of the remainder of one's life in prison; the ignominy and suffering of one's wife and children and other loved ones; the ending of career and ambitions are all vividly present. The brutality and abusive language give a feeling of evilness and of a world turned up-side-down. Worst of all is the feeling of helplessness and despair. Almost always those interrogated are humble people in social terms and sometimes are ill-educated. The detectives seem so confident in their accusations and insinuations and as they are policemen, it is assumed, their word will be believed before all others in a court of law. It is realised instinctively that, if the authorities are so ruthless as to allow institutionalised torture and mal-treatment, the whole law and order system has to be seen in a new light. People who have not been in such a situation are sometimes slow to understand. They are like the little girl who asked her Jewish refugee school chum, "When the Gestapo did those bad things to your daddy and mummy, why did they not tell a policeman?"

A clear cut division exists in the police holding centres between the "confessions" detectives and the uniformed police. The latter disassociate themselves from the former whenever possible and react to their unwelcome presence by an ultra-meticulous observation of rules and procedures. Thus, there are the aspects of Castlereagh reported by Eaton such as the unexpected courtesy of the uniformed guards who look after prisoners while in the cells; the regular offer of meals; and even the relatively senior police officer who visits the cells to ask if the occupants have any complaints although none would know better than he how futile is the exercise.

On the other hand, the "confessions" detectives in the police holding centres must not be dismissed as mere louts and bullies or their methods as mindless viciousness. They are trained men and are applying procedures scientifically evaluated and carefully chosen with the objective of securing a signed confession within a short, specified periods of time without leaving evidence of physical mal-treatment. Persons familiar with studies such as *Beyond Breaking Point* by Peter Deely or *War on the Mind: The Military Uses and Abuses of Psychology* by Peter Watson will recognise familiar patterns in the interrogations to which Samuel Eaton was to be subjected. For example the following is Watson's description of an interrogation making use of "modern" procedures.

The interrogator will work to a three-stage plan. First comes the friendly interview stage, used partly to get basic information about the suspect and his movements and to establish in the mind of the suspect that the interrogator is no ordinary policeman/guard and that he does not have the common attitude to criminals/prisoners. At first any mention of the alleged crime or sensitive information is general enough. The aim is to get across the personality of the interrogator,

180

his professionalism, his humanity. If the suspect does not clam up the interrogator is doing his job properly.

After a while, however, and when the suspect/prisoner is talking readily enough, the situation is dramatically and suddenly changed. The interrogator himself may suddenly change his manner ... Or official looking papers may be brought into him on a secret signal. *The interrogator ... acts as though the whole thing is sewn up, an eyewitness has been found, one of the suspect's accomplices has talked. The suspect may well give himself up. It is a bluff, but it often works. If it does not work, then the interrogator will ... be replaced by ... a verbal bully. This sudden-change tactic works often enough for it to be the most common technique.*

When this technique does not work the third phase is put into operation ... The interrogator moves in close, changes regularly from a friendly to an unfriendly attitude. In this phase he may make use of psychological findings which show that many people have a body 'buffer zone' — an area inside which we do not like other people to come. In most of us it is a circle around us, two or three feet in radius ... All of this, of course, is part of a series of 'interviews', not a one-off affair.*

Omitted from the scenario sketched by Watson is the mental disorientation induced at Castlereagh by physical exhaustion, lack of sleep, overheated cells and over-supply of drugs. Research on such matters has been carried out in many countries although much of it has been in military and similar classified projects with findings withheld from publication. It is understood that the particular procedures used at Castlereagh owe much to the scientific evaluation of earlier methods used in interrogating terrorist suspects in Cyprus and Aden and the IRA suspects whose cases were later taken to the European Commission of Human Rights.

Samuel Eaton and his wife, Dorothy, were awakened by knocking between five and half-past five on the morning of 17th October 1977. It was on the front door and then the back. He went downstairs and called, "Who is there?" The reply was, "Police". He said, "Hang on

*Peter Watson, *War on the Mind: The Military Uses and Abuses of Psychology* (1978), p. 282.

a minute until I get dressed. Are you sure it is the police?" Someone replied, "Yes". He drew on his clothes and opened the front door. A policeman, whose name he later learned was Constable X, flashed his pass. He invited him to come in and he and four or five other policemen entered the living room. Two or three were in uniform and two were detectives in plain clothes. One wore a black, leather jacket similar to that of the paramilitary Ulster Volunteer Force.

Constable X said, "We have come to search your house. Is there anything in it which you should not have?" Eaton replied that there was nothing. He asked if he was sure and he confirmed that he was. He asked if he would like to accompany the police and he replied, "Yes, if you don't mind". A policeman asked how many were in the house. Eaton answered, "My children, my wife and myself". He then requested permission to see if his wife were properly clothed. This was granted and a policeman waited on the landing until she finished dressing in the bedroom.

Samuel Eaton was taken upstairs. Dorothy was asked to stay downstairs where a policeman in uniform searched the livingroom. They would not allow the two of them to be together. A policeman opened a wardrobe in a bedroom upstairs. He said to Constable X, "We have got something. Look at all this money!" Eaton explained that he and two others had won it on the pools. Constable X asked if his wife knew and he replied, "Yes". He went downstairs where Dorothy confirmed her husband's explanation by producing the pools coupon. Satisfied that it was true, he returned and instructed the other policeman to give the money back.

Constable X said to Eaton, "Come downstairs with me a wee minute". He saw Dorothy in the living-room and added, "Come into the kitchen as I want to have a wee talk with you". In the kitchen, he placed his hand on his shoulder and said that he was arresting him under Section 10 of the Emergency Provisions Act and showed him a piece of paper. Eaton retorted that he must be joking. He said, "No, there is the paper. I want you to come to Whiteabbey Police Station with us."

Everyone gathered in the living-room except for two uniformed policemen. A policeman asked if there was a coalshed. He was given the key and there was a search outside.

Samuel Eaton put on his shoes. He was shaking and asked if he could turn on the fire. The detective in the black jacket said he could and he warmed himself at it for five or ten minutes while other parts of the house were being searched.

The police spent over an hour in searching the house and then took Eaton in a police landrover to Whiteabbey Police Station where he was photographed and told that he was to be transferred to Castlereagh Police Holding Centre, Ladas Drive, Belfast. He was placed in another landrover and again was the only person in the vehicle apart from policemen. During the drive to Castlereagh, he chatted to a young policeman in uniform about their respective jobs and the money he had won on the pools. Before he dismounted, this policeman said, "You have heard about Castlereagh. If you do not know anything, you cannot say anything. Just think to yourself — they are not as bad as what the Russians are." His remarks were friendly and as Eaton left he called, "Hope to see you again".

A police sergeant was writing at the reception desk inside Castlereagh Police Holding Centre. He said, "Have you any wishes?" Eaton replied, "I would like to see my solicitor". He asked his name and was told, "Nurse and Jones". He said, "You have no chance of seeing a solicitor in here". He next asked if he wanted to see a police doctor. He replied, "Certainly, I do." He said, "It will be arranged".

Samuel Eaton's money and shoe laces were taken from him, but not his watch as he had left it at home in the stress of leaving. He continued to wear his own clothes. He was conducted up an iron staircase of one flight and through a door at the top. On the other side were two guards in uniform and a corridor of cells in one of which he was locked. It had a single bed and chair. The bed linen was clean. There was no window. A small aperture was placed high on the wall with wire over it. It was square — possibly eighteen inches each way, but no more. The electric light burned all the time. There was no switch with which a prisoner could turn it out. The guards brought a breakfast, but he was too tense to eat it. Shortly afterwards, he was taken down to be examined by a police doctor. The latter gave his name and after the examination asked him to sign a form to confirm that he had no complaints. He did so and was returned to the cell.

DAY ONE

First Interview, Day I

Samuel Eaton's first interview was conducted by two detectives and this was to be the normal pattern. One of them brought him down from the cell where he had been left for a short time after the medical examination. The other one was already seated in the interview room when he entered. They were dressed in civilian suits and ties and did not give their names. This failure to identify oneself by name was to be a feature of all the Castlereagh detectives who interviewed Eaton and was in contrast to the practice of the detectives who were later brought in from Whiteabbey Police Station. Not to do so is contrary to normal police practice in Northern Ireland.

The interrogation room was roughly eight feet by twelve feet. Two walls were made of brick and were painted cream and two were padded with white polystyrene-type material. There was a window obscured with wire and possibly with frosted glass. The light was always good enough to see well, but usually it was electric and possibly flourescent. The room had three or four ordinary chairs. The floor was concrete-type material, painted or stained red.

One detective was aged around forty-five; rather stout and not as tall as the other. He had hair which was becoming thin — in fact, he did not have much hair on the top of his head. He was to do most of the talking and will be referred to as Detective A.

The second detective was aged thirty-five to forty and well built. He will be referred to as Detective B.

One of the detectives asked Samuel Eaton to sit down. Both appeared very relaxed and did not seem pressed for time. There was no hint of maltreatment and Eaton subsequently commented that, if the further interviews had continued to be like the first one, he would have had no complaints. Detective A began the questioning.

DETECTIVE A: Well, what about this?

EATON: Well, what about what?

DETECTIVE A: We will not tell you too much about it, but we will throw you wee hints more or less.

Suddenly, a detective switched the subject with the remark, "What do you think about coming here?"

EATON: I don't know.

DETECTIVE A: You know why you are here?

EATON: No, I have not a clue.

DETECTIVE A: Well, see this form?

EATON: I cannot read or write. I am illiterate.

DETECTIVE A: You are illiterate?

EATON: Yes.

Detective A changed the subject.

DETECTIVE A: Who do you run about with?

EATON: Usually Jimmy Adams.

DETECTIVE A: Where does he live?

EATON: I cannot name the street, but it is around the Diamond.

DETECTIVE A: Who else?

EATON: A fellow called Isaac.

DETECTIVE A: Where does he live?

EATON: In Carnreagh Bend.

DETECTIVE A: You are thinking of people that will not get you into trouble. The rest of your mates are all in here. We have seven of them in here. There is only one that we don't have and you know who he is.

EATON: I do not know who you do not have in.

Samuel Eaton thinks that it was at this stage that he was told the names of these persons who had been arrested rather than in a later interview. He knew well two of the seven named. One of them, George Thompson, had lived next door to him when they were both children. The remaining five, he knew only slightly. He remembers Detective A saying, "Now that we have the rest of them in, you are going to have to tell us anyway".

Detective A returned to the form and said, "It says on the top we are charging you with something. We will give you a couple of wee hints". He added that the job had been done in a place which he named. It was a new housing estate in Newtownabbey.

EATON: I know where that place is. I work on electricity vans doing street lighting in the Newtownabbey area. I work in all the Newtownabbey area and I know most of the places. In fact, I am nearly always on the Glenville Road and in Jordanstown and the general Whiteabbey area.

DETECTIVE A: The job was done on 17th March. It was St. Patrick's night. Where were you on that date?

EATON: I have no idea.

DETECTIVE A: We will tell you. You went to a person's door and you knocked on it and you shot him.

EATON: Not guilty. Definitely not.

DETECTIVE A: If you tell us, we will make a deal with the judge and get you off very lightly. We are always the first to see the judge. We can make a deal with him. We will tell him that you confessed on your first statement and that you were very sorry and could not live with it.

EATON: I am definitely not guilty.

DETECTIVE A: It is a fourteen year sentence. We could get it cut to six or four. Then, with half remission and good behaviour, it would work out at two to three years. That is not bad at all.

EATON: That is not bad at all, but I am not guilty.

DETECTIVE A: If you will tell us, we will write it down and all you will have to do is sign it. We will then do our best for you. If you wait for the second interview, the judge would know that it was not bothering your conscience and would take a serious view.

The questioning was then switched to membership of the proscribed Ulster Volunteer Force.

DETECTIVE A: Are you a member of the UVF?

EATON: I am not.

DETECTIVE A: Do you drink in The Farm social club?

EATON: I have drunk there.

DETECTIVE A: Are you a member?

EATON: No, I am not a member.

DETECTIVE A: Did you know it was UVF?

EATON: I have heard that rumour, but I have never seen any in it. The people in it have always treated me decently and I have no complaint about the club.

DETECTIVE A: Do you drink in the Ardeene Social Club?

EATON: Yes. I have had a few drinks in it.

DETECTIVE A: Are you a member?

EATON: No.

DETECTIVE A: Do you drink in Fern Lodge?

EATON: Yes, I do indeed.

DETECTIVE A: Do you know that a car was stolen from the Fern Lodge for this job?

EATON: I did not. I had not a clue.

DETECTIVE A: You met in the Fern Lodge. You were given guns and had already been told beforehand that your orders were to go and shoot a Roman Catholic whom you believed to be a Provisional IRA officer. Of course, he is not.

EATON: Not guilty.

A DETECTIVE (probably Detective A): Do not say you are not guilty. When you are in here, say you have nothing to say.

EATON: Fair enough, then.

The detectives produced a map with a route marked on it. It began at the Fern Lodge, passed along Doagh Road, Monkstown Avenue, cut into Whiteabbey to the estate where the man had been shot, and ended up at The Farm. They said it was the road Eaton had taken. He replied that he was not there.

Detective A said, "We are putting you in your cell. Think very hard about it and let us know. You can go away for either fourteen years or six years. It is up to yourself." Samuel Eaton did not reply. The interview had probably lasted two hours and he was glad to escape from the room for a rest.

Second Interview, Day I

Samuel Eaton was taken down for the second interview after perhaps half-an-hour in the cell. It was in the same room, but conducted by two new detectives. One was in his early forties and about 5 foot 8 inches in height. He will be referred to as Detective C. The second was aged around thirty, about the same height and well built. He will be referred to as Detective D. Eaton is not absolutely sure about the colour of their hair, but thinks that Detective C had probably fairish hair and Detective D gingery-fair.

He sat in the same chair as in the first interview. Detective D sat on his side of the table and on his right and Detective C sat on the other side of it.

Samuel Eaton had a bad stutter during the three days he was to be in custody. Most of the detectives who interviewed him asked him about it. Some harrassed him on account of it, but not all of them did so. At one stage during his second interview, Detective D slapped him across the back of the head and ordered him to stop his stuttering. He accused him of putting it on.

Detective C began the questioning.

DETECTIVE C: Right, we don't want any more carrying on! We want this information. What about this attempted murder?

EATON: Not guilty, sir.

DETECTIVE C: Don't give me that. Just say, Nothing to say, when you are in here. What about it?

EATON: Not guilty.

DETECTIVE C: I told you before, don't say, Not guilty. Say, Nothing to say.* We know you are guilty. We have witnesses. We do not want these witnesses to lose their lives by going to court to identify you. We do not want people getting killed over you.

EATON: I have nothing to say. I am not guilty.

DETECTIVE D: Look you are not a tough man, son. You will not last the time in here. We will soon break you. Let us get this the easy way first.

EATON: I have nothing to say.

Detective D rose from his chair; stood behind Samuel Eaton‡ and hit him across the back of the head six or eight times. As he did so, he kept saying, "You have plenty to say, son." Eaton moved his head forward, but did not try to protect his head with his hands.

DETECTIVE C: Were you shown this map?

EATON: Yes.

DETECTIVE C: Do you know where it is?

EATON: Yes. I work around the area and know all of it.

DETECTIVE C: Look, do you want these people to have to go in court and maybe lose their lives over you.

EATON: I certainly do not want anyone to lose his life.

DETECTIVE C: Well, if you do not give us the information we want, we will have to use these people and you know that the UVF will deal with them.

*This was good interrogation craftsmanship. If interrogators can force their prisoner to conform to their wishes in a small matter, they have a psychological advantage from then onwards. Also, "Nothing to say" threw an additional strain on persons who felt it incriminating if they were unable to declare their innocence outright.

‡It was mentioned in the extract from Watson's book earlier in this chapter that many people became uneasy when someone comes close to them — or invades what psychiatrists term the personal "buffer zone". Some are particularly upset if the other person stands behind them within the "buffer zone". See Augustus F. Kinzel, "Body buffer zones in violent prisoners", *American Journal of Psychiatry,* vol. 127, July 1970, pp. 59-64. Eaton was not concerned as to where his interrogators stood, but they would not have known that.

EATON: I cannot help it. I am not guilty. I was not there.

Detective D was still standing behind Eaton.

DETECTIVE D: But you are guilty son.

DETECTIVE C: We know who is telling the truth in here and who does not and you are not telling the truth.

Detective D caught hold of Samuel Eaton and pulled him up so that he stood on his feet. He pushed him against the wall and told him to stand against it. He said, "You are guilty, son. You are guilty." Detective C came round the table and started to poke him on the navel with the point of the fingers of a hand held open and flat. Eaton said, "That is sore," and went to raise his hands. He said, "Are you going to hit me?"Eaton replied, "No, but the pain is sore. I am going to be sick." Detective C lifted a wastepaper basket and held it. He said, "Be sick in that". Eaton vomited slightly. He said, "You are not being sick," and kept on poking him on the stomach and repeating, "Aren't you guilty?" Eaton said, "But, I am not guilty," and he retorted, "How many times have you been told you don't say you are not guilty! You say you have nothing to say."

After a time, Detective C stopped poking him on the navel and Detective D ordered him to stand with his arms stretched above his head, finger tips against the wall, feet well apart and head well back. He slapped him on the back of the head and said, "You are guilty, son. We do not want to waste these peoples' lives over an animal like you. You are not a tough man. You are not going to stick this."

The detectives kept Samuel Eaton standing in the special position at the wall until he fell.* He fell because his fingers and legs were aching and he just had to fall. It was possibly fifteen to twenty minutes before he collapsed. Detective D told him to get to his feet or he would knock his teeth down his throat. He got up and he ordered him to resume the position at the wall immediately. The falling down gave relief and he was able to obey.

*A study of 220 American ex-prisoners of war who had been interrogated by the Chinese during the Korean War showed that the most effective form of physical duress for obtaining information is pain which is debilitating and self-inflicted such as prolonged periods of standing. A. D. Biderman, "Sociopsychological needs and 'involuntary' behaviour as illustrated by compliance in interrogation", *Sociometry*, vol. 23, 1960.

Eaton fell down again after some five to ten minutes. Altogether, he was ordered back to the wall four times after having collapsed. Each time he fell down after a shorter period. His head kept falling forward as he came near to the point where he would collapse and Detective D would order him to keep his head back. The detectives (but mainly Detective D) kept saying, "You are guilty, aren't you?" and Eaton would reply, "Nothing to say". He was slapped on the back of the head about twice while in the wall position.

Detective D eventually told him to sit on a chair and the following dialogue took place.

DETECTIVE C: You are going to have to confess because when we take you to court, we are the first ones to see the judge and if you help us we will help you and you would help save these peoples' lives by not having them to go to court. This will help your case by not having these people to go to court and lose their lives over an animal like you. It is not because of you this man is not dead. You shot him and the man has lost an eye.

So what are you going to do about it, son? Are you going to make us take these people to court or are you going to confess? If you confess, you might walk out with only six years and you might have to do four or even three and that is not bad for what you have done.

EATON: Not guilty.

DETECTIVE C: But son, you are guilty all right. We have enough proof. We have witnesses to take you to court. The only reason we are talking to you is to save these lives by not having to take them to court. Don't think that you are going back to your cell to have a rest. You will be interviewed and interviewed all day and all night till we get what we want out of you. We cannot have a person like you running about the streets shooting people.

Eaton thinks that it was probably at this point that he was sent back to the cell. The interview may have lasted about two hours. He thinks that it was when in the cell after it that he was offered food, but he accepted only a cup of tea.

Third Interview, Day I

Samuel Eaton was taken for the third interview after fifteen to thirty minutes in the cell. It was held in a different, but identical room to the one used for the first two interviews and was reached along an L shaped corridor.

Two new detectives were in the room. One was aged about forty and had darkish hair. He will be referred to as Detective E. The other was aged about thrity-five. He was to speak only once or twice. He will be referred to as Detective F.

The detectives sat on one side of the table and Eaton on the other.

DETECTIVE E: What do you think of being in Ladas Drive? You probably thought that you were going to Whiteabbey with the softly, softly boys. I suppose you have heard of the brutality here. I suppose you heard about the fellow who was put in the helicopter and thrown out blindfolded. Would you fancy that? Or would you like to urinate (he used a different word) against an electric fence?

EATON: I work in electricity and I have had a few shocks. I am not that scared of electricity if that is what you mean, but I would not fancy it.

DETECTIVE E: Come on, son! You have had it easy up to now. We cannot have you doing the likes of this and thinking that you are getting away with it. You know your mates in here are beginning to crack up. One has already made a statement naming you and saying that you had something to do with it. Another mate is ready to confess, too. So what are you going to do? Are you going to be the odd one out?

EATON: I am not guilty, sir.

DETECTIVE E: Don't call me sir. And again, don't say you are not guilty. Say you have nothing to say. You have already been told.

Let us see how you can do press-ups. Get down on that floor and let us see you do some press-ups.

Samuel Eaton lay down on the floor as ordered and began to do press-ups. As he was doing them, Detective E said, "Do nine". He did as told and he said, "You have done those well. Let us see you do another nine." He next said, "Let us see you do thirty". Eaton collapsed and he placed his foot under his stomach and heaved him up and down for a number of further press-ups. He then ordered him to get up and to stand at the wall in the same position as in the second interview. It was the same procedure again with the repeated questions, "Aren't you guilty, son? Aren't you going to confess and save yourself all this?" He fell down four or five times.

When Eaton was standing in the position at the wall, Detective E said, "Can you count? Then count the holes in the wall panel. You are supposed to be illiterate so let us see if you can count." Eaton replied, "I can count". He continued, "So we have a mathematician on our hands. Let us see how good you are." He ordered him to count the small perforations on what may have been a ventilation panel — first the number in the top row; then the number in a down row and lastly the total number in the panel. He told him that his answers were wrong and insisted that he re-count them. He taunted him with having claimed that he was a mathematician. Eaton replied that he had not said that — that he had only said that he could count.

Detective E eventually told Samuel Eaton to sit down. He next instructed him to place his back on the seat of his chair and his feet under a pipe which ran along the wall. He was thus supported by the chair in a horizontal position and prevented from tumbling over by the pipe. Detective E placed his knee into his back between the shoulder blades. After a time he said, "What is that like? It is sore, isn't it? It will get a lot sorer."

Detective E took his knee away and came round beside him and, as he lay across the chair, began to poke him on the navel with the tips of the fingers of a flat, open hand. He kept repeating, "You are guilty, aren't you? You are going to confess." Eaton continued to reply, "Nothing to say."

Detective E suddenly said, "You smell, don't you?" and ordered him to stand up. He asked, "When was the last time you had a bath?" Eaton replied, "Saturday night". He continued, "You are stinking, aren't you? You need another one. Don't you?" He then spat on his face as he stood facing him. He added, "you are no good. You are nothing but an animal."*

Detective E next spoke about the danger to witnesses in similar terms to those used during the previous interview. He then said that Eaton's mates had made a statement.

_____

*It should be remembered in connection with this incident that the detective's training in interrogation would have instilled into him that the key to obtaining a confession is to make the prisoner feel humiliated, degraded, isolated and helpless. Pain and physical mal-treatment are usually of limited value by themselves.

DETECTIVE E: Your mates have made a statement. A fellow called Frew has made one. He says that he did it and that you were there. What about this? Are you going to admit it?

EATON: I was not there. I am not guilty.

DETECTIVE E: If we show you the statement, will you admit it?

EATON: I do not know anything about it. I cannot read or write.

DETECTIVE E: Would you like to see the statement?

Eaton was shown a paper. He again said, "I cannot read or write", and Detective E read from it an admission that the signatory had driven Samuel Eaton and another person in a car to a house to shoot a man.* Eaton cannot remember whether it named the other person who it was claimed was present.

Detective E said, "It does not look good for you." Eaton did not reply. He then asked, "Will we get the other statement for you? Would that help you?" He answered, "Yes, I would like to see the other statement". He was told that it was being photocopied and would be ready soon. After a little while, it was brought in and read. The signatory was George Thompson whom Eaton knew well. It was an admission that he and two others, neither of whom were named, had shot a man who was thought to be in the IRA.‡

Detective E said, "If you make a statement, we can put it the same as your mates' so that it will not look bad in front of your other mates who are in here. It will look as though you held out as long as you possibly could." Eaton replied, "I am not guilty". He continued to press him in this way for some time. Occasionally, he slapped him around the back of the head. At last he said, "We are putting you up in the cell again".

It was during the interview which has just been described or the following one (Samuel Eaton reckons that it was during the first day he was in custody) that a detective said, "You say that you are illiterate". He answered, "Yes". He asked, "Can you sign your name?" and received the reply, "Yes, I can". The detective reached him a piece of paper and said, "Let us see how you do it". The paper was white, blank and about foolscap size.

*Brian Frew admits that he signed a confession written by the detectives, but insists strongly that at no time did he mention Samuel Eaton. The confession led to him being sentenced to 7 years imprisonment.

‡This confession resulted in George Thompson being sentenced to 15 years imprisonment.

Samuel Eaton said, "No, I will not sign it. If I put my signature there, sure you could fill in anything. I am signing nothing." The detective next said, "All we want to see is your signature — to see if you can sign it. If you cannot sign your name, you can put an X." Eaton again replied that he would sign nothing. He thinks that the paper was left lying on the table. The incident happened very quickly and he does not remember which detective was responsible.

Also, it was during this third interview or the following one that a detective (Eaton does not remember which one) referred to an incident in which two men — he thinks it was two — were shot in a hut in Ballyduff, Newtownabbey. Eaton said that he had nothing to do with it. The detective asserted that his description fitted one of the men who had done it and asked if he would go on an identification parade. He answered that he did not care as he had nothing to hide. The detective then changed the subject.

Samuel Eaton believes that he was offered food when he was in the cell, but he took only a cup of tea. He rested for possibly an hour or it may have been only half-an-hour before he was taken down for the fourth interview. He had lost track of time by then.

It was during either this interval in the cell or the previous one that a relatively senior police officer visited him. (He was in uniform and had officer insignias on his shoulder tabs.) He told him that his parents wished him to change his solicitor and recommended Mr. Jonathan Taylor. He asked if he wished to accept him and he replied that he would be very satisfied to have him act for him.

The same police officer was to visit Eaton in the cell on possibly two further occasions. One was probably at the end of his second day in custody. On each of his visits the conversation was the same. He asked if he had any complaints and Eaton answered that he had been ill-treated. He did not request details and Eaton did not volunteer them. He asked if he would be making a complaint and was told, "Yes". He then moved on to visit another cell.

Fourth Interview, Day I

The fourth interview was in the room where the first and second had been held. Detective A and Detective B conducted it. There was the smell of drink from them. The dialogue was as follows.

DETECTIVE A: You look tired. What is wrong with you?

EATON: My arms are sore. My fingers are sore and my back is sore. I am tired and sore all over.

DETECTIVE A: What did this?

EATON: The treatment I have had in here.

DETECTIVE A: Have you not been co-operating?

EATON: I have only been saying the truth.

DETECTIVE A: What have they been doing to you?

EATON: They had me against the walls and my back against the seat of the chair and it has been more or less sheer brutality.

DETECTIVE A: We had a nice dinner and couple of nice drinks. What actually were they doing on you that you are in such a state with your arms and all? Show me what they did.

Samuel Eaton demonstrated the position in which he had been forced to stand. Detective A then made him remain in it. He slapped him on the back of the head six or eight times and made remarks such as, "Come on, you are going to have to own up". When Eaton eventually fell, he was made to stand again in the same position. Altogether, he was made to stand in it three or four times, each time until he fell.

Detective A said, "Get those shoes off". Eaton did as told and he trampled on his toes. It was unpleasant, but not very painful and the pressure was not enough to bruise them.

Detective B intervened at this stage. He placed a finger behind each of Samuel Eaton's ears and lifted him until he was standing tip-toe on the floor. It was sheer agony. Eaton was shouting with the pain, but he continued to hold him suspended in that way for a few minutes — Eaton is unable to say exactly how long.

As he held him suspended, Detective B kept saying, "You are guilty, aren't you?" When he returned him to the ground, he stepped back a little and stood behind him. Detective A then said, "You are going to confess and get this off your chest. It will be better for yourself. You are going to have to stick this, not only for three days, but maybe for seven."

Detective B, who was still standing behind Eaton, again lifted him up by means of a finger behind each ear and again he found himself shouting with the intense pain. He said, "You do not like that. Do you? These two fingers — I will stick them right through your brain. You are wasting our time here."

When Detective B returned Samuel Eaton to the ground, Detective A told him to sit on a chair and the following dialogue took palce.

DETECTIVE A: You have seen the statements. Haven't you?

EATON: Yes.

DETECTIVE A: The deal we could have done with the judge will not be so good now because he will look and see that this is the fourth interview and he will not be as lenient. He will say that you do not feel remorse for the deeds that you have done. You will not get off as lenient as the other two, but maybe you might end up with only two years more than they have got. You are going to have to make a statement.

Detective A asked Eaton if he knew a man from Monkstown whom he named. He replied, "Only more or less to see".

DETECTIVE A: He never pleaded guilty and he got life. Do you want that to happen to you. You will have to make a statement for your own good. We know that you have been in the UVF for at least three years. We have a record on you for at least three years. This is not your first one. We leave the rest. We are not pushing for any other — all we want is this one. You know yourself that we are hurting the IRA. We have to put you away too for a few years till the troubles quieten down. We know that we are getting one or two IRA every day. When you get out all will be quiet and you can live your life in peace and quiet the way that it was.

We know that the UVF make you go out and do jobs. If you do not do it, they could shoot you. We know you are in the UVF. The UVF took upon itself to kill so many Catholics for every policeman shot dead. You are only making the troubles last longer. For every Catholic you kill, they kill another Protestant.

EATON: I am not in the UVF.

DETECTIVE A: You know that the UVF will forget about you when you are inside. We would rather have an IRA man in here. I remember when the UVF said they would kill fifteen Catholics for every policeman that was killed by an IRA man. We know that you do not kill policemen like the IRA — that is why we don't hate you as much. You know yourself that you are tired. Do you think that you could last seven days like this? It is only a matter of form for us after three days to get a bit of paper signed and you are in for seven days. This will last all day and all night — this interviewing. You are done out now, son. What will you be like after seven days? We will do it. Don't you think that after this interview you are going up to lie down for an hour because there are another two detectives going to take over and then another two and so forth and so forth until we get what we want. Do you think you can stick seven days of this? Look son, we are Protestants. You are only wasting your time and our time. You have done your duty. Just confess and every-thing will be a lot clearer for you and a lot better for you. You will be able to go to your cell. In the morning, everything will seem much better for you. These interviews will go on all night until we get a statement out of you.

At this point Detective D and Detective E entered the room. The first had taken part in the second interview and the other in the third interview. They took over and Detective A and Detective B left. Samuel Eaton's fifth interview thus took place without him having been returned to the cell.

Fifth Interview, Day I

Detective D began the fifth interview by saying, "Right! No more wasting our time. We are about fed up with you. Get against the wall and get your shoes off." It was the same as before. Samuel Eaton had to stand with arms stretched upwards, fingers touching the wall, feet well apart and head well back. There were also slaps on the back of the head and comments such as, "Come on! You are going to have to confess". Detective D hit him on about two occasions on his ribs on both sides at the same time with the edges of of his open hands (double kidney chops). These blows were acutely painful and Eaton fell down after them. They were administered before he collapsed for the first time from the agony of the wall standing. He was not struck on the ribs during the remainder of the wall standing, but was slapped once or twice on the back of the head. Altogether, he collapsed three or four times from the wall standing.

At one point when Samuel Eaton was in the wall standing position, a detective, who was drinking water, turned him around; poked him in the eye with a finger and said, "Do you know what it is like to lose an eye?" He next pulled his shirt collar back and poured water inside his clothes so that it ran down his back. He said, "Imagine that is blood". He then ordered him to resume the wall standing position.

Eventually Detective E said, "Let us see you doing your press-ups again", and Eaton was made to do press-ups until he collapsed. Detective D then ordered him to get up and sit on a chair.

The two detectives returned to the statements made by Frew and Thompson and asked Samuel Eaton if he had seen them. He said, "Yes". He was asked if he would like them read again. He replied, "I have seen them". Detective D said, "Well, I will read them to you", and he read out both of them.

DETECTIVE D: Well, what about this? Is this fellow lying?

EATON: He must be.

DETECTIVE D: Why should he name you?

EATON: I don't know.

DETECTIVE D: If we let you see George, would that help you? You would then know that we are not making up these statements seeing that you cannot read or write.

EATON: I would not mind seeing George.

DETECTIVE D: It is against our rules. But we will see the Chief and see if we can get him down and let him talk to you and see if he can put any sense into your head.

DETECTIVE E: If we do let him down, you will not start fighting?

EATON: I have no complaints against George. He never named me. George knows I am not guilty.

DETECTIVE E: Say we do let him down — what about it? Will you make a statement after it.

EATON: I promise nothing: but I would like to see him.

One of the detectives went out and came back with George Thompson.* He was left in the interrogation room and both detectives withdrew outside the door. One said, "Don't be fighting!"

Thompson's first remark was, "You look terrible". Samuel Eaton replied, "They say that I have something to do with an attempted

*The police are forbidden in Northern Ireland, as in many other countries, to confront a prisoner with another prisoner during interrogation.

murder, but you know I am not guilty". Thompson said they must be holding him because he was an acquaintance of his. He admitted that he had pleaded guilty. He explained that he had done so under the pressure as he had been promised a light sentence. Eaton said, "I am not pleading guilty because I am not guilty George". The latter answered, "I know that, but they asked me to come down. They said that you wanted to see me and that you were in a bad way." The detectives then re-entered the room and the conversation ended with Eaton and Thompson calling out to each other, "All the best!"

One of them (probably Detective E) began, "Well, what about it?" and the interview continued.

EATON: I am not guilty.
DETECTIVE E: You promised that if you saw George you would see then what you would do.
EATON: I promised nothing. All I said was that I would like to see him. I am not guilty.

Detective E caught hold of Eaton and threw him against a wall. At that point Detective C came into the room. He asked, "Has he confessed yet?" He was answered, "No". He then continued, "What, after us bringing George down to see you! You are wasting our time again. Stand up straight with your back against the wall." He then began to poke Eaton on the navel with the tips of the fingers of a flat, open hand in the same way as he had done in the second interview. He said, "Confess you scum". The more he poked, the more painful it became. He taunted him, "Well, hit us back you coward. You are nothing but a rotten, good-for-nothing coward. At least even a rat would go for you."

When Detective C stopped poking Samuel Eaton on the navel, Detective D and Detective E started to throw him against the padded walls. One of them held him by the upper arm and shoulder and he was thrown so that he hit a padded wall with a shoulder and then the other padded wall again with a shoulder.

He does not know how many times he was thrown against the padded walls. He was just knackered and did not know whether he was living or dead, he explained later.

Detective E grabbed him; pushed him against a padded wall; twisted his right arm behind his back and kept repeating, You are guilty. Aren't you?" Eaton would reply, "I am not guilty". His twisted arm was painful, but not as bad as some of the pain.

While he was pinned thus against the wall with his arm twisted behind his back, one of the detectives turned out the light and Detective D seized a chair and started to hit it against the wall beside him. He has no idea how long this went on. He was shouting with pain. Eventually, Detective C said, "Let him be a moment", and caught hold of him. He said, "Get outside", and took him through a door into the open air.

DETECTIVE C: Do you know why I got you out? Because, if I had not, they would have killed you. You will have to wise up, son. You will never stand all of this from three to seven days. We can make this last seven days if we want. Why don't you just tell me all about it? I will write it all down for you. You can sign it. It will look a lot clearer in the morning. You are tired now. But, if you sign, everything in the morning will look a lot clearer. You will be glad to get it off your chest. Just take a couple of good breaths of air here and calm down. Now what about it? Are you going to sign it?

EATON: I have nothing to say.

DETECTIVE C: Suppose we put you down for the night — would you think about it?

EATON: Yes, certainly.

DETECTIVE C: We will put you down for the night and in the morning we will discuss it again. We will go in and tell these men we are going to put you down for the night.

As soon as Samuel Eaton entered the interview room, a detective shouted, "Get against the wall". Detective C said, "Leave him alone. We are going to put him down for the night. He has promised to think about it." Another detective said, "Back up to the cells", and one of them conducted him up the stairs to the uniformed guards in charge of the cells.

Eaton thinks that the time may have been around 11.30 p.m., but points out that it could have been earlier. He had been awakened that morning in his own home between five and five-thirty and had thus been under constant stress for up to some eighteen hours, including probably about ten hours of ruthless interviewing and mal-treatment.

He was exhausted totally and had taken no food other than cups of tea. Nor was he to eat any food during the two further days that he was to be in custody.

Conditions in the cell

Samuel Eaton lay on the bed and tried to sleep. He was too tired to really sleep and would doze and waken up. The cell was unbearably hot. Once the door was closed and locked, the heat built up until it was so suffocating that he could hardly breathe. He would ask to go to the toilet just to escape into cooler air. At the same time, he was afraid to ask too often in case he would antagonise the guards. He sweated continually. Eventually, he began to keep the polythene cups in which tea was brought so that he could fill them with water at the toilet for drinking in the cell. He slept in his shirt as he was unsure when he would be called.

It should be noted that the oven-like cell is not only a way to undermine a prisoner's will to resist through lack of sleep, but, in addition, the heavy and continuous perspiration causes listlessness and mental depression through loss of body salts as anyone with experience of working in the tropics will confirm.

DAY TWO

Samuel Eaton felt exceedingly tired with sore arms, back, head, and back of head on the morning of his second day in custody.

He was not able to shave or wash either then or at any other time apart from a shower on the evening of the second day.

He was offered breakfast, but did not feel like eating and took only a cup of tea. He does not know what time it was.

Shortly after the cup of tea, he was taken down for an interview. He has difficulty in remembering the exact sequence of the interviews from the second day onwards. He thinks that the one which will now be described was the first on the second day, but is not absolutely certain.

Further Interview, Day II

Detective A and Detective B conducted the interview. As in the first interview of the first day, Detective A did most of the talking.

DETECTIVE A: Sit down. You look tired. Did you not sleep very well?

EATON: No, not terribly well.

DETECTIVE A: I believe you saw your mate, George, last night. Well, have you thought over it?

EATON: I am not guilty.

DETECTIVE A: Don't tell me we are going to have to go through all of this to-day again. Son, do you realise how long you are going to get? Do you want about fourteen years maybe? Do you think that your wife is going to stand by you for fourteen years, waiting on you? Do you actually think that she will stay faithful to you for fourteen years?

EATON: I do not really know.

DETECTIVE A: I can tell you roughly. We know that for a fact, when people are inside, the most that wives last is four years being faithful and that is a good woman. Most of them only last two years. Could you blame the girl if you got fourteen years?

EATON: Certainly not.

DETECTIVE A: That is your family — your marriage ruined. You are not even thinking of your family — you are only thinking of yourself. We will write down the same as your mate, George, says. It won't incriminate anyone else. It will help you. I will not be able to promise that you will get the same time as your mate , George. You will maybe get an extra two years. You never made a statement in the first interview. You must not love your family. What is your wife going to think about this? Look at you! You will never stand this from three to seven days. You are just going to be like a hard man and just say, I never broke down — I never gave in. And you will lose your family over this. Do you want to lose your wife and children? Look at your hands shaking! You are ready to take a nervous breakdown. I can promise you one thing — when you get out you will have no family. The only reason we are talking to you now is to save the lives of these witnesses. I will make you go mad if I have to. You are thinking of nobody, but yourself.

Samuel Eaton began to scream. A detective told him afterwards that he had to hold him down as he was ready to beat his head against a wall.

He does not remember clearly what happened. He felt that his mind was not his own. He was conscious of hearing people talking to him. Someone was saying, "Calm down. Calm down."

Shortly afterwards, he broke down totally. He remembers fighting to hold on to his mind — to hold on to what little reason he had left. He feared that, if he let go, he would lose his mind completely.

He was conscious of voices and not people. One voice said, "We must get a doctor". A new detective entered the room whom he saw banging the table with his fist. He said, "You have brought this on yourself". (A detective told Eaton later that they had even to bring in their boss). One of the detectives gave him some water. He said, "Drink some of this water till we see if we can get a doctor".

Eaton remembers walking out of the room. He remembers two men on the stairs. One caught hold of him — probably to keep him from falling. The older one said, "Calm down, son. You will be OK." His voice sounded in the distance. He does not know who were these two men on the stairs.

He was left in the cell with the door open and a policeman on a chair outside. A little later, he was taken down to see a police doctor.

The police doctor asked Samuel Eaton to tell him what had happened and he did so briefly. He told him that he could not take much more of it. He said that he would have to get him out of the place or he would end up in a mental hospital. The doctor replied that he could not get him out. All he could do, he said, was to give some tablets and to ask the detectives to allow him a rest.

The doctor gave him two tablets and said that he could have more when needed. He wrote down what he had told him and asked him to sign it. He replied that he was terrified to sign it — that the detectives would kill him if he signed anything like that. The doctor remarked that he did not think he could sign it, even if he wanted to, because of the state he was in. He gave his name, but Eaton does not remember it.

The tablets were left with the guards at the head of the stairs which led to the cells with instructions to give them to Eaton when needed. He remembers guards asking him if he wanted tablets, but he cannot remember how often he was asked or how frequently he accepted.*

After the visit to the police doctor, Samuel Eaton was taken to the

---

*The easy availability of drugs in tablet form is a feature of Castlereagh interrogations.

cell and given a rest of possibly a couple of hours, but he is unable to say how long.

He thinks that it was during the interview which has just been described that a detective threatened that his wife could be brought to Castlereagh for questioning. He answered that she was an innocent girl who, like himself, knew nothing and he certainly did not want her brought in.

After the rest in the cell, he was taken for another interview. He thinks that this was the one on the second day conducted by Sergeant Y and Constable X from Whiteabbey Police Station. Also, that this may have been the time when he was taken along a corridor to an interview room in a different block. Both policemen were in plainclothes. They sat on one side of the table and he on the other. Sergeant Y did most of the talking

SERGEANT Y: I am Sergeant Y and this is Constable X. I think you have met him before.

EATON: Yes, I have met him before. (He was one of the policemen who arrested him.)

SERGEANT Y: You need not worry about us hitting you. I will not hit you and Constable X will not hit you.

SERGEANT Y: You are going to have to tell us about this. You cannot have this on your conscience. Do you believe in God?

EATON: I do.

SERGEANT Y: Well, when you die and meet your Maker what will you say then? "Nothing to say." Will you say that to your Maker? You cannot say that to Him because he knows it all. What about your wife? Are you going to lose your family over this?

Sergeant Y talked a long time about Eaton losing his family and then again about religion. He next continued as follows.

SERGEANT Y: Look, if you tell us what we want to know, we could let you see your wife and mother. It would be a terrible shock if they were to read it in the newspaper that you were guilty of attempted murder. I can promise you that, if you were to co-operate with us, I will bring your wife up. She would be glad that you have got this off your chest. She would say that you have done the right thing by telling us. You could do your time and you would then have paid your debt to society. You could then meet your Maker with a clear conscience

EATON: I am not guilty.

SERGEANT Y: We do not bring innocent people in here.

EATON: But, I am not guilty.

SERGEANT Y: We will put you back in the cell. Do you want me to deliver a message to your wife, if I have a chance to-day?

EATON: Would you do that for me?

SERGEANT Y: Certainly, I will do it for you.

EATON: Tell my wife that I love her and that I will see her when I can. Don't be worrying about me. I am OK.

SERGEANT Y: I will give her the message.

The message was not delivered.

Further Interview, Day II

Samuel Eaton thinks that, during this interval in the cell, he was offered a meal. He refused it and is not certain whether or not he took a cup of tea. He cannot remember which interview came next. It may have been one conducted by Detective A and Detective B which will now be described.

DETECTIVE A: We are not going to hit you. I believe that you have been making a complaint about brutality.

EATON: I certainly have.

DETECTIVE A: What have you had — a slap on the back of the head! Sure man, you have been beaten up worse than that outside! I hope that you are not going to blame us two for this brutality. We looked after you when you took the nervous breakdown. Sure, we never did much on you! Sure, you are not going to blame us two!*

*No policeman likes to be subjected to a formal complaint even when he can assume that officialdom will stand by him. In practice, neither detective appears to have been in any danger. Par. 155 of the Bennett Report gives the following relevant information: "A number of prisoners have taken civil proceedings for damages for personal injuries (as well as in some instances for wrongful arrest and imprisonment) alleged to have been caused by assaults by members of the RUC in arresting or interrogating them in connection with scheduled offences ... The records of the Police Authority in September 1978 showed that 119 such claims had been made in respect of incidents

EATON: No.

DETECTIVE A: Sonny, what about this? I don't want to have to talk and waste my voice. It is going in one ear and out the other with you. I am not going to sit here and waste my time. I am just going to sit here and not even talk to you. Just think what you have done. Can you have this on your mind? If you can, you are known as a psychopath. Do you know what a psychopath is?

EATON: I do. It is a fellow who enjoys killing.

DETECTIVE A: We are lucky because we have got you before you have killed anybody.

The detective returned to the subject of saying nothing and letting Eaton sit and think. He then continued:

DETECTIVE A: I would not hit you anymore because I would kill you. You have got me to that state. I am doing this for your own good. What do you do if your children are bad? Don't you smack them.

EATON: Yes.

DETECTIVE A: That is all we are doing to you. We are smacking you to get the truth out of you.

EATON: I am not guilty. How many times do I have to tell you?

DETECTIVE A: I am not going to open my mouth any more. Just sit and think.

At this point the other detective was going to say something, but Detective A said, "No, let him be. Let him sit there and think". He

alleged to have happened since 1 April 1972. 23 of these claims were settled out of court, the latest incident so dealt with having occurred in October 1974. 5 of the claims had been contested in court, 3 successfully and 2 unsuccessfully, these last arising from incidents in January and October 1974. 10 claims had not been pursued. Of the outstanding 82 claims, writs had been issued in 61 cases. The settled and decided claims all arose from incidents which occurred some time ago ... the inference to be drawn from these settled claims is obvious. We need only say that in some of them the allegations were of serious assault; in some the amount of damages paid was high. The comment has been made to us by witnesses that no disciplinary action is known to have been taken within the force against those officers who have been found at fault in civil proceedings." *(Report of the Committee of Inquiry into Police Interrogation Procedures in Northern Ireland* (March 1979), pp. 51-52).

then added some phrase like, "we are only wasting our voices" or "we are only hurting our throats".

Ten or fifteen minutes followed during which no one spoke.*

At the end of that time Detective A resumed as follows:

DETECTIVE A: We are only trying to do you a good turn. We put you away for a few years. You can then go back to your family. Do away with this UVF thing you are in and live as a law-abiding citizen. You are not a criminal. You will never make a good criminal because doubts are written all over your face. For you to sit there and tell us you are not guilty!

What are we going to do with you? We are going to hunt up more records on you. We are going to take your fingerprints. We are going to get something more on you as well as this. You will never get out of jail.

At this point the detectives returned Eaton to the cell.

Further Interview, Day II

Samuel Eaton remembers going for an interview conducted by two detectives whom he assumes were from Whiteabbey Police Station as they introduced themselves by name. (He does not now remember their names). One wore glasses. The other resembled a detective called Stewart who used to live near his home. Next day, he remarked to Sergeant Y and Constable X that he had seen Constable Stewart. They replied that it was not him, but a man who resembled him. The detective with the glasses did the talking and the other said nothing.

DETECTIVE (GLASSES): You have not been co-operating we find. We hear that you have put in a complaint. Why?

EATON: Because I have been ill-treated, assaulted and everything.

---

*This artificial silence episode is another indication of the influence of modern psychology research on interrogation techniques at Castlereagh. Studies of returned prisoners of war interrogated in Korea and Vietnam as well as experimental work in USA, Canada and United Kingdom have shown that for many people silence in the presence of an interrogator is highly stressful. In addition, an accused person often feels that silence on his part is incriminating and is being construed by his interrogator as an admission of guilt.

DETECTIVE (GLASSES): You are guilty. You will have to pay for the crime no matter what you say. You did it. Well, where do you work?

EATON: I work for the Electricity Service.

DETECTIVE (GLASSES): How long have you worked there?

EATON: Eleven years.

DETECTIVE (GLASSES): Do you drink?

EATON: I do.

DETECTIVE (GLASSES): Where do you drink?

EATON: Fern Lodge, Talk of the North, sometimes in the Merville Inn — I have had a couple of beers in the Merville Inn — Coole Social Club and Ardeene Social Club.

DETECTIVE (GLASSES): Did you ever drink in the Electric Club on the Shore Road?

EATON: Yes, I used to drink in it.

DETECTIVE (GLASSES): Who do you know in it? Do you know any of the management committee? Do you know Norman ————?

EATON: I do know Norman ————. In fact, he was my mate for four years.

DETECTIVE (GLASSES): Why do you not work with him any more?

EATON: He was made up to be a jointer.

DETECTIVE (GLASSES): Do you know a fellow called Stewartie?

EATON: I do indeed.

DETECTIVE (GLASSES): They are all decent fellows. Aren't they?

EATON: They are indeed.

DETECTIVE (GLASSES): But you are not a decent fellow. What did you say when you came in here? Did you not ask for a solicitor straight away?

EATON: I did.

DETECTIVE (GLASSES): Do you know that your solicitor has sent a doctor to see you?*

*The authorities were later to forbid the admission of doctors sent by solicitors to visit persons being interrogated in custody. The position was taken that only the registered personal physician of an arrestee could be admitted. In practice, many personal physicians lived too far from Castlereagh to visit it and a fair proportion of those within travelling distance were more than ready to accept police assurances that the prisoner was in excellent health, well cared for and with competent police doctors available on the premises. In December 1978, Sir Robert Lowry, Lord Chief Justice of Northern Ireland, ruled that the authorities had been wrong when they had

The door opened and Constable X came in. He spoke for a moment in a low voice to the detective with glasses. He then turned to Eaton and said, "Do you want to see this doctor? He is Dr. O'Rawe from the Falls Road.* A UVF man going to see a Falls Road doctor! Are you really going to see him?"

EATON: Yes, I do want to see him.

CONSTABLE A: I never thought I would live to see the day when a UVF man would see an IRA doctor. Do you know, this is what he would really love — for you to go and complain about brutality. The next IRA man who comes in here — Dr. O'Rawe will go in to see him and will help get him out. You know you are helping the IRA by seeing this Dr. O'Rawe. What is wrong with your own doctor?

EATON: He is the only doctor that has asked to see me. As far as I know, my own doctor has not even been asked to see me yet.

CONSTABLE X: What are you complaining about anyway?

At that moment, Samuel Eaton could hear thuds from the adjoining interrogation room as though someone was being thrown against a wall. "You are nothing but a thief" and other similar abuse was being shouted. He turned to Constable X and said, "Can you not hear what is going on in that room?" He replied, "That is just a record player". He then turned to the other detectives and said, "Sure, we can hear nothing!"

Samuel Eaton heard shouts, yells and orders like, "Stand up on your feet", on each of the days he was in custody. He found himself ignoring them as he was so preoccupied with what was happening to himself. He is confident that it was no record player.

The dialogue continued.

EATON: I have been thumped and I have been hit and I have had enough of it — that is why I have been complaining.

refused to admit a local doctor when a man from Londonderry City was in custody as his personal physician could not have been expected to travel the entire breadth of the region to visit one patient. Despite this ruling, the practice continued of admitting only registered, personal physicians.

*This is inaccurate. Dr. J. O'Rawe does not live or practice on the Falls Road. He has taken a keen interest in prison conditions and human rights and belongs to a Roman Catholic family.

CONSTABLE X: None of your mates is complaining.

EATON: I know nothing about the others. I have not seen them. The only one I have seen is George.

CONSTABLE X: None of your mates is going to see this Dr. O'Rawe. Are you going to be the only one to go and see him? Can you not see your own doctor instead of the Falls Road doctor? Do you want this place closed because that is what this doctor wants? He is all for the IRA. Do you want to back the IRA?

EATON: I certainly do not. But I want this place closed. There is nothing but brutality.

The door opened and a man who appeared to be the chief detective came in. (He was the one who thumped the table when Samuel Eaton had the nervous breakdown.) He asked. "Is he going to see this doctor?" Eaton said, "Yes, I want to see him", and he left slamming the door. Constable X said, "Then you want to see this doctor after all that I have told you instead of seeing your own doctor! Come on then, we will let you see him".

He was conducted back to the cell and after a short wait was taken down to see Dr. O'Rawe. Another doctor was present. Dr. O'Rawe introduced himself and explained that the other man was a police doctor. No one else was present.

Eaton told Dr. O'Rawe briefly what had been happening to him. He asked if he had seen any other doctors. He replied that he had seen two, but that he had not complained to the first one as he had just been admitted and had not been ill-treated at that stage. He added that he had, however, complained to the second one although he had been too scared to sign it. Dr. O'Rawe said that he need not have worried as what was said to a doctor was supposed to be confidential.

Dr. O'Rawe asked Eaton if he stuttered. He answered, "Only when nervous". He asked if he stuttered at home. He answered, "Very rarely". Both doctors examined him. Dr. O'Rawe asked the other to give Eaton tablets to calm him and he gave him two.

Eaton thinks that he was taken to an interview room afterwards, but has difficulty in remembering. He recollects Constable X saying to him, "You are only after telling that doctor everything I told you here". Whether this was during further interrogation or an isolated remark, he cannot now recall.

Samuel Eaton was again taken to see George Thompson. He may have been accompanied by Detective A and Detective B, but is not absolutely sure. It was possibly eight o'clock in the evening or later as the corridor was darkish when he came out of the room where he was being interviewed. Thompson was in a downstairs cell and the police-man who resembled Constable Stewart was talking to him, but with-drew.

THOMPSON: You are done-in looking.

EATON: I have had it rough.

THOMPSON: I hear you took a nervous breakdown.

EATON: I did indeed.

THOMPSON: Have they beaten you up much to-day?

EATON: I have not really my senses about me. I am too tired.

THOMPSON: Aren't the cells terrible. I asked to go to the toilet just to get air.

EATON: I am suffocated. I can hardly breathe in mine.

THOMPSON: Did you see the wee IRA fellow? He had a rough time.

EATON: I saw a young fellow being dragged along. He is only a child.

THOMPSON: He is supposed to be in for murdering a UDR woman. He is only a kid.

EATON: I am not guilty. I do not know why they have brought me in here.

THOMPSON: I know that.

When Samuel Eaton came out of George Thompson's cell, a detective remarked, "You did not say much in there".

The young prisoner whom Thompson mentioned had been seen by Eaton in a corridor. Two detectives had fetched him from the cell and had found the interrogation room occupied which they had intended to use. They passed along a corridor and through a swing door look-ing for a vacant room. On the other side of the door, they came upon two detectives with a seventeen or eighteen years old prisoner. They were half-carrying him as he seemed to be in a state of semi-collapse and unable to walk. They had one arm over each of them so that they were taking most of his weight with his feet only touching the floor.

The detectives with Eaton halted. One of the two with the other prisoner came up and said, "Can we help you?" (This detective appeared to have a limp). He asked if Eaton was co-operating and was told that he was not co-operating yet. He said, "Fire him in there and I will not be long in making him co-operate". Someone replied, "No, don't bother. He is with us." The other detective then said, "You can interview him in there", and opened the door of a vacant room.

Eaton is uncertain which detectives were with him. Detective A might have been one of them or they could have been Sergeant Y and Constable X.

The detective, who at the end of the second day conducted Samuel Eaton back to the guards in charge of the cells, announced that he was stinking* and that he was to be given a shower. There were two shower cubicles near the toilets. The only soap was a tiny fragment left by previous users. He could not adjust the hot and cold taps so he took a cold shower. It felt good. His mother had left fresh underwear a little earlier and he put it on.

When he had finished the shower, a guard asked if he wanted a tablet and he took one. He asked if he needed water to take with it, but he replied that he had some in a polythene tea cup in the cell.

DAY THREE

Further Interview, Day III

On the morning of Samuel Eaton's third day in custody, he was offered breakfast, but refused it. He accepted tea which he carried down to the interview room in a polythene beaker.

He thinks that an interview conducted by Sergeant Y and Constable X was the first one that day. As before, the former did most of the talking.

SERGEANT Y: I believe that you have not eaten anything since you came here.

EATON: No.

SERGEANT Y: Why not?

EATON: I do not feel like eating to be truthful.

SERGEANT Y: What is wrong you are holding your arms?

---

*This would have been normal because of the perspiration in the overheated cells. In the tropics a daily bath is essential — a fact that visiting Europeans are sometimes slow to realise to the discomfort of local people. In addition, intense emotional and physical stress affects the metabolism of the body.

EATON: My arms are very sore. They are very tired.

SERGEANT Y: Are you not going to confess to this terrible crime? Do you believe in God?

EATON: I do.

SERGEANT Y: When were you last in church?

EATON: A fortnight ago. [It was the christening of his youngest child.]

SERGEANT Y: It did not do you much good. You are sitting there telling us a pack of lies. Aren't you.

EATON: I am telling you the truth. I am not guilty.

SERGEANT Y: If I brought a Bible in here, would you swear on it that you were not guilty?

EATON: I would.

SERGEANT Y: You would swear on a Bible that you are not guilty. Would you swear on your children's lives?

EATON: No.

SERGEANT Y: Why not?

EATON: I do not believe that I should have to swear on my little children's lives.

SERGEANT Y: You are guilty, aren't you.

EATON: I certainly am not.

SERGEANT Y: If I brought a Bible here, why would you not swear on your little children's lives?

EATON: I do not believe that I should have to do that. I would swear on my own life certainly. I will not swear on any child's life. I do not know much about the law, but I do not believe it asks you to swear on children's lives. I do not believe it is even in the Bible.

SERGEANT Y: God will pay you back for all of this. He might not hit only you. He might hit your children or your wife. Do you know a fellow called ————— from Monkstown?

EATON: I do. I know him to see.

SERGEANT Y: You know his little child was knocked down and killed.

EATON: Yes, I was told about it.

SERGEANT Y: He killed people. He is inside doing life for a murder. We know he did more than one murder. This is how God paid him back. When his child died, I went up to see him and told him I was very sorry it happened. He thanked me for coming up. I was sorry it happened to his little child.

EATON: It was very nice of you going up to say that you were sorry to hear about it.

SERGEANT Y: Well, this could happen to your child. God could hit your child, too. Or he could hit you in different ways.

Sammy, you are letting us do all the talking here. Would you like a cup of tea?

Sergeant Y asked Constable X to get Eaton and themselves cups of tea. He replied that he was not sure that the tea place was open and Sergeant Y joked that he would pay if the other would go.

When the constable was away for the tea, Sergeant Y opened the window and asked Samuel Eaton if he would like to go over and get some fresh air. He answered, "Thanks", and did as suggested. On returning to his chair, Sergeant Y said that he could stay and have some more fresh air if he wished. At that point, Constable X returned with cups of tea and the interview continued.

SERGEANT Y: I believe that you are complaining about brutality.

EATON: Yes.

SERGEANT Y: We have not ill-treated you. Sure, we haven't?

EATON: No. In no way have you ill-treated me.

SERGEANT Y: What is my name?

EATON: Sergeant Y.

SERGEANT Y: What is this other fellow's?

EATON: That is Constable X.

SERGEANT Y: Make sure you do not blame us for the ill-treatment.

EATON: No way! You two have treated me fair enough.

SERGEANT Y: What sport do you like?

EATON: I like to watch boxing.

SERGEANT Y: Do you do any boxing?

EATON: No, I just like to watch it and snooker.

SERGEANT Y: Do you play any snooker?

EATON: I do, but I am not great at it.

Sergeant Y asked Eaton about his earnings and home arrangements. Then one of the detectives asked if he should be sent back to his cell. The other answered, "No, wait a bit". He was again asked if he was going to confess and he answered, "In no way". Shortly afterwards, he was taken up to the cell.

Two detectives brought him down from the cell to a special room for fingerprinting. He thinks it was Detective A and Detective B, but is not sure. Prints of his fingers and the palms of his hands were taken. He was asked to sign a form four times. He protested that he was unable to read. The detectives assured him that it was only in connection with the fingerprints and he signed as requested. He was asked after one signature why he had signed it differently. He explained that his arms and fingers were so painful that he had trouble writing at all. The detective looked again and said it was not that different.

Eaton thinks that he had further questioning in the fingerprint room, but cannot remember clearly.

When he was back in the cell, he was offered a meal, but refused it.

Further Interview, Day III

Samuel Eaton was taken for an interview which was conducted by two detectives he had not met before. Remarks which they made indicated that they were from Newtownabbey. The one who did the questioning was probably in his late thirties. He looked like someone who concentrated on muscular sports. He wore a tan coloured suit. The other detective was well-built, but not as fit looking. He said nothing during the interview. Both detectives gave their names, but Eaton does not remember them.

DETECTIVE (TAN SUIT): I am the detective who arrested George after his last offence. Now he is back again. An animal like you won't confess. I hear, too, that you are complaining about brutality. For what you have done, you have a cheek to put in about brutality. I have never hit a prisoner in my life. But, when I meet someone like you, it takes all my strength to keep my hands off you. For what you have done, you have a cheek to complain about police brutality. Is this wee lad Frew a liar? He has named you.

EATON: He must be.

DETECTIVE (TAN SUIT): Why should he tell a pack of lies? Is he holding a grudge against you or something?

EATON: No, not as far as I know.

DETECTIVE (TAN SUIT): Have you ever done anything on him before?

EATON: No.

DETECTIVE (TAN SUIT): Why should he name you?

EATON: I don't know to be truthful. I have not a clue.

DETECTIVE (TAN SUIT): George never named you. I suppose you know this. He made a statement, but he never named anyone. A big, decent fellow, but very foolish. Do you know George's father?

EATON: I think I only met his father once.

DETECTIVE (TAN SUIT): Was his father a policeman?

EATON: I am not too sure to be truthful.

DETECTIVE (TAN SUIT): You are going to let that big fellow go to jail for more than he deserves.

The detective then urged that, if Samuel Eaton did not confess, George Thompson would be given a much more severe sentence. He does not remember his words clearly, but the gist of it was that "George would be thumped" by the judge if he did not confess.

DETECTIVE (TAN SUIT): You are playing the big, hard man. You think that in a few hours you will be released. You will be drinking a pint in [?] hours in The Farm [he specified the number of hours, but Eaton does not remember it] and they will be all clapping you on the back and saying what a great fellow — you never made a statement. I hope you enjoy your pint. Just remember every pint you drink, keep looking around you. I and the rest of the police force will be watching you like a hawk. You will not be able to walk up the Main Drive [main thoroughfare in Rathcoole] without a peeler knowing where you are. I suppose one or two policemen will be shot for this — for bringing all you UVF men in here.*

*This is an example of the fantasy world into which interrogators so easily enter. The records that survive from interrogations by the Inquisition, for instance, occasionally have this fantasy element. During a decade of violence and tension, one policeman only has been shot by a member of a paramilitary organisation of the majority community in Ulster. This happened in October 1973 when a member of the UDA in possession of an illegal sub-machine was suddenly confronted by a policeman. He paniced and fired the gun indiscriminately, killing the policeman and wounding a UDA companion. An earlier shooting of a policeman (Const. V. Arbuckle) in October 1969 was for a time attributed to loyalists, but the three persons accused were tried and exonerated by ballistic evidence of that particular crime.

EATON: I will not be shooting anybody.

DETECTIVE (TAN SUIT): Well, I will be watching my back when you are out. I promise you one thing — and I mean it. If I get the slightest thing — and I mean it — if I get just the slightest thing, I will have you in here quicker than you can say. It will not be for three days, but for seven days. You have my word on that.

Samuel Eaton thinks that it was in this interview that he was told that he would be back in Castlereagh for his Christmas dinner. He was told it on two occasions. It burned into his exhausted mind and haunted him long after he was released.

Although the detective in the tan suit implied that Eaton would soon be out, the others continued to give the impression that he would not be released.

The interview continued.

DETECTIVE (TAN SUIT) How long have you been in the UVF now?

EATON: I am not in it.

DETECTIVE (TAN SUIT) You have been well tutored by the UVF. They have thumped it well into you, boy! I don't know how I am keeping my hands off you! You are telling me a pack of lies.

The penalty for belonging to the UVF is up to ten years imprisonment. A verbal admission of membership in front of witnesses (i.e. the two detectives) would be accepted in the Northern Ireland non-jury courts as sufficient evidence for conviction.

Suddenly, the detective in the tan suit turned round to the other one and said, "Have you got all this written down?" He replied, "Yes". One of them read out a statement. (Eaton does not remember which detective read it out.) It was a confession of having fired the shots in the attempted murder to which George Thompson and Brian Frew had confessed.

Samuel Eaton protested, "I did not say that". One of them turned to the other and said, "Didn't he say it?" The other answered, "Yes".

The detective in the tan suit said, "Sign it". Eaton replied, "I am signing nothing". He said, "But, you are only after telling us. We have got it down here. There it is there."

He threw the confession on the table and continued, "But, you are only after telling us you did it!" Eaton answered, "I never did anything of the sort". He again insisted, "Sign it", and Eaton replied, "I never said that. I am not signing it". He continued, "That is what we have taken down in this interview. What have we been talking about if we have not been talking about this? We have taken it down in writing here." Eaton replied, "I never said that. I am not guilty."

Samuel Eaton was astounded and panic-stricken when the detective read out the false statement. He felt that his word would mean nothing in a court of law if policemen were to claim that he had said what was in it. Also, it was unbelievable to him to find that policemen would do what these two men were doing.

It was obvious that the detectives were hopeful that almost three days of interrogation, physical exhaustion, lack of sleep and food, exposure to drugs and loss of body salts through heat had so disorientated Eaton's mind and destroyed his confidence that he would no longer be able to distinguish between what he knew as reality and what was urged on him by his interrogators.

Why were they hopeful? How many cases had there been at Castlereagh prior to then where men had signed confessions when insane with mental and physical exhaustion? Also, if past experience indicated that persons after less than three days might be in such a state, what chance did someone have of retaining their mental faculties and judgement for the seven days of interrogation to which some have been subjected!

After Samuel Eaton refused to sign the false confession, the detective in the tan suit remarked, "You have been well trained by the UVF. You have had it well drilled into you. You have been longer in it than any of them. You are not like these other wee boys. At that point the second detective left the room without saying anything.

DETECTIVE (TAN SUIT): Do you know why he walked out?
EATON: No.
DETECTIVE (TAN SUIT): If he had not, he would have hit you — he has gone to calm down. For you to sit and tell us a pack of lies and expect us to sit and take it! I am disgusted with you. You must be expecting money for this brutality by the police. You are probably expecting about £700 for brutality. I hope you enjoy it. You will be in here again. Come on before I thump you. I am disgusted with it.

The detective took Eaton out of the room, but outside met another one with a piece of paper. They began to discuss it and he was ordered back into the room. He has trouble remembering here. However, he does recollect when the detective said, "Come on! We will put you back up in the cell."

Also, he remembers that he was getting tablets from the guards between interviews during this third day of being in custody.

Further Interview, Day III

Samuel Eaton's next interview was conducted by Sergeant Y and Constable X. He was asked what had happened to him since they had seen him in the morning. A fairly relaxed and general discussion followed. After a time Sergeant Y said to the other man, "Is the Chief back yet?" He replied, "I don't think that he is down yet", and the sergeant remarked, "I wonder what he is going to do with him."

The general discussion was resumed. Eaton cannot remember much about this interview. The policemen appeared to be filling in time. He was told, "We have done most of the talking so far. Have you any questions? We will just talk about anything." Sergeant Y had said in a previous interview that he was going to have a game of golf. Eaton asked if he had had it. He replied that he had not. Suddenly, he switched the subject.

SERGEANT Y: When you go to Crumlin Road [Prison] — when you see the Governor, will you class yourself as a political prisoner or ordinary criminal?

EATON: I don't really know. I can hardly claim to be a political prisoner when I am not in anything. [i.e. a paramilitary organisation].

Had Eaton been in a proscribed organisation, it would have been a dangerous moment. Lulled into a false sense of safety by the friendly, general conversation, an interogatee could easily have acknowledged being associated with such an organisation and, with the two detectives as witnesses, secured for himself a prison sentence of up to ten years. Political status had been abolished for prisoners sentenced after March 1976. The policemen would have known this fact, but members of the public, such as Eaton, were likely to be ill-informed about it.

Sergeant Y reverted to the casual conversation. Eaton spoke about a fence which he had put up at his house and mentioned that he was laying flags for the children to play on.

Suddenly during the casual conversation, Constable X said sharply, 'You got your workmates set up''. Eaton answered, "What are you talking about?" The constable added, "Your workmates — you got them shot''. The conversation then reverted back immediately to a casual topic without Constable X explaining himself in any way. Eaton was left mystified. He did not know why he had interjected the remark or whether he had been referring to the shooting of the workers in Ballyduff (the incident raised in an earlier interview) or to some other shooting.

Eventually Sergeant Y called an end to the interview and returned Eaton to the cell.

Samuel Eaton thinks it was somewhat later that he was asked if he would like to see a doctor. He replied that he would and was taken down to one that he had not seen before. He gave his name, but Eaton does not remember it.

He told the doctor the story of his interviews the best that he could. He explained that he was so desperately tired that he could not place them in the right order and that he was giving him only rough descriptions. He kept repeating that he could not stand much more of it. The doctor said that it did not matter about the order of the interviews so long as he was telling the truth. He volunteered that he need not worry if he were telling the truth as he would go to court to give evidence.

The doctor examined Eaton and asked him to sign a written complaint. He answered that he was terrified to sign it as no one had any idea of what he had gone through. The doctor said that he should not be telling him, but that once he left the room the authorities would have to charge or release him. He added that they would probably return him to the cell and then bring him down and charge or release him. He said that he could guarantee that there would be no more brutality — that he had his word for it.

Samuel Eaton insisted that he was terrified to sign the complaint — insisted that the authorities would kill him. The doctor told him to sign as they had now to charge or release him and that he could guarantee that they would not touch him anymore. He thinks that he did sign, but is not certain.

He thanked the doctor and was returned to the cell.

After a time, two policemen appeared and told Eaton to take the pillowcase off the pillow and to put the blankets inside it. He replied that he could hardly lift his arms and could not do it. A policeman told him to hold the pillowcase and he placed the blankets in it. He remarked that he should not be doing it. On the way down the stairs, Eaton asked if he was going to be charged or released. A policeman answered that they would not know until they reached the desk.

A policeman at the desk said, "I believe you are making complaints". He said. "Sign your name here and write 'Yes' on both sheets". Eaton asked how to spell 'Yes'. He was too exhausted to remember although normally he can spell that word.

A policeman gave Samuel Eaton his belongings. He thinks they were in an envelope. He said, "I am sure you will be glad to see your wife tonight". Eaton asked, "Am I getting released?" and he answered, "Yes, you are. Your mates are in the other room."

A policeman led Eaton down the hall, opened the door of a room and shouted into it, "Right boys! Come on!" The sergeant at the desk or someone else asked, "Do you need a lift?" Eaton answered, "No". He suspected that his parents would be waiting and anyway was so sick of the place that he would have preferred to take a taxi to accepting transport arranged by the police.

At least four or five men were being released. Eaton recognised some of them. As they walked through the entrance gate, he heard one of them say, "Once we go outside and leave these premises, they can arrest us under that act for another three days". The remark terrified him.

Someone told Samuel Eaton that there were people waiting for him down the road and round the corner. He walked for about a hundred yards and found his parents in their car in a car park. His mother asked what had happened that he looked so awful. She proposed that he get into the back of the vehicle, but his arms and fingers were too painful to open the door. When it was opened, he had trouble climbing in as he was so stiff and sore.

His parents drove him straight home. He himself does not now remember the journey.

18 Like a Man from the Planet of Apes

Dorothy Eaton closed the front door and came into the living room after the police took her husband to the landrover. She noticed that the clock was at half-past six. She drew on a coat, walked to the nearest kiosk and telephoned her sister-in-law, Kathleen, to tell her what had happened and to ask her to tell Samuel's parents.

She returned home. Two of the four children were already up. One said, "There were policemen in my room", so he must have been awakened by the search. She prepared breakfast and in a short time her mother-in-law, Mrs. Elizabeth Eaton, and Kathleen arrived. Two of the children attended school and one a nursery. It was decided to send them as usual and to go at once to Whiteabbey Police Station. They took the youngest child with them and Kathleen drove.

Two policemen were in the entrance office. A heavily built one in shirt sleeves was at the desk. Elizabeth asked if her son was in the station.

POLICEMAN: No. He is at Ladas Drive.
MOTHER: Where is that?
POLICEMAN: Castlereagh Police Station.
MOTHER: Is that where they beat up people?
POLICEMAN: I believe so.

Elizabeth Eaton became a little hysterical.

MOTHER: There was not a mark on him when he left home and there had better not be one on him when I see him.
POLICEMAN: But, you will not be seeing him.
MOTHER: Oh yes, I will because I am his mother.
POLICEMAN: I do not care who you are. Nobody gets into Ladas Drive.

MOTHER: I brought him into the world: I am his mother. Nobody will stop me from seeing him.

POLICEMAN: You go ahead and do what you want, but you will not get in.

Further dialogue appeared pointless and the three decided to return to Dorothy's house. On the way back, they called at Whiteabbey Hospital where Dorothy had an appointment to keep with a doctor as she was recovering from an illness.

Her father-in-law joined them at the house. He had been unable to accompany his wife earlier as he had had to go to his workplace to start the men under him on their assignment for the day. It was agreed that he should return to work as he could do nothing at that time which womenfolk could not do equally well.

Dorothy Eaton and her mother-in-law next visited the Methodist minister, Rev. C. H. Bain, while Kathleen stayed behind to look after her youngest child. The family had been members of the local Methodist church since settling in the district twenty-two years earlier and he had been their minister for the previous four years. The children had always been regular attenders at Sunday school and church. Samuel had been in the Boys' Brigade and the Church Youth Club. Kathleen had been in the Girls' Life Brigade and was a Sunday school teacher.

Bain was much concerned. He had trouble in telephoning Castlereagh Police Holding Centre, but, after some time, succeeded and was told that no one would be allowed to see Samuel Eaton. He asked to be kept in touch as the situation developed and was to call a number of times at Dorothy's house during the time that her husband was to be in custody.

The two women returned home in distress. They were at a loss what to do next to be useful. Elizabeth Eaton made inquiries as to who was the best solicitor and was told that there was no one better than Jonathan Taylor. She telephoned him and he agreed to act. She also contacted Castlereagh Police Holding Centre and asked that her son's consent be obtained.

A telephone was being installed that day at Dorothy's house. The work was completed about half-past three and Elizabeth Eaton telephoned Castlereagh Holding Centre at intervals during the remainder of the day. Next day she did not go to work and again telephoned at intervals. About six o'clock, she and her other daughter, Lilian, took underwear, shaving gear, tooth brush, toothpaste and a hair brush and set off for Castlereagh. They took a taxi part of the way and then changed to a bus.

At Castlereagh Holding Centre, they were directed to a small office. The policemen in uniform were courteous and considerate and accepted the items brought for Samuel. His mother asked if she could see him for five minutes. She was in tears. A police said, "Sorry. In no way." She asked, "Do you know whether he is taking food? You know he is a vegetarian." The policeman replied that there was nothing that he could do about it and advised her to ring the PO. She asked if there was a telephone near and he directed her to a garage.

She and Lilian went to the garage, but an attendant told them that the telephone was not for public use and suggested a public call box at a distance. They walked a long way without finding it. They decided to go home and were standing at a bus stop when they noticed a public house on the other side of the street. Elizabeth telephone Castlereagh Police Holding Centre from inside it and asked for the PO. She was told that he was busy and to 'phone back later.

She and Lilian took a bus to Belfast City Hall where she again telephoned from a call box. A man answered. She told him that her son was a vegetarian and asked if he was eating food. He replied that there was no cause for worry as Samuel was eating his food and that he would see about him being a vegetarian. He assured her that he was very well — that he was doing well and sleeping well.

Elizabeth Eaton was reassured. She rang her daughter Kathleen to tell her it was all right about his food. She and Lilian then returned to Rathcoole and called Dorothy before going to their respective homes. By then it was about half-past midnight.

On Wednesday, 19th October, the third day of Samuel Eaton being in custody, Dorothy telephoned Castlereagh first thing. The man who answered was "ever so nice" and assured her that her husband was all right. She went to the shops to make some purchases and met the mother of one of the other men who had been arrested. She told her that his wife had telephoned Castlereagh that morning and had been told to 'phone back at one o'clock when she would find out whether her husband was to be released or charged.

Dorothy told her mother-in-law at her place of work. She returned home with her and both waited in great tension until one o'clock.

Elizabeth Eaton made the call to Castlereagh as Dorothy could hardly go near the telephone. She was told to ring again at four o'clock when she would be told whether her son was to be released or charged. She was also warned that he could be held on a special order for up to seven days.

After the children came home from school, Dorothy accompanied her mother-in-law to her house. At a quarter to four, both went to a neighbour's house and again her mother-in-law telephoned. She was told that Samuel was still being held for questioning and that she should ring again between eight and nine o'clock. She said, "Do you realise that we have been 'phoning all day and have been put off?" The reply was, "Well, you will know between eight and nine".

Dorothy returned to her house to make supper for the children. Her mother-in-law joined her after six o'clock and they sat and waited. At about half-past eight Elizabeth Eaton telephoned. She was told that her son was to be released and could someone come and collect him? She then telephoned a friend who contacted her husband and he soon arrived in his car. She left with him for Castlereagh and Dorothy remained behind with the children. It was about nine o'clock and the journey took some forty minutes.

The Police Holding Centre is on a dark, lonely stretch of street. The Eatons were unsure of the building and, when they slowed down in front of it, a policeman on guard duty ordered him to keep moving. They drove on some yards and climbed out. At the entrance gate office, they said that they had come to collect Samuel Eaton who was due to be released. A policeman checked some papers and telephoned someone. He said, "In about a quarter of an hour", told them to take their car to the car park which they would find at the bottom of the road. He said that someone would bring their son to them. They did as instructed and waited in their car in the car park until half-past ten or a quarter-to-eleven.

Samuel's mother saw him come round the corner. She barely recognised him. He kept his head down and was carrying his arms in an awkward way. He was like someone in a daze. He came up to the car and slumped against it. He said nothing. He was unable to open the door and there was trouble getting him into it as he was so stiff. His breath was foul and he sat on the back seat for a time in total silence. His mother was so shocked that she began to weep. At intervals on the journey home, he would repeat, "I shall never forget this.

You people do not know what I have been through." He would also repeat in an hysterical way, "You have to be in there to realise". His parents tried to calm him and to change the subject, but it made no difference.

Dorothy heard the car returning. She went to the front room and saw her husband get out of the back of it. He staggered as if drunk. His head was down and he seemed unable to hold it up. He moved into the light of the street lamp which is about thirty feet from where she was standing at the window. She remembers saying, "Oh God, look at him!" It just was not him. Any other time he came home, he walked confidently with head up. He was hunched up. As he came up the steps, he lurched over like a drunk man.

She went to the door and opened it. He was up the steps and fell against the porch pole with one arm slumped around it. He did not reach out to catch hold of it. She stood looking at him. He walked straight past her with his head down. He said nothing. He walked up the hall and collided into the wall with his right side as he went to go through the open door into the living-room.

The police at Castlereagh had been so nice on the telephone that Dorothy had been reassured that Samuel was being reasonably well looked after. She was greatly shocked when she saw him leave the car. As he came through the front door, she began to cry and she does not cry easily. She gasped, "What happended? What has happened?"

His parents caught up with him and helped him to sit down. He sat on the settee with head slightly down and eyes staring. His hands were held with the palms and fingers resting on the knees and he was shaking to the point where the hands were almost drumming them. Neither his parents nor his wife had seen him sit like that before. Immediately he sat down, he cried quietly. Dorothy was not sure whether there were tears, but she knew by the agony on his face that he was weeping. He would cry a little and then say, "They are coming back for me. They told me they would be back." He kept looking at the door as though expecting someone. On one occasion, he muttered, "Nobody has any idea!"*

Dorothy sat and looked at Samuel while his parents tried to calm

*An intense dread of being re-arrested is characteristic of all persons on release after interrogation at Castlereagh. Some have even emigrated.

him down. They would say, "You are all right now. You are home now. Here is Dorothy." They tried to draw his attention with remarks about the children, but he ignored them. Again and again, he would say, "They are coming back for me. They said that they would be back." Dorothy made a cup of tea and a couple of tomato sandwiches. He made no effort to take the cup from her and she left it on the arm of the settee. Later, she took it away undrunk.

Samuel Eaton's parents rose to go home. His mother said that she would see him in the morning and that he would be all right after a good night's sleep. He made it clear that he did not want to stay in his own house that night and so they decided to take him home with them. He had the overwhelming dread that the police would return to take him back to Casltereagh and he wished to be away from Dorothy and the children when they came as he felt it would be preferable to stab himself to death.

At his parents' home an aunt and uncle come in and he remembers his uncle trying to cheer him up. He asked for his grandmother, who lives in the same street and was seventy-eight, to be fetched. Ordinarily, he is a considerate person and would not have dreamt of having the old lady disturbed at that hour of the night. He would complain occasionally about the back of his head, neck and ears. More frequently, he would place both hands on his ears or the back of his head or the back of his neck. He would make no comment, but it could be seen that they were painful. All his remarks were about Castlereagh and that the police would be back again inside three weeks.

He did not want anyone to go home. He remembers wanting company: wanting people around: being reluctant to be alone. His grandmother got up to go, but he insisted that she stay. It was probably half-past two before she left. Eventually, his grandmother, aunt and uncle, one by one, edged out and went home.

Both parents were needed to take Samuel Eaton upstairs. His legs dragged and he kept complaining about his arms. He protested when his father touched him. His mother gave him a sedative and his father put him to bed. He does not remember his father doing so, but he remembers weeping to himself before he fell asleep and feeling awful.

He was awakened by knocking on the front door and assumed it was the police. He remembers trying to get up and being dead drowsy, tired and weak and he remembers going down the stairs as he was afraid that his parents would react violently to the police on his account.

His mother had already opened the door. It was his sister Lilian who had called to ask about him before she went to work. (It was about half-past six or a quarter-to-seven). She saw him as he stumbled down the stairs. She burst out, "Oh, my God, look at our Samuel!" and began to cry. He started to talk about the police coming back for him and she tried to calm him, but with no success.

He said that he would have to get home to Dorothy and his parents drove him back in their car. He was drowsy, tired and shaking and cannot remember much about going back. He was like a man in a daze and still walked with his head down. He ate nothing and was sore all over. He stuttered very badly and kept returning to the theme that they had said that they would be coming back for him.

He remembers hardly anything of the first two days at home. He was extremely nervous and had bouts of weeping. The horror would keep returning to him of the occasion when the detectives produced the false confession and pressed him to sign it. He remembers vaguely people calling in, but not who they were. He remembers his own doctor sitting in the room, but nothing else of his visit. He remembers on another occasion his mother saying, "I will get my doctor". He does not remember his visit except for him standing at one end of the room.

At one point during the first morning after Samuel Eaton return home, he rose from where he was sitting in the living room and walked into the hall where a crescent-shaped table with a glass top was fixed to the wall. He wrenched it from its supports; threw it unto the hall floor; returned to the living room and sat down. His wife was greatly astonished, but said nothing. His parents who were in the living room were no less surprised, but they, too, did not comment. His action was a mystery as nothing had been said or done to annoy him. When his parents told him later, he could not believe he had done it.

Probably that first day or the next one (it was certainly in the first few days after he returned home) his wife smacked a child upstairs. It cried slightly. Samuel heard it and shouted, "Leave him alone". She came downstairs. The tone of his voice and a staring look made her fear that he was going to hit her. She had never known him to speak or look like that before. In fact, she had never known him to be violent at any time. He had a strong aversion to it.

Dr. Robert McElderry is the family doctor. He was telephoned early on the first morning and arrived during the course of it. He examined Eaton, made notes and wrote a prescription. He also left some tablets to calm him until the prescription could be obtained from the chemist. While he was writing, someone knocked loudly at the front door. Eaton's knee and arm shot up into a defensive posture and he curled into the arm of the settee. The doctor's face showed strong surprise.

Samuel Eaton's mother was extremely worried that first morning. She telephoned the office of Rev. Dr. Ian Paisley, the member of Parliament and asked to speak to him. The secretary of the party, Peter Robinson (now member of Parliament for East Belfast), told her that he was in America. He offered to do what he could to help and gave his telephone number. She, however, was disappointed that Dr. Paisley was not available and did not give many details.

A little later, she telephoned the Peace People. A man answered. She told him that she wished to speak to either of the leaders of the movement, Mrs. Betty Williams or Mairead Corrigan. Mrs. Williams came to the telephone. She listened sympathetically and took notes. She said that she knew how she felt — that she dealt with that sort of thing every day. Elizabeth Eaton began to tell her about the press-ups and wall standing and that her son threatened to kill himself if the police came to take him back to Castlereagh.

Betty Williams cut her short in a nice way. She said that she heard the same thing almost every day and fully believed that it happened.

MOTHER: Can the Peace People do anything to help? You know that we are not of the same religion as yourself.

MRS. WILLIAMS: It does not matter which religion you belong to as I am here to try to help anyone. Three Protestants from the Shankill who had been released from Castlereagh came to see me. You might not believe it, Mrs. Eaton, but they were like men from the Planet of Apes.

MOTHER: I would believe it. After seeing my son, I would believe anything. He went in a man and he came out a wreck.

If the police come again as they said they would, who should we turn to for help?

MRS. WILLIAMS: You have got the 'phone number. No matter what time of the day or night that the police call to arrest Samuel, you ring the number. We will be at Ladas Drive before they are there.

Elizabeth Eaton thanked Betty Williams and her last words as she rang off were, "Do not forget. If you need me ring back".

Samuel Eaton became worse. He took possession of a long-bladed breadknife and said he would stick it in himself if the police came. Dorothy had gone to visit a local shop, but his mother pleaded with him and he gave it to her.

He sat quietly for a while, staring into space. He seemed not to pay attention to anyone. Dorothy returned and, when his mother left, Kathleen stayed with her. For the next number of days, it was always arranged for someone to be with Dorothy so that she did not have to cope on her own. Usually it was Kathleen.

Elizabeth Eaton's physician is Dr. Paul McKeown. She has much confidence in him and, on the second day after his release, she asked her sister who lives close to him to call and ask if he would see her son as a private patient. He was just in from the surgery and having his tea, but came as soon as he finished it.

Samuel Eaton was sitting in an armchair beside the fire and Dr. McKeown sat down near him on a pouffe. He kept saying, "Sir, you do not know what I have come through", and, "Sir, I had a terrible time in Ladas Drive". He also began to weep again.

The doctor, said, "They made you do push-ups, son, and they made you stand against a wall with your feet apart and arms stretched up". Eaton answered, "Yes" and went to tell him more, but he said that he knew about it as he had been in Castlereagh Police Holding Centre the other day.

Eaton said that they were going to come back for him. Dr. McKeown said he had to try to get that out of his mind and assured him that the police would not be back. He stayed for some time and gave him a thorough examination. Eaton kept addressing him as "Sir". It was unlike him to speak in such a deferential way and he also had a bad stutter.

As the doctor was leaving, he stopped Dorothy in the hall and said that if the police were to return, she was to contact him immediately. He left tablets which caused her husband to fall asleep almost at once and he slept well into the next day.

While Dr. McKeown was seeing Eaton, Miss Anne Colville called on behalf of the Peace People. She said that she could see the state that he was in and that she would not ask him anything at that time. She called again the next day (Saturday) and possibly twice during the following week. She also telephoned once or twice. She left the names of two ladies to contact, if needed. One lived in Rathcoole and the other in Graymount. The latter, she said, had a car and, if necessary, could run messages for Dorothy. In practice, their help was not needed.

For the first few days after Samuel Eaton came home, he kept repeating obsessively that they were coming back for him and for some weeks the fear of being re-arrested kept recurring in his remarks. A number of times he spoke of suicide should the police return. One night he left the long-bladed breadknife on the floor beside his bed. Dorothy ignored it, but stayed awake. She feared that someone might knock on the front door during the night and he would assume it was the police.

Eaton could recount small happenings fairly sensibly after he was home a few days, but it was some weeks before he could tell the whole story of his experience in coherent form. It was all he talked about. He remembers that he had the feeling that he had to hold on to his senses. He was convinced that, if he let go, he would never get them back. At night he had terrifying nightmares in which he dreamt that he was again in Castlereagh Police Holding Centre. He would keep saying in them, "Not guilty, Not guilty." He dreaded night because of the horrors of the nightmares and because he could not forget that the police came during the night to arrest him and that the night or early morning arrest is their custom. He was reluctant to go to bed. He would sit up talking until one or two o'clock and invariably it was about what happened to him at Castlereagh. He would urge visitors to stay when they went to leave in order to have company. When they left, he would sometimes go out himself. The first time that his mother knew that he was beginning to recover was one evening when he noticed that it was nine o'clock and remarked that she should be leaving for home.

When he came back from Castlereagh, he stammered very badly. In fact, he stammered on nearly every word and it took him quite some time to tell anything. Even a long time after his release, he still stammered more than was usual for him.

His boss in the Electricity Service and a workmate called one day and urged him to return to work. He allowed himself to be persuaded, but did not feel cabable in his own mind for a long time. His workmate would sometimes point out that his mind was not on the job and the he was doing the work incorrectly. Also, he was sometimes off work for a day, especially after a bad night of nightmare.

Samuel Eaton began to improve about the end of the second week or beginning of the third. He could not shake off the dread for a long time that the police would return as the detectives had threatened. The terrifying "Castlereagh" nightmares became less frequent through time. Nevertheless, three months later, he still had them about twice a week and, a year or more later, he continued to have them occasionally.

Five months after Eaton signed the complaint form at Castlereagh Police Holding Centre, he received a letter from the Office of the Chief Constable. It stated that his complaint had been recorded and investigated in accordance with Section 13 (1) of the Police Act (Northern Ireland) 1970 and that the Director of Public Prosecutions for Northern Ireland had directed that there should be no prosecution of any police officer.

19 Regardless of Party in Office

The advent of the Labour government in February 1974 made less difference to the intelligence and undercover services than they themselves could have anticipated. They may have curtailed voluntarily some of the more flamboyant and irresponsible illegalities, but the basic pattern of their influence and activities remained as before. Nor did the change of government at Westminster mean any change in the privileged immunities available to them. They were still able to secure official protection regardless of which party formed the cabinet. For instance, it was a Labour attorney general who decided that the men responsible for the shooting of William Black were not to be prosecuted.

Highly placed officials continued to order assassinations some of which, as in the Black case, have been to protect the intelligence set-up against exposures. They ordered them under the new Labour administration of Harold Wilson just as previously they had ordered them under the Conservative one of Edward Heath and just as more recently they have continued to order them under the renewed Conservative one of Margaret Thatcher which came to office in May 1979.

One of the more recent instances was the assassination in the summer of 1980 of a woman of considerable personal prestige and social standing and whom an Irish republican terrorist organisation regarded as its intellectual patron. The killing caused acute apprehension in at least one section of the security forces where it was feared that it had placed the leaders of the terrorist organisation in a postion where they would feel that they had no alternative but to retaliate by the counter-assassination of the government's most prestigious woman, Margaret Thatcher, the prime minister. A parallel was drawn with the CIA's assassination plots against Fidel Castro and other Soviet protégé national leaders which had placed the persons who ordered the assassination of President Kennedy in a position where they felt that they had no alternative. Airy Neave, Margaret Thatcher's colleague and intelligence expert, had been assassinated in the previous year and no one doubted that she could be equally vulnerable.

One or two "dirty trick" occurrences after Labour came to office can be discounted as of small consequence. Others were more sinister. Leafllets, for instance, were distributed with lists of names and addresses of persons whom, it was asserted, had been responsible for assassinations. One had thirteen names and addresses. Some claimed to be from a new loyalist organisation, the Ulster Citizens' Army. These carried both the loyalist red hand symbol and the plough stars symbol of the Official IRA and on that ground alone were attributed to army intelligence by many who received them, including local newsmen. In the same category was an attempt to smear William Craig, leader of the Vanguard Unionist Party, in connection with a kidnapping and murder. The German magazine *Bild* printed the allegation and he was awarded compensation in a libel suit.

In the period immediately before the UUAC general strike of May 1977, there were four explosions at emotive buildings in quiet districts. The number was small and damage slight, but they were reminiscent of the ones in the weeks prior to the general election to the Whitelaw Assembly in 1973.

There was also the mysterious unexploded bomb found in Lisburn Orange Hall after the local Official Unionist association had held a bring-and-buy sale. Enoch Powell had been the main platform speaker and the date was 16th April 1977, a fortnight before the UUAC general strike commenced. Next day — a Sunday — a man telephoned a Belfast newspaper. He said that he spoke for a proscribed loyalist organisation and that it had planted a bomb in the Lisburn Orange Hall prior to the Official Unionist function. Enoch Powell, he added, was on the organisation's death list. The police checked the hall and found a three pound bomb hidden behind a curtain on a staircase leading to the platform. The building had been thoroughly searched prior to the function and there was no sign of a break-in.

During April 1977, relations between the leaders of the Official Unionist Party and those of the other loyalist parties were tense. The latter desperately wanted the Official Unionists to back the UUAC general strike (which would commence on 2nd May) in the same way as the anti-Faulknerite Official Unionists had backed the UWC general strike three years earlier. Most of the Official Unionist leadership, and especially the Westminster Parliamentary group (including Enoch Powell), on the contrary, were resolved to throw their weight behind the Northern Ireland Office in its confrontation with the strikers. At the same time, they knew that the concept of the strike had substantial backing among the rank and file of their party — backing which subsequently showed itself during the strike by resolutions of support; several substantial donations to strike funds from branches and, in one instance, by a resolution to remove the picture of Harry West, the party leader, from the walls of the room where a branch met.

Anti-strike Official Unionists seized on the bomb find in the Orange Hall as a heaven-sent expedient with which to discredit the other loyalist parties and demoralise the pro-strike people within their own. The leader of the Official Unioinst MPs at Westminster issued a statement in which he described it as a very sinister development and added that it was known that a certain loyalist political party wanted to frighten Mr. Powell. Dr. Ian Paisley construed the remarks as implying that he and the DUP were responsible for the bomb and demanded an apology. Ernest Baird and the UUUP were equally incensed and he, too, demanded an apology. The members of both parties were seething with a feeling of outraged innocence as their entire wish at the time was to patch up a working relationship with the Official Unionists for the purposes of the coming strike. Many insisted that the only loyalists who could have had a rational motive for planting the bomb were the anti-strike leaders of the Official Unionists. Some suspected Enoch Powell himself for no reason other than that he had served with military intelligence during the Second World War and had reached the rank of brigadier in it.* The suspicion was without a shred of evidence.

A day or so later the police placed the Orange Hall find in a new

*Enoch Powell received his commission in April 1940. By 1941, he was a general staff officer in intelligence with 9th Armoured Division. Later that year, he was assigned to Intelligence and Plans Division in Cairo and became secretary to the Joint Intelligence Committee, Middle East. In May 1943, he was transferred to India as secretary to the Joint Intelligence Committee for India and South-East Asia Command.

light. They were satisfied, they said, that the bomb had been made by a Provisional IRA bomb maker with whose style of workmanship and design they were familiar. One or two newspapers jumped to the conclusion that the Provisionals must therefore have planted the bomb. Few persons with a knowledge of Ulster affairs did so. The Provisionals are noted for their indifference to constitutional politics and for their ignorance of inter-loyalist politics. Also, logic would have told them that, if an unexploded bomb would trigger a bitter, loyalist internal feud, an exploded one would trigger a vastly more bitter one.

The issue thus narrowed down to the question, "Who other than the Provisional IRA might have in their possession a Provisional manufactured bomb?" The obvious answer was the army bomb disposal men and through them the government organisations which liaise with the army. So once again the finger of suspicion pointed to the British intelligence services.

A number of small explosions and other terrorist incidents during 1978 were claimed by the Irish Freedom Fighters which purported to be a new Irish republican secret organisation. It was suspected at once of being a British army intelligence enterprise devised by someone recently arrived in Ulster. The name was clearly modelled on the feared Ulster Freedom Fighters. The public and press assumed that the latter was a genuine loyalist terrorist organisation, but the IRAs and other Irish republican extremist groups had long believed it to be linked with British undercover and probably controlled by it. No new Irish republican organisation would have selected a name for itself resembling it. After a time, the Provisionals denounced the IFF as a government operation and no more was heard of it.

When Roy Mason, secretary of state for Northern Ireland, had to admit that the troop reinforcements brought in for the UUAC general strike were to be returned to the mainland and Germany, he had assured the public that SAS-type undercover operations would be intensified. The assurance made little difference to the level of such activities, but it may have given a new unwholesome confidence in certain quarters. The Provisional IRA continued to murder and maim members of the security forces in cowardly, sneak-thief attacks. It was heartbreaking and desperately frustrating for soldiers at all levels and especially as they knew that, if they could "get away with it", they had a remedy in the type of reprisal which the Provisionals would understand and respect.

On the afternoon of 12th December 1977, Colm McNutt, a member of the Irish Republican Socialist Party, a group sympathetic to the aims of the small terrorist organisation, the Irish National Liberation Army, was shot dead by someone who stepped from a motor car in an Irish republican district of Londonderry City. An army spokesman later stated that the man had been shot by a plain clothes military patrol when he had tried to hijack their car. A death notice inserted by the IRSP in a local newspaper confirmed that he had been one of their members. During the first half of the following year, 1978, five acknowledged Provisionals — Paul Duffy, Denis Heaney, James Mulvenna, Denis Brown and Jack Mealy — were shot dead in confrontations with army anti-terrorist units. Three of them were shot outside a post office depot in Belfast when they arrived carrying bombs. The authorities had learned of the plan and soldiers were waiting. They were cut down in a hail of automatic fire which, in addition, killed an innocent passerby. One of the bomb carriers was hit by sixty-three bullets. On 11th July, John Boyle, a sixteen years old schoolboy was shot dead by SAS soldiers beside an arms cache in a cemetery in North Antrim. On 30th September, James Taylor, a twenty-three year old civil servant, was shot dead near Coagh in Co. Tyrone by an army undercover squad in cililian clothes who saw duck-shooting equipment in the back of his parked car and assumed that he was a Provisional. In the following month, on 25th September, fifty year old Patrick Duffy, whom the Provisionals afterwards claimed as an auxiliary member, was shot dead by six soldiers lying in wait in a house in which a store of arms had been hidden in Londonderry City. His family asserted that he was hit by eighteen bullets.

These various incidents built up into a persuasive indictment that authorisation had been given at a high level within the army command for a "tit-for-tat" revenge vendetta against the Provisional IRA.* It also became clear that no protest would be forthcoming from the public at the shooting dead of Provisional IRA members. Even the shooting of Patrick Duffy, claimed by the Provisionals as an

*There had been earlier killings which many suspected were army undercover "tit for tat" retaliations. For instance, there was that of Mrs. Margaret Gamble who was followed home and stabbed to death on 4th April 1976. She was a sister of Mrs. Roisin McLaughlin who had been named by the police as a prime suspect in connection with the cold-blooded murder of three soldiers lured by girls to a supposed party in a flat in Belfast.

auxiliary member, caused no serious outcry. He had driven up to the house with his daughter and grandchild. The soldiers claimed that they had fired in self-defence when he had attempted to seize one of the hidden guns. His family, in reply, urged that he could not have attempted to seize anything as a recent stroke had paralysed his left arm and made him incapable of rapid movement.

The shooting of John Boyle, the schoolboy, and James Taylor, the young civil servant, caused intense and critical public reactions in contrast to the public indifference to the deaths of the IRA adherents.

The Boyles were a respected Roman Catholic family. The boy had gone to the cemetery beside his father's farm to search for the grave of a forebear. He saw objects wrapped in plastic in a cavity under a heavy, fallen headstone. He suspected it was a terrorist cache, but did not interefere lest it was a booby trap intended to kill members of the security forces. He told his father who informed the police who contacted the army. Next morning, he set off on his father's tractor to join his brother who had already left to begin hay-making. As he passed the cemetery, he yielded to curiosity and went in to see if the police had removed the objects. At the spot where they were hidden, he was shot dead from twelve yards by two SAS soldiers with blackened faces.

James Taylor was shot on a quiet country road. He and two friends had been duck shooting. When they returned to their car, they found that the tyres had been let down. They walked two miles to his uncle's home and returned with him in his car. Several men in plain clothes were standing near the parked one. Taylor asked if they had let down the tyres. There was a moment with no reply and then, it is alleged, he was shot dead. Two days later, the army issued a statement. It admitted that one of its undercover units had killed Taylor in a tragic error and extended its sympathy to the bereaved family.

The police report on the death of John Boyle was submitted to the Director of Public Prosecutions. He transferred it to the Attorney General in London as had happened earlier with the report on the shooting of William Black. An inexplicably long delay followed which led to the suspicion that the government was resolved to prevent the case from coming before a court. Public concern grew rather than diminished as the months passed. The police forensic report was leaked to the press on 1st February 1979 and given front page coverage. Questions were tabled in Parliament demanding to know what action the DPP had decided to take. The authorities were in a delicate and embarrassing position. The shot boy was a Roman Catholic and, in Ulster terms, Jim Callaghan's Labour government was as Protestant as an Official Unionist one of the destroyed Stormont Parliament. The outcome was that the two SAS men who had fired the fatal shots were committed to trial for murder.

The trial was in July 1979 with Sir Robert Lowry, Lord Chief Justice of Northern Ireland, as judge.* The father of John Boyle afterwards summed up the basic difficulty when he remarked, "There were only three people who knew what happened. John is dead and the other two were there. It was their word against the word of a dead boy." Sir Robert Lowry, in a summing-up in which he acquitted the soldiers, made the same point, but in different words. He said, "The only way in which the defence of self-defence can be defeated, once the medical evidence has had to be discounted, is if I, as the tribunal of fact, were confident enough to say: 'I simply do not believe this evidence about pointing the rifle and, therefore, I am satisfied that A and B [the two SAS soldiers] deliberately shot the deceased without any question of a rifle having been pointed by him [John Boyle] in their direction.'

"This could, indeed, be the truth, but how can one possibly be sure? The more heinous the charge, it is traditionally said, the more cogent must be the proof, if one is to eliminate the possibility of a reasonable doubt."

The police report on James Taylor's death had, for a time, a history similar to that on John Boyle's. It went to the Director of Public Prosecutions who transferred it to the Attorney General. Delay followed and someone eventually leaked the autopsy report to the press. Taylor's death, it stated, had been caused by three bullets fired from behind at him. In addition, his two companions, who had been present, were available as eye-witnesses. If the two soldiers who had shot young Boyle could be committed to trial, it appeared inconceivable that the ones who had shot Taylor should not be tried. Nevertheless, such was the decision. It was announced on 19th April 1979 that the DPP had ruled that no one was to be prosecuted.

---

*During the trial a disturbing fact emerged which was ignored by the press apart from brief mentions in *The Guardian* and *Ballymena Guardian*. This was that several items had been deleted from the written statement of Constable Miller, a police witness, after it had been received by the Director of Public Prosecutions.

20   The Grand Design

Military strategists have accepted since about 1975 that the international balance of nuclear terror is becoming increasingly unstable and will probably collapse into a World War Three of unimaginable destructiveness in the mid-eighties. During this same period, Britain's military planners have had thrust on them the nightmare of having to plan against nuclear attack from both east and west. Previously they had been able to assume that, in a war between the Warsaw Pact countries and NATO, the nuclear threat to Britain would be solely from the east with Norway, Denmark and West Germany providing a protective screen.

First came the Soviet Backfire bomber with a range that enables it to attack Britain with nuclear bombs by an Atlantic route. A little later the cruise missile, which was not even mentioned at the Strategic Arms Limitation Talks at Vladivostock in 1974, was a reality. It has a nuclear warhead; is cheap to make; can be launched from land, aircraft, ship or submarine; flies at tree top height and thus cannot be detected by ordinary radar; and is accurate to within a few yards at long ranges. Further, there is the incredible fact (first reported to the American Congress by Dr. G. Heilmeier, director of the Capital Defence Advanced Research Projects Agency) that a research breakthrough has been made which will enable laser or charged particle beams to be developed capable of destroying nuclear weapons, including rockets in flight, while still thousands of kilometers distant.* More recent still is an invention which makes objects, including aircraft, invisible both to radar beams and infra-red rays and which, it is reckoned, will be in wide use within a few years.

The Irish Republic, like Switzerland, prides itself in being neutral during wars and in being uninvolved in military alliances. All of the political parties subscribe to the dogma and much of the population.

*The United States has confirmed that its satellites now incorporate devices to protect them against laser attack. The confirmation came after rumours that American satellites had been disabled by Soviet laser beams.

It was neutral in World War Two and is outside NATO and the EEC military arrangements. The sole external military involvement since the state was founded has been to contribute troops on three occasions to United Nations peace-keeping forces in Africa and the Middle East.

The Irish defence forces are well-disciplined and formidable for their size, but totally unequipped for a role in modern, semi-space age warfare. The country is thus an undefended approach route for attack on the United Kingdom from the west. Backfire bombers can at present release stand-off nuclear bombs aimed at Liverpool or English midland cities while still over Irish territory. **Thanks to Irish neutrality, it could well be that the first indication of a nuclear attack would be enemy bombers seen with the naked eye over the English countryside or the roar of enemy cruise missiles over English house-tops.**

On the other hand, if the Irish Republic were part of the NATO alliance, it would be a long, broad shield and early warning platform to protect England and Wales from the west.

Previously, British defence policies had been based on the premises that incorporation of the Irish Republic into NATO was a long-term aspiration to be brought about by tactful diplomacy following political and military withdrawal from Ulster and the appeasement of the Irish territorial ambition. **The Backfire bomber and cruise missile changed the time-scale and strategy. Britain's defences have to be extended westward to include the Irish Republic as swiftly as possible. The development can no longer wait on a probable, long-term mellowing of Irish attitudes in return for an act of political generosity.**

The United States, too, has been increasingly worried by Irish neutrality. The plan for holding an invasion of western Europe by Warsaw Pact armies depends on speedy, mass transport by air of immense numbers of troops from North America. An air base in Ireland, such as the international airport at Shannon, would reduce the area of the Atlantic where the transport planes would fly unprotected.

The development of the threat from the west to the United Kingdom and to the American air bridge to Europe coincided with a new, less rigid attitude towards Britain in political and official circles in the Irish Republic. The Ulster Workers's Council general strike of

A Labour Party secretary of state for Northern Ireland *(centre)* and his deputy *(right)* give thought to an Ulster problem in addition to their parliamentary duties as MPs for English constituencies. The third person *(left)* is a civil servant.

Century Newspapers, Ltd.

William Black — at heart a countryman.

The front door from which William Black escaped. The cottage has since been demolished.

The yard at 128 Middle Road, Tully-West where William Black, Jim Birch, William Birch and Joe Patterson chatted.

Arrow A. The window of the bedroom where the SIB gunman waited with the silenced sub-machine-gun.

Arrow B. The outhouse where the water tank was stored. The one in which the stolen goods were planted is not included in the photograph.

John Orchin.
Pacemaker Press, Ltd.

Andrew Beattie and his wife on holiday shortly after his Long Kesh ordeal.

Samuel Eaton at home.

Senator Frank Church, chairman of the Senate Select Committee on Intelligence, holds a dart gun uncovered during an investigation of the use of lethal poisons by the C.I.A.

Popperfoto

1974 was even more traumatic in its psychological impact in Dublin than in London. It drove home for the first time that Ulster in its present mood would not allow itself to be incorporated into the Irish Republic. The previously unchallenged orthodoxy that the British government was the main obstacle to the political unification of the island no longer carried conviction. More flexible attitudes began to emerge towards Britain and to institutions such as NATO which have her as a member. There was even some thankfulness that the British government had not succeeded in handing over Ulster as it could now be seen that the result would have been civil war. Car bombs in Dublin during the UWC general strike underscored the point and in political terms those bombs still reverberate through the corridors of the Irish parliament. They killed thirty persons and injured over one hundred and, it is suspected, were exploded by a loyalist para-military organisation which had declined to join officially in the strike because of the insistence by the UWC on non-violence.

Irish neutrality threatens both the United Kingdom and the United States and they have come together in a grand design to ease the Irish Republic out of it and into the western alliance. The British Foreign Office and D16 and the American State Department, FBI and CIA are playing the main roles and the scale, complexity and deviousness of the undertaking is without precedent in a western country of the modest size of the Irish Republic.

The starting point was the new recognition that the British government had tried to hustle Ulster towards political union with its neighbour. The failure, it was unobtrusively but patiently emphasised, was because earlier Irish governments had alienated the Ulster public by neutrality in peace and war, irresponsible sabre-rattling, reactionary social policies and ambivalence towards IRA terrorism. A politically unified Ireland was still possible, but only when the Ulster people had been reassured by new policies and attitudes and especially by comradely association with Britain within the EEC and North Atlantic communities.

The chanceries of the allies of Britain and the United States have been pressing the same message on the Irish Foreign Office. The substantial and influential Anglophil minority of the Irish population has required no persuasion. Irish politicians with EEC ambitions and persons with EEC commercial interests have become speedy converts. Officers in the armed services, bored by home garrison duty, are attracted by the prospect of European service as part of the western alliance.*

D16 is responsible for intelligence and covert operations in the Irish Republic and has numerous agents and informants, including many at high levels in the civil service, police and armed services. The territory had been part of the United Kingdom until 1921 and even to this day Irish governments do not have full legitimacy in the eyes of some citizens. Feuds from the civil war that followed independence linger on. Political bias in appointments is common and breeds the type of jealousy that erodes loyalty to a regime or even to the state itself. D16's problem has never been to find agents, but to limit them to those with the best contacts and most promise.†

D16 expanded its anti-IRA organisation in the Irish Republic as the Ulster crisis developed in the early seventies. The Anglo-American operation to manipulate the country into the western alliance meant a further expansion with the emphasis on swinging over key individuals; on influencing public opinion and on endeavours to ensure that the reins of government would eventually end up in the hands of politicians other than those of the hard-line, neutralist Fianna Fáil Party. The news media in particular has been infiltrated at all levels, including ownership, by either British or American intelligence. A number of experienced agents were transferred to Dublin, including one who earlier had played a vital role in a D16 "dirty trick" episode and who now is the prime mover in what will ultimately be seen as the most ambitious and effective covert operation to destabilise the Fianna Fáil Party and the present Fianna Fáil government. The American FBI and CIA have co-operated closely, but "in the field" have usually left the initiative to D16.

The Irish operation has been large and ambitious, but, in the main,

---

*For example, Lt. General Seán MacEoin, former Irish Chief of Staff, asserted in Nov. 1978 that "Ireland would have little option but to become a participant in a European defence union". He added, "Soldiers are soldiers and I would find it difficult to believe that our military people would not gladly relish participation in a cause in which they believe and which they consider must be honoured." See also leading article, *An Cosantóir* (Journal of the Irish Defence Forces), January 1980.

†The other side of the coin is that the Irish Republic has had its undercover agents in Northern Ireland and possibly also the mainland. Micheál Ó Móráin, a former Irish minister of Justice, admitted in March 1976 that he had 15 police undercover agents in Northern Ireland when he was in office in 1970.

no different from manipulative operations undertaken by Britain and America in areas such as the Middle East and Latin America. Even the incredible Byzantine deviousness and complexities are not new. Iran, for instance, has known it all. As with contemporary Ireland, that country is regarded as strategically vital to the west. (It is oil-rich and provides a barrier to the expansion of the USSR into the Indian sub-continent, the Gulf and eastern Africa.) As in Ireland, British intelligence is strongly placed because of historical factors. The country was occupied by Britain in World War Two and an extensive network of agents was left behind when the military forces were withdrawn. Again, as in Ireland, British intelligence dominates with American co-operating closely. When the socialist Dr. Mohammed Mossadegh declared Iran neutral in the east-west confrontation and prepared to nationalise the mainly British-owned oil wells and refineries, D16 planned a coup to overthrow him and only when all British nationals (including D16's station director) had either been expelled by him or withdrawn did the CIA take over and implement the scheme.* Again, when in 1979 the right-wing revolution associated with Ayatollah Ruhollah Khomeini led to the imprisonment of the American embassy staff, intelligence information continued to flow to Washington much as before while the British embassy remained open.†

The new strategic importance of Ireland led the Soviet Union to ask the Irish government for permission to establish an embassy in Dublin with an unusually large establishment. The British Foreign Office and American State Department encouraged it to consent. They knew that it would be forced to depend on them for the technology and expertise to keep under surveillance a large, modern Soviet embassy and that, once that situation developed, they would

*Kermit Roosevelt, grandson of President Theodore Roosevelt, was CIA Chief of Bureau in the Middle East and station commander in Tehran with responsibility for carrying out the coup. He has written a book detailing the role of D16 and of persons such as Sir Anthony Eden, the British prime minister. Publication has been delayed by the CIA's insistence on deletions.

†Ayatollah Ruhollah Khomeini knew what was happening, but delayed for a time taking action against Britain as he believed he needed her diplomatic presence to help discourage the USSR from expanding its occupation of Afghanistan to include Iran. He may also have been influenced by the fact that D16, sensing that the Iranian revolution was about to break, approached him in exile in early 1979 with suggestions for a *rapprochement*.

gain a measure of influence over other areas of Irish intelligence.

The Soviet Union is unlikely to have created an intelligence network in Ireland comparable to that of Britain or even the United States. Nevertheless, it has clearly some well-placed agents. For instance, items appear from time to time in the Dublin news media with strong indications of a Moscow origin. An alleged example was a detailed description at the height of the Afghanistan invasion crisis in early 1980 of the location and raio communication arrangements of the underground military and civil headquarters in Northern Ireland for use in a "doomsday" nuclear attack. The item coincided with the publication in London of descriptions of the locations of the prime minister's "doomsday" national control centre and of the mainland regional headquarters. It is alleged that only the Kremlin could have provided such information and co-ordinated its appearance in two different capitals and that the motive was to induce a sense of reality into the British government which had been making jingoistic noises about its military effectiveness.

Not all Soviet activities in Ireland are covert. The Kremlin is as conscious of the military potential of Shannon international airport as is the Pentagon. In the spring of 1980, it ordered Aeroflot to use it as a refuelling base and constructed an aviation fuel tank farm. It is a nonsense in terms of airline operating logic, but establishes a physical presence. The United States responded by deciding to station permanently thrity American customs and immigration officials at Shannon. It is the largest block of officials to be sent to Ireland since 1941 when President Franklin Roosevelt sent navy technicians, dressed as civilians, to Londonderry in Ulster to construct naval and radio facilities in preparation for America's probable entry into World War Two.

The current rivalry between the USSR and China has extended to Ireland. The establishment of the Soviet Embassy has been followed by the opening of one by the Peoples' Republic of China in September 1980. The ambassadoress is Madam Gong Pusheng. Her sister was at one time director of the Department of Intelligence at the Chinese Ministry of Foreign Affairs.

Political tranquility is needed if the Anglo-American covert operation against the neutrality of the Irish Republic is to succeed. Violence and tension cause public and politicians to lapse back into entrenched attitudes which in the Irish Republic means hostility to

Britain and neutrality towards the alliances of which she is a member. There are some twenty million Irish-Americans in the United States. Since the days of the Fenian raids against Canada to the present, they have not been an influence for tranquility in Anglo-Irish relations. They are one of the most experienced political pressure groups in Washington. They have been the main source of money, arms and explosives for the Provisional IRA and their most effective propagandists. In Ireland, their influence is considerable and invariably on the side of polarisation and confrontation in relations with Britain.

Thanks to the Irish-American lobby in Washington, efforts to prevent the export of supplies to the IRAs had been perfunctory until the realisation in the mid-seventies that the conflict in Ulster was a threat to the vital American air bridge to Europe. After that action was vigorous. The small unit of the FBI in London was expanded and FBI officials began to visit Ulster to liaise with British intelligence and the RUC. Gun-runners were convicted in American courts and supplies for the Provisionals slowed to a trickle.

The Irish-American political lobby is a more serious menace than the gun-runners. A speech or other happening in Congress or Senate can raise the political temperature in Ireland more than the dispatch of arms and explosives to the Provisionals. An incident of small consequence in early 1980 is an indication. The RUC had ordered pistols from an American company. President Carter, in deference to Irish-American murmurs in an election year, blocked their export. Indigation waxed strong in Ulster and was echoed in the Westminster House of Commons.

The problem with the Irish-American political lobby is emotionalism, misty sentiment, ignorance of Ireland and deep ignorance of Ulster. When persons in high places are a menace through ignorance rather than ill-intention, a high-powered seminar or conference can be useful in supplying some of the needed education. Most modern governments use the device from time to time. So, too, do international bodies. The present writer once acted as an observer on behalf of the International Association of University Professors and Lecturers at a United Nations seminar of that kind. It was convened primarily for senior officials from Latin American and Caribbean countries. Persons such as the Swedish ombudsman and the director of the Civil Liberties Bureau of Japan were added to give additional prestige. The theme was "The Effective

Realisation of Civil and Political Rights" — a subject not inappropriate for certain of the countries from which the officials came.

It was recognised that the Irish-American lobby would need more than a seminar or conference to cure its propensity for international mischief-making. A decision was made to take the seminar concept a stage further and to involve the congressman responsive to the Irish-American ethnic vote in a direct intervention into the Ulster problem on the principle that burnt fingers provide a better understanding of the nature of fire than verbal description. One or two congressmen created a Congressional Ad Hoc Committee for Peace in Ireland with the declared object of bringing about a peace settlement. The Irish National Caucus, a nation-wide body strong on Irish unification sentiment and strident in anti-British pronouncements, has been infiltrated at the top by FBI agents to the point where they control its political direction* — a situation fairly easy to achieve with a large amorphous body of that kind. These used the lobbying expertise of the organisation to persuade congressmen that the Ad Hoc Committee was responding to the strongly felt views of Irish-Americans. Membership has grown to one hundred and thirty which, it is claimed, is the largest in the history of the Congress. A smaller group of senators and congressmen, with at least some understanding of the Ulster complexities, declined to become involved. They included T. P. O'Neill, speaker of the House of Representatives, Senator Edward Kennedy and Senator Daniel Moynihan. Invitations to a "Peace Forum" to be held in Washington in May 1979 were sent to the political parties in Ulster and to the Provisional IRA and loyalist paramilitary organisations. All refused to attend. No political party would attend if representatives of terrorist organisations were to be present. The Provisional IRA, on the other hand, declared that the Irish National Caucus is CIA controlled (they were wrong: it is FBI controlled) and the proposed gathering CIA inspired.

The "Peace Forum" was put back until the autumn and then post-

---

*The present writer deposited an early draft of part of this book with the FBI. I found one of its agents in the Irish National Caucus in a position where he could not refuse to agree to arrangements to accept it. I next allowed D16, who had already purloined the text, to learn of the arrangements and finally handed over the draft in the presence of an American consul-general. I knew that in the American post-Watergate climate, the FBI, being themselves implicated by the presence of the unwanted draft, would be a restraining influence if D16 were planning anything unpleasant for me although a Canadian citizen. The draft did not include the present chapter which was not written at the time.

poned indefinitely. The Ad Hoc Committee continues in existence and, no doubt, further educational activities will be found for it from time to time. It and the Irish National Caucus institutionalise Irish-American energies so that they are channelled into activities least troublesome to the grand design to ease the Irish Republic out of its neutrality. There is a parallel with the youth leader who organises his charges into football teams to channel their energies away from vandalism. **Also, it is a gross breach of American constitutional propriety for the State Department, CIA and FBI to conspire with their counterparts in Britain, a foreign power, in order to manipulate Congress regardless of the American democratic process.**

On one occasion, the very success of the Ad Hoc Committee – Irish National Caucus covert operation led to an embarassing crisis. Charles Haughey, the Irish prime minister who came to office in December 1979, was impressed by its apparent vigour and militancy and decided to align his administration more closey with it. (He has been remarkably ill-served by his intelligence officials both in Ireland and abroad.) The decision was made that this could not be permitted as it was likely to unbalance the carefully constructed arrangement for neutralising Irish-American grass-roots wrong-headedness. Haughey's plan included the replacement of the Irish ambassador to Washington. News of the impending change was planted in the American press and commentators, who some hours earlier were unaware that there was such an ambassador, pontificated on the unwisdom of the change. The news media in the United Kingdom also carried the story with the BBC intervening at one stage apparently in an attempt to dispel an assumption that the British government had leaked the news. At least two influential American senators telephoned the Irish prime minister and warned that, if he transferred the ambassador, he could no longer rely on their sympathetic support. They explained that his removal would be seen as a victory for the extremists of the Ad Hoc Committe and Irish National Caucus and magnify their influence dangerously at the expense of persons like themselves who knew something of the real issues in Ireland. Next day the Irish minister for Foreign Affairs issued a statement to confirm that the ambassador was to remain in Washington and added that press speculations that he was to be moved were "entirely without foundation".

Events in Ulster are vital if the Anglo-American operation is to

248

suceed in manoeuvering the Irish Republic out of its neutrality. The
Conservative government formed under Margaret Thatcher in 1979
appointed Sir Maurice Oldfield to a new post called "co-ordinator of
security in Northern Ireland". After only eight months he was
replaced by Sir Brooks Richards. Sir Maurice was director-general of
DI6 from 1972 to 1975 and Sir Brooks was co-ordinator of intelligence and security to the cabinet and a former ambassador. The
appointment of persons of such standing caused astonishment and
government spokesmen added to the mystery by insisting that the title
of the post was an accurate description of the duties.* The truth is
that the post is primarily to co-ordinate the Anglo-American covert
operation against Irish neutrality and touches only marginally on
security activities in Ulster. It needs someone able to meet on equal
terms the most senior diplomats, intelligence chiefs and military commanders in Washington or other NATO capitals. It also has to be a
man with a thorough knowledge of intelligence and diplomacy. Sir
Maurice Oldfield had been both intelligence officer and diplomat; he
had been director-general of D16 and he knew well most of the senior
American intelligence fraternity. Sir Brooks Richards fills the require-
ments in a similar way. As a former co-ordinator of intelligence and
security to the cabinet, he was familiar with intelligence matters at the
highest level. His previous career was no less relevant. He had been
British representative to West Germany, ambassador to Saigon and
ambassador to Greece and each appointment had been at a time of
intense British or British-American intelligence activity in the particular country. Sir. John Killick is alleged to have been the alternative
choice for the post when Sir Maurice accepted. This again underscores
its nature and importance. Sir John is British ambassador to NATO
where the main work is to liaise with the American military and intelligence establishments plus those of other NATO allies.

Sir Maurice's interest in day to day security work in Ulster was minimal despite the title of his post and this appears to be equally true of Sir
Brooks. The Royal Ulster Constabulary has been given more responsibility against common terrorists and this has extended to its Special
Branch. The latter has been strengthened by a number of new, competent persons. The step was perhaps unavoidable, but has its risks.
Men and women intelligent enough to catch Provisional IRA and

*One spokesman explained that the aim is "to have someone in Ulster to sandpaper
down the edges between the British army and the RUC".

INLA terrorists are equally capable of asking among themselves unwanted questions about the actions, past and present, of the other intelligence services. They noted that at the same time as more routine
anti-terrorist chores were relinquished to the RUC, the other intelligence services began to step up their political activities, including the
bugging of politicians and of the police themselves. They are
exasperated to find them conducting surveillance of persons already
under RUC Special Branch surveillance. Sometimes this leads to com-
plications, ranging from competition for strategically placed surveillance positions to tense moments until it can be ascertained whether
persons acting suspiciously are terrorists or from a rival intelligence
organisation. On at least one occasion in the summer of 1980, a RUC
Special Branch surveillance unit on political work found itself in competition with no less than two other units. Only one of them was
identified quickly and it was army intelligence.

The RUC Special Branch tends to be the last of the intelligence services to receive equipment involving advances in technology. Unlike
military intelligence, they have few micro-wave personnel detectors
and have to send men out in hazardous areas with dogs as their
means of warning against ambush. Another grievance is that the
RUC is refused direct access to the new telephone tapping device, RF
Flooding. It was developed at the Royal Signals and Radar Establishment at Malvern in Worcestershire for use in Ulster and is operated
from the army's Landline Interception Centre in Belfast.

Ulster is a critical area in the Anglo-American covert operation. The
latter is a scheme to entice a donkey in the form of the Irish Republic
out of its neutrality by dangling in front of it the carrot of Irish
unification. It is thus vital that the British government keep the carrot
fresh and enticing. A large part of the Ulster public would prefer to be
ruled directly from Westminster (despite the concomitant criminalities
and mainland indifference) if the alternative is a form of government in
which Irish republicans would have a part either directly or though a
veto. When the Conservative administration came to power in May
1979, a number of English and Ulster politicians urged permanent
direct rule. The political parties in the Irish Republic were alarmed and
each emphasised that that policy is unacceptable as it would lock the
door permanently against the political unification of the island. The
reaction made clear, even to a new government, that to continue direct
rule would wither and destroy the Irish unification carrot — the one

thing which neither London nor Washington dare allow to happen.

Humphrey Atkins, an unknown Conservative MP, was appointed as secretary of state for Northern Ireland and instructed to prepare the political ground for a form of limited, devolved government which, on the one hand, would not provoke a third general strike by the Ulster majority and, on the other, would placate Irish republicans and keep healthy their hope of Irish unification.

A preliminary conference was arranged to which selected Ulster political parties were invited. The response within the loyalist parties was cool and, as on certain earlier occasions, an "opinion poll" result was concocted to help persuade hesitant invitees that the public wanted them to attend. On the date proposed for its release, the majority of people had not heard of the conference and many of the remainder were indifferent — an awkward fact conveniently ignored as figures were selected to total one hundred per cent. In the event, no representative attended from a loyalist party apart from the unpredictable Dr. Ian Paisley and one of his colleagues.

Other preparations were cautious and thorough. They were also sometimes misdirected as it was assumed that the Ulster public has the political sophistication of foreign office officials and is impressed by speeches and statements from prestige sources. The visit of Pope John-Paul II to the Irish Republic provides an example. It was preceded by intense lobbying of the Vatican by Foreign Office officials and others in liaison with it. A very senior prelate in the English Roman Catholic Church is alleged to have been a particularly effective channel in ensuring that the government's proposed devolution initiative was kept to the fore as the Pope's Irish speeches were being drafted. Nor was it a coincidence unconnected with lobbying that, during the Pope's visit, the Protestant World Council of Churches issued an appeal for political co-operation in Ulster in terms remarkably close to those which he used.

The Pope condemned terrorism and appealed to Irish republicans and loyalists to co-operate to bring about a new harmonious political arrangement. He also disassociated the Vatican from Irish annexationist claims to Ulster by speaking of "Northern Ireland" the term which acknowledges that it is part of the United Kingdom. The crowds and TV audiences were delighted by his friendliness, smile and outgoing personality. His political remarks passed them by unnoticed. So, too, did the appeal of the World Council of Churches.

At the other end of the political and religious spectrum, Radio Moscow denounced Provisional IRA terrorism and urged the Ulster factions to come together in fraternal co-operation. The jargon was standard Moscow (lackeys of western imperialism, exploitation of the workers, etc.). Decoded the message was the same as that of the Pope and World Council of Churches.

This intervention into Ulster affairs in support of the British government was not unique. There had been several earlier ones of which the most important was a denouncement of the Provisional IRA and its terrorist methods carefully timed to give the Provisionals the maximum feeling of isolation as they went into the "Feakle" negotiations at the end of 1974. It is also true that at no time has the USSR given the Provisionals arms or other supplies. Soviet weapons have turned up in Provisional hands, but they have always come from an Arab or other source over which the Kremlin had no control.

The explanation of such helpfulness to Britian by the USSR is complex. The Biafran rebellion against the Federation of Nigeria overlapped into the Ulster crisis by some months. The British government knew from that experience how skilful propaganda on behalf of the starvation beset Biafrans had sent deep emotions surging around the world with the most serious repercussions, including trade boycotts against Britain even by an ally such as the Netherlands. It knew that the outcome could have been a Biafran victory had the Soviet Union not sided with the Federation of Nigeria and withheld from the Biafran cause its formidable, world-wide facilities for propaganda and political agitation. The Biafran episode intensified the sensitivity of the British government to bad international publicity on Ulster and helps to explain the exceptional deference paid by it to the Soviet Union and other Warsaw Pact countries. An illustration of the latter was the transfer of Howard Trayton Smith (now Sir Howard) to the Northern Ireland Office in 1971. He was ambassador to Czechoslovakia at the time and earlier had held the rank of councillor in the Moscow Embassy. Later he was to be ambassador to the Soviet Union and (thanks to his considerable intelligence experience) is now director-general of D15.

However, the Biafran experiece is no more than part of the explanation of British attitudes towards the Soviet Union. For a more complete understanding, one has to go back to the Cold War years that followed World War Two when the United States, Britain and certain of their allies endeavoured to forment revolt and unrest in the Soviet satellite countries and even among Russian national minorities such as the Ukranians. The moment of truth came when the Hungarians broke into insurrection in 1956. America and Britain found that they could either intervene and precipitate a nuclear World War Three or stand aside ignominiously and allow the Hungarians to be crushed. The lesson was painful and remembered. It was that the **great threat to world peace is not Soviet might, but unstable areas prone to crises which bring the great powers into collision despite their mutual wish for peaceful dètente.** When the Kremlin decided in 1968 that Czechoslovakia had to be occupied by an armed invasion, Washington was allowed to learn of it in advance. It gave its tacit consent and halted large-scale troop movements which were in progress near the Czech frontier in case the Soviet command might misinterpret them.

When civil turmoil broke out in Ulster in 1969, the Kremlin realised that it could use the situation to secure the United Kingdom as an ally or accomplice in dealing with its own malcontents. Strangers began to appear in Belfast and other parts of Ulster. British intelligence recognised them as mainly east European agents already known to it in Cyprus and to a less extent in other areas. Men from military intelligence with previous experience of them were brought in and soon most were identified. (The present writer subsequently became acquainted with one of the men. He had had previous experience with military intelligence in Cyprus.) The Soviet news media launched an anti-British campaign and threatened that the USSR would support the sending of an international peace-keeping force to replace the British "army of occupation".

The Foreign Office was greatly alarmed. It assumed that the Soviet Union was preparing to make very serious trouble. It was thus in a receptive frame of mind when its Soviet counterpart proposed an understanding whereby the Soviet Union and United Kingdom would help each other to eliminate political subversion. Tsar Alexandra I had tried to persuade British statesmen to agree to a remarkably similar proposal a century and a half earlier and been rebuffed. This time there was acceptance. The understanding was limited to Europe. In other areas, Britain, more often than not, has joined with the USSR's opponents. Thus, in Angola in 1975, the CIA, DI6, South African BOSS, French SDECE and Chinese intelligence service co-operated to help UNITA and FNLA in an unsuccessful attempt to prevent the Soviet-backed MPLA from winning the civil war.

It was not long before the first British request for assistance arrived at the Kremlin. It arose out of the deepening Ulster crisis of 1969. A number of persons, including part of the Irish army command and certain ministers in the Irish cabinet, became involved in a plan to seize Northern Ireland by military force. (The soldiers (and the army intelligence section in particular) were the main-spring of the plot and provided most of the brains.) It was based on the premises, first, that the government at Stormont, helpless in the face of "civil rights" marches and rioting mobs, would be incapable of effective armed resistance and, second, that the Westminster government would not dare to use military force against Irish troops because of one million Irish voters in Great Britain, some twenty million Irish-Americans in the United States and a formidable pro-Irish and pro-small nation international lobby.

The plan required an obvious and dramatic justification for Irish military intervention to disarm and divide opposition in Great Britain, to rally the pro-Irish international lobby and, most important of all, to enable the Irish government to carry with it a majority of its public. Find or engineer such a justification, the plotters reckoned, and Ulster could be taken over with possibly even less bloodshed than eight years earlier when India overran and annexed the Portuguese territory of Goa against the wishes of the majority of the population. "Civil rights" marches and stone-throwing mobs were not sufficient, but by August 1969 Irish republican activists had begun to speak of "liberated areas" in districts where the police had stopped patrolling. These already had local committees. If they could be given armed militias, they could be represented as *de facto* independent territories with the essentials of independent governments, including their own armed forces. A call for military intervention from them would have an element of international credibility. It would also leave the Stormont authorities little choice but to respond with physical force to prevent the armed militias from expanding the "liberated areas" indefinitely. Once the shooting began, the latter would scream that they faced extermination. It would be the ideal pretext. The Irish army could be ordered to the rescue with overwhelming support from the Irish public.

On 12th August 1969, a long, violent confrontation with police took place in Londonderry City which was mishandled to the extent that the mob was allowed to remain in occupation of a section of the town. The massed stone-throwers and ineffective baton charges filled

TV screens across Ireland. "The Bastille has fallen" brand of euphoria swept through the Irish Rerpublic and the Irish republican areas of Ulster. Next day, the Irish cabinet met in a highly charged atmosphere. The proponents of Goa-type annexation dominated it. (They were helped by the fact that some of the less astute members did not grasp that there was more afoot than boisterous sabre-rattling to impress the Irish electorate.) A statement was drafted which the prime minister read on Irish radio and TV in the evening.

The prime minister's statement dovetailed well with the needs of the Goa-style annexation scheme. It asserted that the RUC was no longer accepted by the people of "the north" as a police force. It thus opened the way for recognition of an armed militia (or community police) in republican districts. It claimed the right to inverene in Ulster with the sentences, *The Stormont Government is evidently no longer in control of the situation . . . The Government of Ireland can no longer stand by and see innocent people injured and worse.** Having asserted the right of the Irish government to intervene, the statement denied it to the United Kingdom. *The employment of British troops is unacceptable nor would they be likely to restore peaceful conditions – certainly not in the long term.* These strong words about the use of British troops are understandable. Their presence in numbers would mean that the Irish army would be able to occupy only "liberated areas" close to the frontier, such as Londonderry City, and perhaps not even them if the British government were to muster enough will to use its troops to establish a physical presence in those districts. This claim of the right of the Irish government to intervene was underscored by the information that the Irish army had been ordered to set up field hospitals close to Londonderry City and at other points on the frontier. The prime minister's statement called for a United Nations peace-keeping force – a shrewd move as it would enable the Irish government to claim that it had sent its army into Ulster only because the United Nations had failed to act.† Finally, the statement called on the British government *to enter into early negotiations with the Irish Government to review the present constitutional position of the six counties of the north of Ireland.*

*It is noteworthy that four days later *Pravada* wrote that the Irish government was entitled to aid the "patriots" in Northern Ireland by means "short of invasion".

†The Irish government shortly afterwards tried to raise at the United Nations the issue of a peace-keeping force for Ulster, but the United Kingdom blocked the attempt.

The British government's response was swift. Even before the Irish prime minister had delivered his statement on the media, a large contingent of troops had been ordered to be air-lifted into Ulster. They were, however, withheld from establishing themselves in the Irish republican districts and so the way remained open for the setting up of "liberated areas" or "no go districts" as the local people came to term them. While these areas existed, a Goa-style intervention continued to seem feasible to those in the plot in the Irish army command and Irish cabinet.

The Goa-style annexation scheme depended on an armed militia being formed in the "liberated areas". The problem was the arms. They could not be obtained from the Irish defence forces as that would be political dynamite at home and brand the government abroad as an *agent provocateur*. Also, a substantial consignment was needed and as quickly as possible. An order to an arms dealer appeared to be the answer. About three weeks after the prime minister's truculent TV and radio statement, two men, one of whom was the brother of a cabinet minister, met a contact in London who claimed to represent an arms dealer. They released after a time that they were being shadowed by British intelligence and went home. Towards the end of the following month, October, the brother of the cabinet minister accompanied by a member of the IRA (which at theat time had not split into Official and Provisional) returned to London and re-met the contact. Again, there was obvious surveillance and both went back to Dublin, but not before they were introduced to a Peter Markham Randall who claimed to represent an arms dealer. He was invited to Dublin to continue the negotiations. There he offered the IRA member money to act as an informer. His organisation decided to have him shot in the Gresham Hotel where he was staying and sent for an assassin to Belfast. An officer in Irish army intelligence who had been assigned to help with the arms procurement learned of the plan and prevented the killing.

The London disappointments turned thoughts to the Irish-Americans, the traditional source of illicit arms. Two members of the IRA, including the one who had gone to London, were sent to the United States to re-activate the arms sources and smuggling routes used in an earlier, ineffective terrorist campaign in the fifties. They made excellent progress thanks partly to help from a former American senator. The nucleus was formed of the organisation which was to develop into the formidable money-raising Irish Northern Aid and contacts were renewed inside the longshoremens' union in New York. Alarm prevailed in London as the extent of the progress emerged from intelligence reports. The situation in Ulster was continuing to deteriorate and here was militant Irish republicanism laying the foundation for long-term money and arms supplies. The decision was made to try to divert attention away from the United States by dangling the hope of immediate arms from a European dealer. An approach was made to a minister in the Irish cabinet through a continental acquaintance. The response was brisk. A negotiator was sent to Dortmund where he was introduced to the contact man of a Hamburg arms dealer.

In the meantime, the Foreign Office and DI6 had called on their new comrades against subversion in the Kremlin and were promised full co-operation, including co-operation by the Soviet dominated Czechoslovakian authorities.

The arms offered were mainly Czech which reassured the Irish buyers as they assumed that hard-line Warsaw Pact Czechoslovakia was irreconcilably hostile to NATO Britain and hence correspondingly dependable. The deal as concluded was for 50 general purpose machine-guns; 84 light machine-guns; 200 sub-machine guns; 150 FN rifles; 200 pistols; 200 percussion grenades; 250,000 round of ammunition; and 70 flak jackets. The cost was a modest £35,000 of which somewhere between £26,000 and £28,000 was paid, the money being obtained from a sum of £100,000 approved by the Irish parliament for "the relief of distress in Northern Ireland".

The types of weapons chosen is in itself evidence that they were for holding towns or territory. Machine-guns and percussion grenades are not suitable arms if the purpose is to enable local residents to defend themselves against lawbreakers in the absence of police.

While the quest for arms was being pressed abroad, other steps were being taken in the Irish Republic. The Irish troops were brought home from the United Nations' peace-keeping force in Cyprus and the army reserve was called up for full-time service. At the end of September, a number of civilians from Londonderry City were given weapons training for a week at Fort Dunree, an Irish army camp in Co. Donegal, but the scheme was discontinued when the press began to ask questions.

The Irish Minister of Defence issued a directive on 6th February which he gave to the Chief of Staff of the army in the presence of the Director of Army Intelligence. It read: *The Government have instructed me to convey to the army a directive that plans be immediately put in train for operating in Northern Ireland, in the event of the situation (in the opinion of the Government) warrants interference. The Government further directs that training and planning programmes be directed to cater for such an eventuality.* Two months later on 2nd April 1970, five hundred redundant army rifles were transferred to Dundalk, a town within easy distance of the frontier. During a subsequent court trial the Minister of Defence was unable to give any explanation to counter the allegation that they were intended for use Ulster.

The deal with the Hamburg arms merchant was concluded at the end of January 1970 and delivery should have followed within a short time. DI6, with the co-operation of its Soviet and Czech counterparts, had other ideas. The arms were to be sent by ship to a point near the Kish lighthouse outside Dublin where they were to be off-loaded into small boats. The small boats were sent out three times, but each time no ship appeared. A member of the Irish cabinet urged that enough time had been lost and that a regular cargo ship should be used with the arms passed through customs by a secret arrangement. The officer in army intelligence who had been assigned to assist with the arms deal and importation* approached another member of the cabinet who arranged for them to be cleared through customs as mild steelplates. The ship selected was the m.v. *City of Dublin* and arrived on 25th March. The total consignment consisted of "six bales of garments" which were found to be Czech flak jackets. A telex inquiry to the continent brought the reply that the arms had been stopped by Belgian customs officials as there was no export licence. Eight days later, the Irish army intelligence officer met the Hamburg merchant on the continent and arranged for the arms to be sent on a chartered aircraft on 7th April. The agreement was not carried out. Ten days later, a message arrived that 3,000 kilos of pistols and

*The officer was Capt. James Kelly. In July 1980, he wrote in the press, *The arms importation was official government policy, with the statutory authority, Mr. Gibbons* [Minister of Defence], *having been kept in touch with its development from the very beginning on the basis of reports submitted by me through Colonel Heffernon* [Director of Army Intelligence] *initially and, later, by direct reporting by me to the Minister in his office.*

ammunition were being sent on an Aer Lingus (Irish Airlines) passenger plane on a normal flight. The airline officials pointed out that the plane could carry only the pistols, but not the ammunition as that would be contrary to IATA regulations. The arrangement to fly the ammunition was cancelled. This left the pistols to travel alone, but that, too, was cancelled when it was learned that they would be caught in a security check at Vienna airport. Aer Turas, an Irish air charter company, was approached. A senior official became suspicious and reported the approach to Peter Berry, the head of the Irish civilian state security system. He was resolutely opposed to the plot and at last in a position to take action. Dublin airport was surrounded by Special Branch police. The men behind the attempt to import the arms quickly learned of it and the charter idea was abandoned. Berry was under no illusion as to the magnitude of what he was up against and took the unprecedented step of reporting the plot to the Irish president, Eamonn de Valera. The step was decisive. The plotters were placed in a position where they had either to abandon the attempt to import arms or else precipitate a constitutional crisis with incalculatable consequences. A day or so later, the army intelligence officer, who had gone to Vienna (the western city most convenient to Czechoslovakia), received a telephone call to inform him that the scheme was not to be carried further.

In the autumn of 1971, DI6 undertook a further, similar operation in conjunction with its Soviet and Czech counterparts. The purpose was to locate sympathisers of the Provisional IRA in the British Isles. It was based on the premises that the nature of a person's dedication to a cause is shown by how he or she reponds when asked for money in an emergency.

A stranger walked into the office in Kevin Street, Dublin of the alleged political wing of the Provisional IRA and asked to be put in touch with the organisation.* He was an American; said his name was Freeman; and offered to set up arrangements for a deal with Omnipol, the state-owned arms manufacturer in Czechoslovakia. The Provisional leaders responded with vigour. David O'Connel, probably the most influential member of its Army Council, travelled to the continent where he obtained a Czech visa in Switzerland and was

*See Maria McGuire, *To Bear Arms* (1973) for an account of this episode by a Provisional IRA participant.

joined from Dublin by Maria McGuire who spoke fluently French, German and Spanish.

Four and-a-half tons of arms were ordered from Omnipol. They included bazookas, rocket launchers and hand grenades. The cost was £20,000 of which £10,000 was an initial deposit. As DI6 had calculated, the Provisional IRA fund raisers were hard pressed to find the money quickly and contacted (sometimes by telephone) an ever-widening circle of sympathisers. As they did so, a picture was built up of whom the Provisionals themselves believed to be their friends or whom they assumed could be pressurised into parting with money. When the agreed sum was about reached, O'Connel was offered a much improved deal for an extra £2,500. He fell to the bait and the Provisional money raisers were forced to cast their nets in yet wider circles thus providing British intelligence with even more names.

The arms were to be flown from Prague to Amsterdam international airport where they were to be transferred to await shipment to Ireland. A Cork businessman who had promised the use of a warehouse had cancelled the arrangement, but a Dutchman had conveniently materialised and provided O'Connel with an alternative one.

The plane arrived on 17th October 1971 as arranged and the one hundred and sixty-six crates of arms on board were promptly seized by the Dutch authorities. O'Connel and McGuire heard the news on the radio. They immediately went "on the run" and returned to Ireland via France. The Netherlands and Belgium are members of NATO and the authorities in neither had any wish for a political trial or that too many details should transpire of the Czech role or of the "accidental" discovery of the arms by the Dutch authorities* In Amsterdam, the Dutchman who had so conveniently materialised with the empty warehouse now no less conveniently asked O'Connel and his companion, "Would you like to stop at my house tonight?" At one stage on their train journey through Belgium, two plain-clothes policemen sat in the same carriage. They flashed their police identification cards so that they could not miss seeing them and talked loudly about the "Amsterdam arms case". It was one way of suggesting that they did not loiter in the country.

*The official version as given to the media was that the arms were discovered at Amsterdam international airport when a crate accidentally burst open during unloading.

The Kremlin initiated the understanding with the Foreign Office (and DI6) on co-operation against subversion and it has insisted on and received good value in return. It is particularly sensitive about foreign broadcasts aimed at Warsaw Pact populations. They had been one of the causes of the Hungarian insurrection and, although the western allies had subsequently been careful not to transmit incitement to revolt, they were adept at deflating Moscow's versions of events. The matter was raised with the Foreign Office under the anti-subversion understanding. A difficulty was that, if BBC broadcasts were to exclude material carried by the Voice of America or West German transmissions, their credibility would be undermined without the Soviet authorities receiving any benefit. The first task was thus to persuade the United States and West Germany to join in a joint mellowing of broadcasts. The latter was the more easy convert. Bonn was contemptious of the political dogma on East German and other Warsaw Pact broadcasts, but reports in depth of private and institutional scandals could wreck the prospects of a political party or individual politician or civil servant and an arrangement which curtailed the hazard was not unwelcome. Eventually, the United States succumbed to the argument that, as all western broadcasting to the east had been subdued since the Hungarian insurrection, some additional restraint was worthwhile in the interest of Britain's Ulster problem and the western alliance as a whole. By the autumn of 1973, the Kremlin was sufficiently satisfied to discontinue jamming.

Georgi Markov, a Bulgarian defector employed as a broadcaster by the BBC's Bulgarian service was walking to his office in Bush House in central London on 7th September 1978 when he was prodded on the back of the right thigh by a well-built man who apologised in a heavy foreign accent and disappeared in a taxi. Five days later, he died in hospital. The umbrella appears to have been a disguised air gun which discharged painlessly into the leg minute metal pellets filled with a deadly poison extracted from the castor oil plant. Three weeks earlier, a similar attack had been made in Paris on Vladmir Kostov, another Bulgarian defector well-known to Markov. He had survived probably because he was wearing thick clothes.

The Bulgaria of communist Premier Zhivkov has a number of sturdily independent, strong personalities in its ruling circle who insist on having their own way in Bulgarian internal matters even in defiance of clearly expressed preferences by Moscow. These persons have been the frequent target of BBC broadcasts which have shown an uncanny intimacy with details of corruption and nepotism involving them or their departments. Markov had known some of them before he defected and although that had been nine years earlier, it was concluded that only he (helped by men such as Kostov) could have the range of top level contacts to secure information of that kind. This was the explanation given by British officials who investigated the murder and there seems no reason to doubt it. The Bulgarian authorities were tragically wrong about Markov. They overlooked the fact that the men who were the BBC's targets were the same ones whose stubborn independence was exasperating Moscow and it did not occur to them that the BBC could have in the KGB a more thorough source of information than was possible with a defector in exile even if he had succeeded in maintaining old contacts.

Early 1980 was a traumatic time for the Anglo-Soviet anti-subversion understanding. President Jimmy Carter had decided that the public response of the United States to the military occupation of Afghanistan would be an international boycott of the Olympic Games which were to be held in Moscow in mid-summer. It was election year for the presidency and the degree of success of the boycott would influence his national standing. Washington placed the British government under intense pressure to support it; the British public was receptive to the idea and the government knew that it would strengthen its popularity by doing so. The first official pronouncements suggested that no British athletes would be taking part, but the Kremlin quickly warned that their absence would mean the end of the anti-subversion understanding and the beginning of an international campaign orchestrated to cause Britain the maximum embarrassment on the human rights and other aspects of its Ulster administration. The point was underscored by the despatch to Ulster of front organisations with the publicly avowed purpose of investigating human rights infringements. One was a fact-finding deputation from an international youth group. Another was a solidly Marxist orientated professional body which the Northern Ireland Office treated with exceptional deference.

Caught between the Washington pressure and the Moscow ultimatum, London wavered briefly and then capitulated to the latter. The Foreign Office was instructed to issue athletes with their travel documents at the same time as Margaret Thatcher, the prime minister, rhetorically appealed to them to stay at home. They ignored her call without exception as everyone knew that they would.

21 Who are Responsible?

Who are the persons ultimately responsible for the activities outside of the law as illustrated by the cases recounted in preceeding chapters? This question is what this book is about. The present writer hopes that an independent judicial commission of inquiry may be appointed. Its task will be difficult. The historian, David Irving, has demonstrated that there is no clear documentary proof that Hitler knew that the extermination of six million Jews was taking place under his rule. This should not surprise anyone. Ordinary law breakers endeavour to leave no written or other evidence of their deeds and the highly placed do not act differently. The European Commission of Human Rights could use its powers under Article 28 of the Convention to lay bare the truth, but it will not dare allow itself to become involved.

The chain of responsibility can often be traced without difficulty when the authorisation or initiation of an illegality is a political decision made at a political level as, for instance, with the creation of the Castlereagh special interrogation team. On the other hand, when intelligence organisations (DI6, DI5, Army Intelligence, Special Branch, etc.) are involved, the question of responsibility is as complex and shrouded in ambiguity as the workings of the criminal world itself.

On paper, the chain of command of an intelligence organisation looks as precise and logical as in an army division or a civil service department. It should thus be easy to pinpoint responsibility for specific covert operations. The reality is different. Each organisation has elaborate cut-out arrangements to ensure that within it as few individuals as possible know about any one covert undertaking.

Most of the matters presented in this book have arisen out of the Ulster crisis. When examining the question of responsibility, one has to bear in mind that a special intelligence arrangement and command may have been set up for Northern Ireland with its own director of operations responsible to none of the senior officials of the London based organisations, but using certain of their personnel and facilities, including those in London and other parts of the mainland. On the political side, it is possible, too, that much intelligence liaison has been via the Northern Ireland Office.

The "David" who endeavoured to suborn the Waters at the Commodore Hotel outside Edinburgh had an aircraft at his disposal. This fact suggested that he was with DI6. It has had such a facility for many years. Even in the early years of the World War Two when aircraft were in desperately short supply, it managed to retain a pale blue Dove machine. It is understood that, in contrast, DI5 does not have an aircraft. On the other hand, it is possible that "David" was an official in a special intelligence structure for Northern Ireland with either its own aircraft or the use of a military one.

David Blundy, writing in *The Sunday Times* in November 1977, described intelligence headquarters in Ulster in an article on the murder by the Provisional IRA of Captain Robert Nairac, VC. He did not take up the question of the overall organisation or how many of the important decisions are made in London. His picture is of the situation at the operational level.

Intelligence work in Northern Ireland, Blundy wrote, *is run from a dingy corridor behind an electronically-operated steel grille on the first floor of army headquarters at Lisburn. At the time Nairac arrived* [he arrived in early 1974 and thus shortly after the shooting of William Black], *that intelligence, though often brilliantly successful was, to put it mildly, unco-ordinated. One of Nairac's colleagues puts it more bluntly: "It was a bloody shambles. Nobody knew what anyone else was doing. The army didn't trust the police; the police thought, rightly, that the army bungled operations."* ...

Even the denizens of the corridor often had little idea what their neighbours did. There was for example, the enigmatic middle-aged Scotsman who affected a Tam-o-Shanter with a pom-pom and a gnarled stick. His office was listed as "political secretariat". He was in fact the resident MI6 man, drafted in from the Foreign Office. In the same corridor were the SAS, the Intelligence Corps, the Military Intelligence officers and the Special Duties team. There was also an MI5 intelligence co-ordinator from the Home Office sitting in Stormont Castle; and most important of all, there was the RUC Special Branch.

264

Each group had its rivalries. One army intelligence man who ran a valuable agent across the border was ordered, for example, to report not to army intelligence but directly to MI6. The main problem, however, was rivalry between police and army. Yet the police had a virtual monopoly of informants. One of Nairac's first tasks was to tout for information from Special Branch officers in Portadown.

Sir Findlater Stewart, in his report to Parliament on DI5 in 1945, remarked of the office of director-general that "having got the right man there is no alternative to giving him the widest discretion in the means he uses and the direction in which he applies them". This comment is equally true of officials and agents at many levels of an intelligence organisation. G. D. K. McCormick (pseudynm R. Deacon) in a discussion on agents in *A History of the Secret Service* wrote that the critical moment is when an agent "sees the path ahead clearly, appreciates the objectives and, ignoring the rules, drives ahead on his own". "In espionage", he explained, "there should be cautionary rules, but no others; whether a government likes it or not, if the end justifies the means, all should be forgiven." He cited the example of the British agent who burgled the safe of Sumner Welles, the American under-secretary of state, and obtained documents with important information.

An example of a similar type of initiative may have been a small bomb which wrecked an empty Orange hall in Co. Antrim in 1975. It exploded in the attic. A government spokesman claimed that it had been caused by illicit gelignite which had self-ignited through heat from the sun shining on the roof. The explosion, however, had been in the cool of the late evening and a stranger had been seen leaving the building a short time earlier. Several organisations use the building, including one or two legal paramilitary units. The more probable explanation is that the explosion was the work of British undercover in order to set the users of the hall speculating on their telephones. It would then be easy to learn quickly the names of the members of the paramilitary units together with local assessments of their views and militancy.

Intelligence organisations by their secrecy and systems of information cut-outs within themselves provide the conditions for buccaneering activities at all levels, including the most senior. An incident in 1945 is an example of the latter. Konstantin Volkov was a nominal Soviet vice-consul in Istanbul. In reality, he was area head of Soviet Intelligence. He contacted the man who, he believed, was the DI6 area head at the British embassy and offered to provide specific information* in return for safe transit to Cyprus and £27,500. Kim Philby, who was a Soviet double agent and head of DI6's Soviet section, arranged for himself to take charge of the case and instituted delaying tactics, including a visit which he made to Turkey. Volkov was prevented from handing over information in detail. Some weeks later, he was bundled unconscious into an aircraft, which landed briefly and without permission at Istanbul airport, and was flown back to the USSR, no doubt, to be executed like Colonel Oleg Penkovsky and other Russians who have defected and been caught.

Unauthorised activities by individuals are a factor in the intelligence scene, but it would be a great mistake to attempt to explain too much in that way. The overall picture is of complex, co-ordinated operations. For example, the episode of William Black indicated complex decisions and responsibilities at many levels. No maverick individual was responsible for planting the stolen goods and illegal weapons; the dispatch of the SAS officer from Hereford for the attempted assassination; and the wide range of subsequent activities, including details such as the opening of letters from the European Commission of Human Rights to William Black and the present writer over a period of six years.

Every country has myths which the public accept with little question. In the United Kingdom, one such is the belief that the important decisions in the governing of the country and its relations with other countries are made by the prime minister or by him and the members of the cabinet either collectively or as individual ministers. The truth is that the senior civil servants, more often than not, are the real shapers of policy. It would not surprise anyone that weak or inexperienced ministers frequently rubber stamp the decisions placed before them by their civil servants. However, strong-willed ministers with determined views may still find themselves implementing the wishes of their senior civil servants instead of their own.

*The information included addresses and descriptions of KGB buildings in Moscow with details of burglar alarm systems, key impressions and guard schedules; registration numbers of all NKVD (subsequently renamed KGB) cars; a list of Soviet agents in Turkey with their methods of communication and the names of three Soviet agents in government departments in London.

Civil servants have much greater technical knowledge and expertise than the minister. His term of office with the department may have been short and, at most, will rarely have been more than two or three years. They are woven together by personal frienships and long acquaintances. They are highly intelligent, educated at the best universities and collectively can have a will of their own more resolute and enduring than an individual minister or even, in the long run, of a cabinet. Their craft, cunning, sense of timing and even deviousness are formidible in advancing policies of which they approve and in thwarting those of which they disapprove. During the sterling crisis of March 1976, Joe Haines, the prime minister's press officer, remarked to an official of the Treasury that the chancellor of the Exchequer did not appear to know about everything that had taken place.

"That's right," he said. "All this is classified 'Top Secret'."

"So?" Haines queried.

"Oh," he said cheerfully, " 'Top Secret' means you don't tell the Chancellor."*

Of all the departments, the Foreign and Commonwealth Office is the most determined, ingenious and ruthless in obtaining its own way. Its members have served together in little groups, often in tense and trying circumstances, in every part of the world where Britain has embassies or high commissions and the resulting self-confidence and *esprit de corps* places them in a class by themselves among civil servants.

A good illustration of the unwillingness of the senior men of the Foreign Office to be subject to the instructions even of the prime minister is provided by an occurrance in February 1969. Joe Haines who experienced it at first-hand has described what happened.† The United Kingdom had still not become a member of the EEC at the time, but the Foreign Office was determined that it must join. General de Gaulle proposed in an interview with Sir Christopher Soames, the British ambassador to France, that the United Kingdom initiate a new European Economic Association to replace the EEC and to render NATO superflous. He emphasised that his remarks were made in the strictest confidence. The Foreign Office was totally un-

*Joe Haines, *The Politics of Power* (Coronet edition, 1977), p. 68.
†Joe Haines, pp. 74-81.

interested in the proposal that the EEC should be brought to an end even before the United Kingdom became a member. It was, however, much interested in using de Gaulle's initiative to discredit him with the other EEC governments and the State Department in Washington. The obstacle was Harold Wilson, the prime minister. He, too, was opposed to de Gaulle's ideas, but he emphasised that his remarks had been made in strict confidence and that the confidence had to be honoured.

Six days later, Wilson, had to visit Bonn. He mentioned to Dr. Kiesinger, the West German federal chancellor, that he had received a recent communication from de Gaulle, but did not indicate its radical content. Thus confidentially was preserved while due respect was shown to the West German ally.

During Wilson's absence in Bonn, the Foreign Office, in defiance of his clearly expressed wishes, provided the governments of the EEC countries, other than France, and of the USA with an extensive although incomplete account of de Gaulle's interview with Soames. This was done in the knowledge that it was certain to be leaked to the press by some of the recipients. The leak came in a garbled version in *Figaro* and *France Soir* some days afterwards. The Foreign Office was not happy with the garbled account and came up with a scheme to leak the text to *Il Messagero* in Rome. The United Kingdom, it was reckoned, would not be suspected if the new leak was in an Italian newspaper. Harold Wilson vetoed the plot immediately he heard about it. However, he had to attend a political rally in Felixstowe that evening which meant that he could not be contacted until his return some hours later. He left Downing Street at 4.20 p.m. and shortly afterwards the Foreign Office gave a press conference and released the text as already provided to the governments. Within hours it was public knowledge around the world and the French government was preparing a bitter protest note.

The key officials in the Northern Ireland Office have been senior Foreign Office men on secondment. Also, the Foreign Office has been primarily responsible for matters with a bearing on the Irish Republic. The wilfulness, insubordination and deviousness of the Foreign Office may thus be relevant to understanding events in Ulster and specially relevant may be the acceptance by so many of its officials that covert activities are normal and valuable. Geoffrey McDermott, the former head of the Permanent Under-Secretary

Department of the Foreign Office and Foreign Office adviser to DI6, sketched the situation with disturbing frankness in his book *The New Diplomacy*. The DI6 men posted to British embassies, he wrote, "naturally had direct contact with their head office in London; and they would be saints, rather than human beings, if in the occasional burst of inspiration, or of exasperation with the official diplomats, they did not deploy a little private enterprise. The traditional British ambassador used to regard all this activity as ungentlemanly and a waste of time and money. But the traditional British ambassador is, happily, fading into a well-merited oblivion. Most of our heads of mission to-day, and their younger colleagues who will be the ambassadors of to-morrow, have a proper respect for the activities of the SIS [DI6], so long as they are kept reasonably well-informed — and the enterprises yield results."*

McDermott does not define what he means by "reasonably well-informed" nor does he indicate how many ambassadors would prefer not to be informed at all if it meant being told about the kind of activities which have happened in Ulster. Nor, yet again, does he mention the occasions when persons who are as much DI6 men as diplomats are appointed ambassadors as happened when Christopher Ewart-Biggs† was sent to the Irish Republic in 1976.‡ His remarks, too, convey the impression that DI6 is really a peripheral organisation and its activities peripheral. This was once true, but, in more recent years, it has come to exert power and influence second to none. This is true of the intelligence services in most countries. In the United States, the director of the CIA is an ex-officio member of the president's inner cabinet. In the USSR, the KGB has equal status with the Soviet External Affairs Department in the conduct of foreign affairs with both answering only to the Politburo. The British DI6, DI5, GCHQ and Service Intelligence have been more successful in maintaining a low

*Geoffrey McDermott, *The New Diplomacy* (1973), pp. 142-3.

†He was assassinated in Dublin by the Provisional IRA only twelve days after he took up his appointment.

‡Chapman Pincher in *Inside Story* (p. 25) told how George Brown (now Lord George-Brown of Jevington) asked to be shown the headquarters of DI6 shortly after he became secretary of state for Foreign Affairs in 1966. The DI6 officials insisted that he should not travel from the Foreign Office in the official limousine lest it should be recognised and arranged for him to be collected from his house in a "cover" car. The intelligence man who called for him with the car was Christopher Ewart-Biggs.

profile. The result has been that few have realised that they, too, have come to occupy a position of similar power. Further, the power is more uncontrolled and arbitrary than is exercised by the CIA and possibly even the KGB. Unlike the CIA, British Intelligence organisations have no Committee of Forty to bear in mind. The more rigid libel laws of the United Kingdom protect them from the kind of journalistic and legal developments which made possible the Watergate exposures. They are safe from even a question in Parliament let alone investigations such as the CIA received from the Church Committee of the Senate or the Pike Committee of the House of Representatives.

The director-generals of DI5 and DI6 report to the prime minister. This suggests that he is responsible and in control. The reality is different. A prime minister can have close co-operation from a director-general and much uncensored information, if they mutually agree on objectives and methods. At the other extreme, if there is no such common ground, he may well be fed only such "sanitized" information as the intelligence service thinks appropriate. Even the cabinet co-ordinator of intelligence is no better placed, if an intelligence service wishes to deny him information. Again, there is the contrast with the CIA. The Pike Committee came to the conclusion that the CIA "had been utterly responsive to the instructions" of the president and his Assistant on National Security Affairs. Dr. Henry Kissinger testified to the committee that every CIA operation of consequence had been approved by the president in office at the time.*

Few British prime ministers, apart from David Lloyd George and Sir Winston Churchill, have taken a close interest in the intelligence organisations. Harold Macmillan was not untypical. "I don't expect the gamekeeper", he said, "to come and tell me every time he kills a fox". Some prime ministers may have been genuinely indifferent: others may have preferred not to know too much as knowledge of what is being done brings responsibility for allowing it to continue.

*Kermit Roosevelt was the CIA Chief of Bureau in the Middle East in 1953 at the time of the CIA engineered coup in Iran which overthrew the regime of Mahomet Mossadeq. He has stated that President Eisenhower was briefed on the operation before and after it took place and that it was authorised by John Foster Dulles, Secretary of State; Walter Bedell Smith, Under-Secretary of State; and Allen Dulles, Director of the CIA. *Los Angeles Times News Services,* 30 March 1979.

It is known that Sir Harold Wilson during his penultimate period as premier rarely met Sir Martin Furnival-Jones, the director-general of DI5,* and he himself has confirmed that normally a prime minister does not meet the director-general of DI6.† Lord Wigg, whom Wilson appointed co-ordinator of DI5 and DI6 in 1964, resigned after three years partly because of difficulty in gaining access to him past his private secretary. Such a situation could not have prevailed if Wilson had been much interested in intelligence matters.

The main hold of the prime minister over the intelligence organisations is that he appoints the replacement when a director-general retires, which is normally at the age of fifty-five in DI5 and DI6. It is usually less significant than might be expected. The choice of the new man has, in practice, to be acceptable to the intelligence services as a whole and, also, be agreeable to the American CIA and NSA. In 1965, Harold Wilson wished to appoint Colonel Eric St. Johnston, chief constable of Lancashire, as director-general of D15 in succession to Sir Roger Hollis. The intelligence services quickly let him know that they did not care for the idea and he dropped it.

An all-prevading, inhibiting factor in the prime minister's dealings with the intelligence organisations is that they are the channel for Anglo-American co-operation in intelligence gathering. The United Kingdom depends overwhelmingly on American intelligence. Satellites are now the main source for information and the United Kingdom has none. Radio surveillience is also important and the most effective radio listening centres in Britain have been built by American money and are manned by employees of the American NSA. In fact, the discrepancy between American and British intelligence gathering capabilities is now so huge that the British intelligence organisations, Foreign Office and military establishments would go to almost any extreme to protect the present close co-operation and no prime minister would care to collide with them on the subject.

It is conceivable that a director-general may himself be in a similar position in relation to his own subordinates as the prime minister is in relation to him. The remark of Sir Findlater Stewart that "having got the right man there is no alternative to giving him the widest discretion in the means he uses and the direction in which he applied

*The Observer, 17th July 1977.
†B. Penrose and R. Courtiour, The Pencourt File (1978), p. 9.

them" is equally true of many appointments within an intelligence organisation. A subordinate may be running an operation on his own or in conjunction with a section of another intelligence organisation or the CIA. The "need to know" rule, whereby no one is given information unless he cannot perform his assigned task without it, means that he and the operatives under him may be the only persons in the organisation with any knowledge of what is afoot. Thus he can give or withhold information from the director-general as he judges expedient. Miles Copeland, the former senior official of the CIA, has emphasised that even the director of the CIA is "protected" by need to know regulations which keep from him all information that is not essential to his job. He added that this would be almost all the detailed information in the organization.*

Intelligence organisations, too, are large, complex and divided into specialised departments. A director-general who has not himself spent any of his career in clandestine operations is in a weak position to enforce detailed accountability on a subordinate who is in charge of such a department. There are also the administrative pressures and conventions which can isolate senior officials from knowing what is happening under their authority. Shortly after David A. Phillips became Director of the Western Hemisphere Division of the CIA, he spent a Sunday investigating personally a report that a CIA official had defected with knowledge of CIA operations against the government of Salvador Allende in Chile. Next morning, it was pointed out to him that he was now a manager and not an operator. He commented, "The Division Chief had to delegate even the most intriguing cases and allow others to enjoy the excitement of running operations".†

Nor should the network of well established personal relationships within an intelligence organisation be underestimated and the consequent ability to thwart interference from above. Miles Copeland has described the reaction within the CIA to the unpopular reorganisation attempted by James Schlesinger during his brief sojourn as director. Senior men whom he wished to dismiss were kept on the books under "funny names" and most of the espionage branch went to ground thus crippling his ability to run the organisation.‡ A

*Miles Copeland, *The Real Spy World* (1974), p. 26.
†David A. Phillips, *The Night Watch* (1977), p. 240.
‡Miles Copeland, *The Real Spy World* (1974), p. 301.

secret trial within the British DI6 in 1952 ended in a "not proven" verdict for Kim Philby, suspected of being a Soviet agent. Sir Dick Goldsmith White, who was present as a member of DI5, was, nonetheless, convinced by it that he was one. When he was transferred to DI6 as director-general four years later, he found that Philby was still an official and about to be posted to Beirut, thanks to the stubborn solidarity of his colleagues.

A most dangerous possibility is that a number of like-minded men may conspire together in one or more intelligence organisations to use the contacts and facilities under their control to achieve an agreed objective, political or non-political, without reference to or interference from director-general or anyone else. The so-called Lavon affair in Israel in 1954 is an example. The British and American governments (including the relevant section of the CIA) had swung to the view that Britain had to withdraw from the Suez Canal Zone in order to secure permanent Egyptian goodwill and to strengthen the Egyptian strong-man, Lieut.-Colonel Gamal Abdel Nasser, as a bulwark against Soviet expansion in the Mediterranean. Israeli observers realised that, once British troops would withdraw, Egypt would occupy the canal and close it to Israel. A number of key individuals within the Israeli intelligence organisations, Mossad and Shin Beth (equivalent of DI6 and DI5), hatched a covert operation to harden the British and American publics against Egypt and to sew doubts as to Nasser's ability to maintain law and order. Several small bombs were to be exploded in American-owned buildings such as the US Information Offices. An informer tipped off the Egyptians. Eleven Israeli agents were arrested. Two were executed and the remainder given long prison sentences.

In the recriminations that followed the plot, Phinhas Lavon, the Israeli minister of defence, was accused of having been responsible, but six years later a cabinet committee concluded that he had neither known that it was to be implemented nor had he authorised it. The truth was that there had been a conspiracy by persons in Mossad and Shin Beth who were confident that they knew best what action should be taken and assumed that they would "get away with it". It was the kind of internal intelligence conspiracy for which parallels are likely to be found when the day comes for Ulster covert happenings to be scrutinised.

A number of like-minded men, closely knit together by long

association and with formidable resources under their control for which they need be accountable to no one other than themselves, are not to be regarded lightly. If, as in British intelligence, they have themselves taken part in or watched their American counterparts take part in the making, manipulating and overthrow of governments from Iran to Chile, they are likely to have had thoughts about applying similar techniques within their own country. Finally, if they are staunch patriots by inclination and made doubly so by the nature of their occupation, it should not surprise if, from time to time, they may have gone beyond thoughts and entered the realm of action.

APPENDIX

The United Kingdom Intelligence Organisations

The intelligence organisations of the United Kingdom consist of DI5, DI6, Special Branch of the Metopolitan Police, Service Intelligence and Government Communications Headquarters, Cheltenham. DI5 and DI6 are abbreviations for Defence Intelligence 5 and Defence Intelligence 6. Until a few years ago, they were named MI5 and MI6, the abbreviations for Military Intelligence 5 and Military Intelligence 6. DI5 is also sometimes called the Security Service and DI6 the Secret Service. In addition, DI6 continues to be referred to by another earlier title, Secret Intelligence Service or SIS. DI5 operates in the United Kingdom and DI6 abroad, but in practice the distinction is not always clear cut. An old, inexact definition of their roles is that DI5 catches foreign spies in Britain and DI6 plants British spies abroad. Neither organisation has executive powers and legal searches, arrests and prosecutions are undertaken on their behalf by the Special Branch. DI5, DI6 and SI are headed by director-generals, each of whom has the right of direct access to the prime minister. The Co-ordinator of Intelligence and Security in the Cabinet Office is responsibile for seeing that their activities do not overlap, but has no authority over their internal affairs. He, too, has direct access to the prime minister.

The official justification for the existence of the intelligence organisations is "defence of the realm" by the methodical gathering of information on external threats from foreign powers or internal threats from subversive or potentially subversive groups and individuals. Part of their activities are covert and are sometimes conducted outside of the law. They are often much wider than the information gathering which is officially admitted and include covert interventions designated to influence the course of events.

The United Kingdom intelligence organisations have a freedom from public accountability unknown even to the Central Intelligence Agency (CIA) of the United States which has to bear in mind the

Committee of Forty and Congressional inquiries. In Parliament, they are never referred to by name and ministers do not discuss their activities. The fact that they cannot be mentioned by name is in itself an obstacle to worthwhile debate which no verbal ingenuity can overcome.

Parliament approves in the national budget a sum known as the Secret Vote for the financing of DI5 and DI6. The real cost is some eight times the Secret Vote and is concealed in defence and other estimates. A parallel situation exists in the United States where the committee of inquiry, chaired by Congressman Pike, discovered that the foreign intelligence budget is three to four times more costly than Congress is told and that the domestic intelligence one may be five times more costly.

DI6, in addition, sometimes receives American money. It is usually for projects which the CIA wishes carried out, but hesitates to undertake for fear of political repercussions in post-Watergate Washington. GCHQ is even more indebted to the United States for subventions although usually in the form of advanced equipment and technology.

The Defence Intelligence Committee has a general oversight of the intelligence organisations. It is a cabinet sub-committee with representatives from each of them and from the Foreign Office. It prepares the "national intelligence estimate" and is expected to keep a special watch on strategic operations with political ramifications. It has been described as the board of directors of British intelligence. The nearest equivalent in the USA is the US Intelligence Board.

DI5

DI5 has its headquarters in Curzon Street, London and other offices at Grosvenor Street, South Audley Street, Great Marlborough Street, the Euston Tower Building and Mount Row, Mayfair. It also operates a surveillance and bugging centre in conjunction with DI6 and the police at Grove Park, Camberwell.* It is affiliated to the Home Office and is the largest of the undercover organisations. It is

*Articles by Duncan Campbell in *New Statesman,* 1st and 8th Feb. 1980, give details of the main premises of the intelligence services, including ones used in connection with bugging and telephone-tapping. His estimate of the numbers of personnel employed based on the area of office space in use supports the figures in this book which were obtained in a different way.

276

understood to have around 5,000 full-time employees and many times that number of part-time and occasional. It is divided into Counter-espionage Branch, Protective Security Branch, Counter-sabotage Branch, Counter-subversion Branch, Scientific and Support Services Branch and the Registrary and Administration Branch. The branches are divided into sections and the latter into sub-sections or "desks". The registrary is reported to have files on over four million persons.

DI5 is under the umbrella of the Home Office for civil service descriptive purposes, but it is independent and self-contained. The director-general has the status of deputy under-secretary. He may liaise with the permanent secretary who heads the Home Office, but he does not accept direction from him or provide him with information other than he himself thinks expedient. Nor has the secretary of state for the Home Office or any other minister the authority to require him to divulge information unless he himself chooses of his own wish to do so. The directive which is the written basis for MI5's non-accountability spells this out clearly. It was issued by Sir David Maxwell-Fyfe when Home Secretary in 1952 and reads: "You [the director-general] and your staff will maintain the well-established convention whereby Ministers do not concern themselves with the detailed information which may be obtained by the Security Service [DI5] in particular cases, but are furnished with such information only as may be necessary for the determination of any issue *on which guidance may be sought.*"*

DI6

DI6 has its headquarters at Century House, 100 Westminster Bridge Road, London and has about 1,000 full-time employees at home and abroad. It has its principal training centre at Borough High Street, London and a "field craft" training one at Fort Monkton in Gosport, Devon. Its computer centre is on the third floor of an annexe adjacent to Century House. It is closely intermeshed with the Foreign Office of which it is part and has the same structure of regional and administrative departments. DI6 personnel frequently serve abroad under diplomatic cover and the transfer of regular Foreign Office personnel to serve for periods with DI6 appears to be increasing. The Foreign Office Adviser to DI6 is supposed to act as a

*Quoted in *Lord Denning's Report*, Cmnd. 2152, 1963.

day-to-day link and his consent is normally secured before significant operations are launched. Mail is addressed to Box 850 or to a non-existent Mr. G. H. Merrick, Foreign Office.

Special Branch

The Special Branch has its headquarters on the top floor of Scotland Yard, Victoria Square, London. It supplements the work of DI5 and DI6 by gathering low level information on individuals and organisations singled out by the intelligence services as subversive or potentially subversive; prosecutes for espionage, treason, offences against the Official Secrets Acts and Public Order Act; watches at ports and airports for persons who are regarded as undesirables; provides personal guards for visiting dignitaries; monitors aliens and vets applications for naturalisation. A central part of the work of the Special Branch is thus to act as the police arm of DI5 and DI6, which as has been noted, have no executive powers of their own. Its officers make the arrests, prepare the evidence and participate in the trials.

The annual report which the Metropolitan Commissioner submits to Parliament through the Home Secretary contains no indication that such an organisation exists. Its budget is secret. In 1968, it had only 300 officers and was entirely London-based. Today, it has close on 1,400. 409 officers are in the metropolis; 850 are distributed among the forty-one police authorities in England and Wales other than the Metropolitan and about 80 in the eight police authorities in Scotland. The Metropolitan Special Branch has an Irish Squad of 70 and smaller units, specialising in Irish matters, exist in cities with large Irish populations and in ports of entry from Ireland. A police Anti-Terrorist Squad, based in London, is drawn partly from the Special Branch and partly from CID detectives. It had 220 men for a couple of years. By the autumn of 1977, the fear of renewed bombing in England by the Provisional IRA had receded and it was reduced to 30. The remainder were assigned to other duties, but are available for recall as, for instance, during a temporary resumption of terrorist incidents in 1979.

Special Branch men and women are recruited from the regular police after they have completed the normal two years probationary period. The provincial squads usually range from eight to twelve. The minimum is six. There are reports that the overall competence has declined because of the rapid expansion of recent years. Also, the quality of the recruits attracted is not improved by the increasing amount of degrading work expected of Special Branch police such as posing as courting couples over long periods of surveillance.

The Special Branch registry contains information on about three million persons, including a special computerised file of 600,000 key persons in political parties, trade unions, commerce, industry, etc.

Northern Ireland has its own Special Branch of about 280 officers. It has a relationship with the Royal Ulster Constabulary similar to that of the Special Branch with the Metropolitan Police. However, during most of the period covered by this book, both the RUC and it were held at arm's length by the Westminister administration in Ulster.

Service and Army Intelligence

Service Intelligence is a section of the Ministry of Defence. It performs the functions of the former military, naval and air intelligence services and has "listening posts" in key military areas of the world such as Europe, Hong Kong, Cyprus and the Persian Gulf. It is primarily concerned wth strategy and defence policies. On the other hand, army intelligence in normal circumstance is an integral part of the army. A battalion of 550 men has an intelligence section of three officers, six NCOs and twenty-five men. A brigade has an intelligence unit of about twenty under a major and an army headquarters a larger number under a lieutenant-colonel or colonel. In special situations, such as Ulster, the importance of army intelligence can escalate dramatically and it can assume an authority and independence which the ordinary soldiers are unable to challenge. Officers from it have had a strong influence in deciding policies in Ulster. Army intelligence had a part in training the Special Interrogation Unit at Castlereagh and it has men stationed permanently on the premises. On the ground, soldiers have done much information gathering. The registry and computer at Northern Ireland Headquarters, Lisburn now have information on some 65 per cent of the adult Ulster population.

GCHQ

General Communications Headquarters is on Prior's Road, Cheltenham. It is formally under the control of the Foreign Office and is the British equivalent of the American National Security

Agency. It employs over 2,000 full-time persons at home and abroad, including a substantial contingent of men from the army's Royal Corps of Signals. Monitoring foreign radio communications is its main work and the fact that it has three times as many employees as DI6 indicates its importance. Another indication is that Sir Leonard Hooper, who was Co-ordinator of Security and Intelligence in the Cabinet Office until early 1979, was director of GCHQ prior to that appointment. It has close agency-to-agency relations with the American NSA to the extent that there is an NSA station inside the GCHQ monitoring complex at Cheltenham.

A department of GCHQ specialises both in the sureptitious placing of hidden devices to monitor conversations by electronic, laser beam and other means and in the protection of government premises from them.

An organisation is only as good as the men who operate it. Undercover organisations have difficulty in recruiting persons of other than average ability. None of the intelligence successes of World War Two was due to DI6. Every one of its agents in Germany and German-controlled territory was arrested. On one occasion, Himmler named every chief officer in DI6 from the director-general downwards. A wartime sister organisation, Special Operations Executive, was responsible for economic and general sabotage in enemy territory. For three years, it conducted radio communication with the German counter-intelligence organisation in the belief that it was with its own agents in the Dutch resistance. Almost every new batch of agents which it parachuted into the Netherlands during that period were promptly rounded up by the Gestapo and shot. Also, dropped to the waiting Germans were twenty-eight thousand pounds of explosives, three thousand sten guns, five hundred revolvers and large sums of currency.

Trevor Roper, who subsequently became Regius Professor of Modern History at Oxford, served in D16 during much of World War Two. He described the permanent officials as part-time stock brokers; retired Indian policemen; agreeable epicureans from the bars of White's and Boddle's; jolly, conventional ex-naval officers and robust adventurers from the bucket-shop.

Recruitment was somewhat widened in the post-war period, but the problem of quality remained. Captain Henry Kerby, who was with DI6 until he entered Parliament in 1964 as Conservative MP for Arundel and Shoreham, described it as diluted by an influx of "unfrocked dons, misfits, oddities, queers and drunks" none of whom was properly vetted. Bruce Page, David Leitch and Philip Knightley have expressed the problem a little more tactfully. They described it thus: "Unlike the normal civil service, the secret departments did not impose intellectually rigorous entrance qualifications. How could they? — the jobs could hardly be advertised. Both departments [DI5 and DI6] therefore recruited via the ramifications of personal introduction ... The armed services compensated for the flexibility of their entrance qualifications by the tradition of 'get promoted or get out' applied with varying degrees of vigour throughout the first half of the century. The civil service compensated for its security by its entrance standards. Lacking either civilian or military self-discipline, it was easy for the upper echelons of the secret departments to become havens of mediocrity or vapid eccentricity."*

The defection to the USSR in 1952 of two DI6 officials, Guy Burgess and Donald MacLean, caused widespread misgivings that the organisation was inadequate, if not incompetent, and the fear that it might still be harbouring other traitors. In 1956 came the *Ordzhonikidze* fiasco and shortly afterwards Sir Dick Goldsmith White was appointed director-general. He was a career officer from DI5 and had been director-general of it for the previous three years. He had been educated at the universities of Oxford, Michigan and California and made a number of overdue reforms. More persons were recruited with university training and with a wider range of expertise. His successors have continued most of White's innovations. The last few years have seen a partial return to recruiting more persons from the services. Young officers about to end short-term commissions and with no immediate employment are a better hunting ground for individuals with ability than the graduates of univeristies with minds already set on the normal professions.

Nevertheless, the basic problem remains. Gifted and ambitious men and women are normally repelled by the prospect of careers in

*Bruce Page, David Leitch and Philip Knightley, *Philby* (Sphere edition, 1977), pp. 137-138.

intelligence. Perhaps, it is partly reluctance to be swallowed up in the twilight world of undercover work with no prospect of proper recognition for achievement outside one's immediate colleagues. David Atlee Phillips, the former Director of the Western Hemisphere Division of the CIA, mentions in his book, *The Night Watch*, that it is often a relief for children to learn that their father is an intelligence officer.* "For the first time they are disabused of the notion that their father is an unsuccessful business nomad who can't seem to hold a job or settle into a career. Or, they will understand why he has not become deputy chief of mission or an ambassador, enjoying a long black car with flags flying from the fenders."

Phillips emphasises, too, the strain on intelligence officers as they maintain their assumed identities. "They — and their families — must lie constantly. They cannot tell the truth to bankers, neighbours, lodge brothers, or delivery boys." He himself, he added, had even lied to the Boy Scouts organisation when filling in application forms to be a scoutmaster. Not surprising, the divorce rate is higher than in most professions. Phillips admits that this is so in the CIA and it can be assumed to be true of other intelligence organisations.

There have been exceptions to the rule that intelligence organisations do not attract the ablest persons. One such was Vice-Admiral Sir Reginald Hall, Director of British Naval Intelligence in World War One. Kim Philby, the Soviet double agent in DI6 in more recent times, was possibly another. But, in general the rule holds good and the phenomenon is not peculiarly British. For instance, the American CIA has the same problem. The average CIA man has a less impressive academic background than his diplomatic colleagues from the State Department. The traditional stigma associated with spying as a profession is alive even in the supposedly materialistic and egalitarian society of the United States. In American embassies, the social tension between the officials of the State Department and their wives and the CIA men and their wives can be formidable.

DI6 has traditionally held DI5 in disdain. It has been described as the disdain which a guards' officers' mess has for that of the military policemen. It long regarded DI5's emphasis on the painstaking filing of information, item by item, month by month, as unimaginative, bureaucratic labour. DI5, in turn, has had its disdain for DI6 as an organisation with too many poorly-vetted men and too much reli-

*David Atlee Phillips, *The Night Watch* (1978), pp. 187, 202, 269.

ance on intuition and the methods of the gangster. In the past, there has been much friction and working at cross purposes between them, but this is possibly less pronounced since the changes introduced by Sir Dick Goldsmith White. The impression that there is a marked social distinction between the senior personnel in DI6 and DI5 is inaccurate. The top officials in DI5 are as likely to have as impressive family connections as in DI6. This is not primarily because of social snobbery, but because social status is useful in the work of both organisations. It gives an entré to important political and social circles and a deference useful in itself. The CIA, too, is aware of the uses of social status and it is no accident that so many of its senior men have been educated at Ivy League universities.

The "old boy network" is a feature in recruitment with all undercover organisations, including the British DI5 and DI6, American CIA and Russian KGB. Someone who volunteers his services is immediately suspect. The alternative is to choose from those who are personally recommended. In DI5 and DI6 this even extends to the secretaries and the girls who file the information in the registries. They tend to belong to well-connected or service families.

Intelligence work has become increasingly dominated by technology. GCHQ towers over the other intelligence organisations in expenditure and importance of information obtained. DI5 and DI6 employ many technological specialists and the latter is respected abroad for its competence in industrial espionage. The technical and scientific employees of the intelligence organisations are as good as those in other civil service departments. However, such persons are like the NCOs of an army. They carry out instructions, but seldom form policy.

When one turns from the officers of DI5 and DI6 to the full-time and part-time agents in the field, there is no criteria for recruitment other than usefulness. They range from prominent businessmen and correspondents of respected newspapers to ex-convicts, including a small number of expert safe-blowers. Among those identified in Ulster are a well-known barrister, an unknown solicitor, three persons in institutions of higher learning who were recruited at earlier stages of their careers for industrial espionage in the United States, a shipping agent recruited when overseas in similar employment and a former senior member of the Official Unionist Party. After each of the intelligence fiascos of recent years, such as the failure to detect the impending attack on Israel by the allied Arab countries in October 1973 or the Turkish invasion of Cyprus, it was discovered that the information had been available but had gone unnoticed by the American and British analysts. In order to prevent the recurrence of that kind of failure, British intelligence in Ulster has been using a small number of local people to help evaluate information. For instance, the former member of the Official Unionist Party has been listening to tapes of bugged conversations of Ulster political leaders.

Service Intelligence and the intelligence branches of the armed forces have their older hands, some with experience that includes one or more of the anti-insurgency campaigns in Malaya, Kenya, Cyprus and Oman, but, in the main, they find their officers by drafting in promising regulars for a three year stint. A few find it their métier, but most regard it as an unwelcome interference with their service careers. A problem is that so much time is spent on boring work such as compiling house details in places like Andersonstown, Belfast, including colour of front door or wallpaper pattern in a particular room and the names of better-known dogs. Recruitment of the rank and file has equally its difficulties. Peter Watson reports that army intelligence often attracts the "James Bond" type and that army psychologists now grade applicants on a scale of 1 to 5 according to how much of a "cowboy" they are. Only grades 1 and 2 are accepted.*

David Cornwell (John le Carré) in one of his novels makes the director-general of what is unmistakably DI6 remark, "I would say that since the war, our methods — ours and those of the [Eastern Block] opposition — have become much the same. I mean you can't be less ruthless than the opposition simply because your government's *policy* is benevolent, can you, now?"†

The ruthlessness of the British undercover organisations, however, extends back long before the onset of the cold war. The first assassination, about which information is available, appears to be that of Alexander Szek in 1917 during the First World War. He was an Austrian employed by the Germans in a radio station in Brussels. His parents and two sisters lived in England. Agents of MI 1c (the name

*Peter Watson, *War on the Mind: The Military Uses and Abuses of Psychology* (1978), p. 370.
†John le Carré, *The Spy Who Came in from the Cold* (1963), p. 19.

by which DI6 was known until the 1930's) threatened to have them interned and thus blackmailed him into providing sections of the German radio code. These enabled British intelligence to decode a telegram sent by the German foreign minister, Alfred Zimmermann, to his representative in Mexico instructing him to urge that country to attack the United States if it should enter the war against Germany. The text was passed to President Woodrow Wilson who published it. Soon afterwards German intelligence began to make inquiries at the radio station. Szek feared that he would be found out and made a bargain with MI 1c that he would be conveyed safely to London in return for the remaining section of the German code.

MI 1c had him smuggled out of Belgium. Vice-Admiral Reginald Hall, the Head of Naval Intelligence, was in charge of the German code operation. He realised that once Szek was found missing at the radio station, the Germans would assume that he had stolen the code and would substitute a new one. He ordered him to be murdered by a Naval Intelligence agent and the body smuggled back to Brussels where it was arranged for it to appear that he had been run down by a motor car in a street accident near his lodgings.*

British Security Co-ordination, the body which in World War Two co-ordinated the British intelligence operations in America and liaised with the FBI, assassinated in the United States various enemy agents and the occasional British traitor. "Disposal squads" were maintained to arrange suitable "accidents". William Stevenson's biography of Sir William Stephenson, the director, is based on official BSC papers. In it he notes, "The normal formula was that the victim 'had departed for Canada', a fate more final than it seemed when written on a police blotter."†

One of the earlier victims was a British seaman who was providing Germany with information about shipping. He was found dead in the basement of an apartment building in New York. Another was a German secret agent, Captain Ulrich von der Osten. He was knocked down in March 1941 by a motor car while crossing Broadway at Times Square in New York and then run over by a second car.

Nor were all victims relatively minor individuals. William Rhodes

*Donald McCormick (pseud. Richard Deacon) records these details of Szek's death in *History of the British Secret Service* (p. 216). He was told them by a former agent of MI 1c.
†William Stevenson, *A Man Called Intrepid: The Secret War* (1976), p. 278.

Davis was an American oil magnate from Alabama who had also a refinery in Hamburg and was involved in shipping oil to Germany. He held the confidence of John L. Lewis, the isolationist leader of the CIO [Congress of Industrial Organisations], and had visited Berlin with his backing on a peace mission a day or two after the outbreak of war. The BSC papers record that Davis' many deals with Nazi Germany included "a project to ship oil through Mexican charter vessels to hidden fuel depots in the Atlantic and Caribbean among lesser-known islands where the German U-boats could prey upon merchant vessels along the American eastern seaboard without the need to return to Europe to refuel. The swiftest way to put a stop to this scheme was to remove Davis from the scene." William Stevenson adds the further information, "The cause of death was given as 'a sudden seizure of the heart', and further police inquiries were discouraged by the FBI at BSC's request."*

The extent to which British undercover organisations in recent years have been involved in assassination outside of Ulster is difficult to determine. They have a bad reputation in intelligence circles for assassination and are reputed to be partial to the use of poisons. Arabs insist that one killing in London was a reprisal for the shooting of a British agent by the intelligence service of a Middle Eastern country. A former senior officer of the Shah of Iran admits that another murder in London was by the Iranian intelligence organisation, but insists that it was carried out with the concurrence of its British counterparts. Chapman Pincher, defence correspondent of the *Daily Express,* has been told that the police chief of Premier Mohammed Mossadegh of Iraq was killed by an agent acting on DI6's behalf. He has also written that he knows details of arrangements made to kill President Gamal Abdel Nasser of Egypt during the Suez crisis of 1956.† It is interesting, too, that a former DI6 officer has expressed surprise that Kim Philby was not liquidated after he had become suspect and had been transferred to Beirut. A KGB officer, who defected from the Soviet Embassy in Helsinki, had confirmed that Philby was a double agent and it was understood that the Lebanese security service was willing to kidnap him.

Charles Senseney, a former employee of the United States Special Operations Division at Fort Detrick, during evidence to a Senate

*Stevenson, p. 295.
†Chapman Pincher, *Inside Story* (1978), p. 90.

committee inquiring into toxic agents, stated that he was a specialist on poison dart launchers and similar weapons and that he had been on temporary duty in England in a "collaborative effort" with the United Kingdom. Stan Newens, MP for Hounslow, learnt of Senseney's evidence and submitted a question in the House of Commons. The minister of Defence answered on 10th July 1979. He said that his department was not involved in any project connected with toxic darts and that Senseney had been seconded for work on defence against biological warfare.

Newens' question was a futile exercise as it brought no-one any nearer the facts. Denial is the most common response by intelligence authorities. An earlier minister of Defence had assured the Commons that the report about the shooting of William Black "was absolute nonsense". Or again, after the murder of Captain Robert Nairac by the Provisional IRA, the authorities had denied that he was either an intelligence officer or in the SAS. Only when his army colleagues and members of his family confirmed that he was both, were the denials discontinued.

The intelligence services and other bodies protected by "national security" classifications are absolutely safe from any inquiry into what was involved in the "collaborate effort" to which Senseney testified. The futile question by Newens went to the limit of what is possible. In the United States, where official secrecy is tempered by ethics and public concern, Senator Church's committee of inquiry had already in 1975 discovered that the CIA had enough shellfish poison and cobra venom to kill thousands of persons and an arsnel of specially developed devices for administering poison, including a specially designed pistol and a gadget known as the M-1 which could be fired from a fountain pen, cane or umbrella. It also uncovered buttons filled with compressed bacteria and parts for car engines that would give off poisonous fumes when hot.

If British intelligence has resorted to assassinations on various occasions, it will cause no surprise that it has used every other dubious and criminal expedient. As with the intelligence services of practically all countries, British undercover relies heavily on blackmail for recruiting agents and for procuring information. Physical and psychological threats, physical violence, theft, burglary,*

*Two journalists and a former agent of the Swedish intelligence organisation, the IB, were imprisoned for a breach of Swedish "official secrets" legislation in 1973. They

forgery, planting and dissemination of false information have all been used. Instances of stealing of papers and photographing of papers are legion. The interception and opening of mail is constant and the tapping of telephones extensive. All cables to or from the United Kingdom are monitored at Cheltenham.

Rank or position is no safeguard. When it was asserted in 1977 that Harold Wilson's offices had been bugged by an intelligence organisation while he was prime minister, many refused to believe that such a happening was possible. An occurrence in the less buccaneering days of 1936 should persuade such persons that these organisations are rather more enterprising and less respectful than they assume. Neville Chamberlain was prime minister. He distrusted and disliked the Foreign Office and exchanged letters with Edward Daladier, the French prime minister, by courier in order to by-pass it. Unfortunately for his intention, the courier was in the pay of DI6 and his letters were photographed by it at St. Ermin's Hotel, Westminster.

Forgeries by British intelligence organisations have ranged from letters such as those from "Anna" in 1941 which resulted in the execution by the Germans of General Alous Elias, prime minister of the puppet state of Slovakia, to a comparatively recent document designed to cause internal dissension in an Ulster political party.

False information planted in the media is an old expedient. Rigged opinion polls are a more recent one. Possibly the first such poll sponsored by British undercover was in November 1941 at the National Convention of the CIO in Detroit. The aim was to strengthen the hands of Franklin D. Roosevelt and other Americans who felt that the United States could not remain neutral indefinitely. As noted above, a number of opinion polls conducted during the Ulster crisis have been suspect.

DI6 has been more aggressive in illegalities and crime, but DI5, too, can come up with' a "dirty trick" when it wishes. In World War Two it was responsible for explosions in various places partly to convince the Germans that agents, who had been captured, were still at large and partly to alarm the British public into greater security

---

claimed during the trial that IB and DI6 had co-operated in a joint break-in at the South African legation in Stockholm. Such co-operation against a target of common interest to two national intelligences services is in no way unique and is an indication of the extent to which such activities are regarded as normal in intelligence circles.

vigilance. They included explosions at the de Havilland aircraft factory; an electricity generating station at Bury St. Edmund's; a food storage dump at Wealdstone; and army huts in Hampshire.* More recently, certain information gathering burglaries and thefts during early 1977 were widely suspected of being the work of DI5. They involved seven members of a defence committee set up to fight the deportation of the American writers Philip Agee and Mark Hosenball and another defence committee to fight the cases of Crispin Aubrey, John Berry and Duncan Campbell, three Englishmen charged under the Official Secrets Acts.

Even the Special Branch, the "man Friday" of the intelligence services, is not above irregular methods, including *agents provocateur*. A well-documented instance is the case of Kenneth Lennon, a Provisional IRA informer, whom the Special Branch blackmailed, outrageously exploited and left exposed and unprotected.† Some claim that it was also responsible for his murder in a Sussex country lane, but present evidence does not eliminate the possibility that his death was a revenge killing by the Provisionals.

The UKUSA Pact of 1947 made permanent the British-American co-operation on intelligence gathering which had evolved during World War Two. (Britain accepted responsibility under it for radio and electronic monitoring of Europe west of the Urals and Africa.) The co-operation between British and American intelligence organisations, however, has a vitality independent of any formal agreement. It is based partly on a large measure of similarity in outlook on world problems (e.g. Cuban activities in Africa); partly on a mutual need of one another's assistance (e.g. CIA advice in Washington will be reinforced if it is known that DI6 is urging the same views in London); and partly on professional solidarity.

*Sir John C. Masterman, *The Double-Cross System* (1972), Chapters 6, 7 and 9.
†For a detailed examination of the case, see G. Robertson, *Reluctant Judas* (1976).